Ritual and Semiotics

Critic of Institutions

Roberta Kevelson
General Editor

Vol. 14

PETER LANG
New York • Washington, D.C./Baltimore
Bern • Frankfurt am Main • Berlin • Vienna • Paris

Ritual and Semiotics

edited by
J. Ralph Lindgren and Jay Knaak

with an introduction by
Roberta Kevelson

PETER LANG
New York • Washington, D.C./Baltimore
Bern • Frankfurt am Main • Berlin • Vienna • Paris

Library of Congress Cataloging-in-Publication Data

Ritual and semiotics / J. Ralph Lindgren & Jay Knaak (editors); with an introduction by Roberta Kevelson.
p. cm. — (Critic of institutions; vol. 14)
Includes bibliographical references and index.
1. Semiotics (Law). 2. Ritual. I. Lindgren, J. Ralph.
II. Knaak, Jay. III. Series.
K213.R5 340'.115—dc20 96-30662
ISBN 0-8204-2805-1
ISSN 1068-4689

Die Deutsche Bibliothek-CIP-Einheitsaufnahme

Ritual and semiotics / ed. by J. Ralph Lindgren & Jay Knaak; With an introd. by Roberta Kevelson. –New York; Washington, D.C./Baltimore; Bern; Frankfurt am Main; Berlin; Vienna; Paris: Lang.
(Critic of institutions; Vol. 14)
ISBN 0-8204-2805-1
NE: Lindgren, J. Ralph [Hrsg.]; GT

Cover design by Nona Reuter.

In Memory of Jay Knaak

Teacher, Scholar and Friend

Contents

Introduction

Roberta Kevelson*

I.

Jay Knaak's early death shocked us. We knew he had been sick, but had seemed to recover. He had expected to be able to complete this volume on *Ritual* and had been working on it. We, his friends and colleagues of this Round Table, will miss him. Jay Knaack had been a most valued member of our annual colloquium for more than a decade. This volume, *Ritual*, was his special contribution to this Series, *Critic of Institutions*. The volumes as a whole represent a network of relationships on a variety of topics in Legal Semiotics. Thus this Series stands for a realization of what Peirce calls a "community of inquirers." The first volume, *Codes and Customs: Millennial Perspectives* (R. Kevelson, ed., New York: Peter Lang, 1994) consists of contributed essays by each of the editors of the subsequent volumes of this Series, on their respective key areas of interest.

Most but not all of the books forecast in Volume One are out; Jay's book goes out among them. I am gratified to be able to also say that some of the contributors to this, Jay's volume, have organized a special session to commemorate him, which will be part of the 1996 Law and Society meeting, to be held in Glasgow.

II.

Jay had initiated this collection and had invited the contributors. Thanks to the devotion of his wife and of his close friend Terry Prewitt, secretariat of the Semiotic Society of America, (also at the University of West Florida with Jay) the manuscripts were carefully boxed and sent to the Center for editing. And it is through the great generosity and hard work of our mutual friend and colleague, Ralph Lindgren, that these papers have been brought into readiness for the publisher. Any appreciation expressed to Ralph can be at best an understatement. J. Ralph Lindgren is Emeritus Clara H. Stewardson Professor of Philosophy of Lehigh University.

III.

Before he came to Philosophy and ultimately to Legal Semiotics Jay had been an off-Broadway actor. His first paper at the Round Table Colloquium was on the Oedipus Rex and ancient law as seen from a semiotic perspective. His concern with Ritual here is further, continuing concern with drama, with ceremony, with patterns of human interaction interpreted as symbolic. I take the opportunity now to recall Jay's paper in the first volume of the Critic Series: "Ritual, Law and Reform of Institutions." (*Ibid.*, 177–188).

Here Jay shows that despite spiritual erosion in the modern world a reconciliation appears to be taking place between the sacred and secular institutions in our society. He discusses a late 19th century phenomenon which held that "historical progress" was merely a "delusion . . . ritual, as well as all art, law, education, economics, and culture in general, were looked upon as ways in which obsessive and pathological behavior was expressed in order to sublimate psycho-social conflict, and as ways to reconcile those conflicts." (*Ibid.*, 180–181).

In contrast, Knaack says, "Today students of ritual and analyses of rituals are highly sophisticated, varied and dynamic. Ritual is looked upon as a fluid field in which a multiplicity of human concerns and aspirations can be publicly dramatized." (*Ibid.*, 186).

IV.

The interdisciplinary nature of semiotics, together with the fact that semiotic investigation brings together a variety of topics into new relationships, alerts one to the significance of metaframeworks, even in introductory classifications of parts of a volume such as this. I have therefore kept editorial impositions to a minimum, and choose instead to present contributors in a "neutral" style, by alphabetical rather than any alternative order. The following introduction of contributors and their work is in this unmarked order:

Denis Brion writes in "The Ritual of Judicial Opinion" on the controversial subject of indeterminacy in law. He opposes indeterminacy to a traditionalist notion of law as formalistic and formulaic. Brion argues that the Legal Realists in the United States, influenced by leading assumptions of Pragmatism and Semiotics, advocated a law which was antithetical to "formalistic structure." The position of the Realists was revolutionary in

American law. This revolutionary trace, he shows, is central in recent arguments of the Critical Legal Theorists. The anti-ritualism of Realism is discussed by Brion who carefully describes and interprets the transformation of legal ritual under the influence of powerful arguments on indeterminacy.

From a different position and perspective Antoine Garapon proposes to investigate legal systems which seek not only the nature of a "law" native to a given society, but he proposes also to detect alien, residual strains that survive within an apparently homogeneous system. This argument hinges on the rejection of wide-spread assumptions, namely, that members of a given society assent to values that law reenforces. Garapon further shows that the origins of values in a society are not one-to-one connections with the apparent values promulgated by the particular legal system in power. He says that old, formative rituals which are hidden are nevertheless informing upon a present system. It is important, then, to attempt to recover these underlying value-systems through semiotic inquiry so that current rituals in law may be examined, and reaffirmed or revised or rejected.

David Kertzer's paper focuses on ritualistic struggle in Italian law. His paper is "The Hammer and Sickle in Court Symbolic Struggle in the Italian Communist Party." Kertzer says that language and emblem interact in the creating of a powerful symbolic party myth replete with rituals, legends, fantasies. Kertzer reconstructs the historical events which constitute the frame of the Communist Party's "staging," through the 1980's. He goes on to show that far from being formal repetitions of established patterns of behavior, the kind of ritual represented by the dynamics of the Italian Communist Party are self-creating.

Ralph Lindgren's "Semiosis, Ritualization and Magic" challenges the idea that belief systems are acted-out patterns of prevailing and/or underlying social values. In contrast to mythologies which become canonized into explanations of a causal nature, ritual remains flexible and an open sign-system. Semiotics emphasizes the process of beliefs being acted out, i.e., dynamically ritualized rather than as static mythic referent structures.

Lindgren discusses how the semiotic investigation of ritual may provide access to a dynamical process of social beliefs in flux, and may thereby provide a means of examining interpretations by law and by related social systems. Lindgren's special focus here is on the effects between ritualized social practice and such practice acted into law. He also examines the efficacy of "magic" as a causal force that influences modification of ritual and which, he suggests, in turn influences the law.

The general topic of Ritual is differently approached by Emily Salus in "Aladdin and the Law." She points up a practice of disowning values. In point, the law interprets shared fictive beliefs in a society in different ways, depending on the social class in question. Emily Salus' paper is a close reading of the nursery tale of Aladdin and the Forty Thieves. She highlights her reading by underscoring the role of the sovereign. i.e., the Sultan in this case. The Sovereign, she finds, has the ability of and power to impose change upon existing law by utterance only; whereas, those with lesser power need to have the back-up of the written word. Implicit in this paper is the fact that injustice does not invalidate law but is distinguished from just law.

Under the category of Ritual, Peter Salus discusses several semiotic approaches to the broad problem of taboo: laws of the forbidden, and particularly laws governing incest. Salus focuses on those pre-Mosaic laws in which different kinds of incest are distinguished, and thus lead to different kinds of penalties. From the perspective of a Peircean semiotics one might say that incest between different kinds of relations *means* differently, and the consequences are appropriately different. Peter Salus shows that these differing interpretations of incest find their way into competing, coeval methods of psychiatric practice and into different approaches to remedies by opposing systems of law as well, he suggests.

Agnes Schreiner's paper, "So this is how it is done . . . ," investigates the ritual procedures — rituals of civility, perhaps — that people are expected to act out in business procedures, in conveyances of goods of all kinds. Certain "superlegal" rites are performed above and beyond the requirements of the law. Such acts bring about a quality of social order that is not obligatory but is voluntary and by custom stands for a sign of free action. This free or willed rituality has a cohesive force that contributes to the continuity of social interaction through voluntary customary acts.

Schreiner calls such ceremony "ritual order." She sees it as a "gift" that the ancients built into the civil law. Ritual order is not representative of the natural, organic world. Rather, it signifies representation of social, *made* values. Schreiner examines the significance of selected ritual orders in this paper and raises the question: What do such rituals "mean"? She finds that ritual is not a belief system, but rather functions as a design for action and interaction in human societies which are relatively open.

In Christopher Stanley's "Si(g)ns of the Flesh: Law Violence and Inscription upon the Body," we are brought to a perspective on ritual which inquires into a kind of exchange between "the body of law and the body of the individual." What ways may signify the cross-reference between these two kinds of bodies? Which is referent? Which is predication? Stanley recalls to mind, although he does not discuss this allusion, Roman Jakobson's notion of "shifters" in semiotic precesses. The classic problem of inner and outer is explored by Stanley in this study, especially as this problem relates to interaction between the personal body and the body of the law upon the place of juridical and jural space. Stanley draws upon a wide range of critical work, including Nietzsche, Foucault, Deleuze and others associated with contemporary critical studies.

One moves from Stanley's paper to that of James Ware with a shock of dissociation, and finds a kind of unifying theme which analogizes the interplay of bodies in Stanley with a cross-reference between discourses in comparative study of religious texts. Ware's paper, "Legislating Religious Rituals: How Communion is Regulated in Some Protestant Denominations," opens from the assumption that power acts in ritualistic manner. It is ritual which effectualizes power. Ware closely examines evidence for this thesis by interpreting the major rites and rituals of several Protestant denominations. His main objective is to show "how legislative processes shape the ritual of Communion." This focus — the ritual Communion — discusses significance and symbolism of covenants, of fellowship, and of closed community within the canonical frame of Christian Protestantism.

We move from church to state and to the concluding paper of this remarkable collection by Willem Witteveen: "Enacting Law: Ritual Performances in Dutch Political Culture." Witteveen's work, well known and esteemed among legal semioticians, is remarkable for its ability to turn commonplaces around and to present for fresh investigation unfamiliar faces of a subject. In this paper he takes the position that rituals are not the hardening of performances. On the contrary, they are the means or mediums which transform ordinary actions into symbolically -charged procedures. Such procedures are sign-functions. Rituals facilitate, *as means*, the process whereby the actions in question come to be seen as symbolic. Such acts may be those of law, or of religious, political, or other types of system-specific activity. In this paper Witteveen selects four special "ritual performances" that are integrated within "Dutch political culture." This complex, detailed study draws upon the work of Mary Douglas. Witteveen notes that it is the vital ritual component of political culture, in the Netherlands in particular, that provides exemplary resource material for his own thesis. The particular thereby becomes a general example for possible continuing inquiry into legal-political cultures elsewhere.

V.

This volume will act as an introduction for many to Jay Knaack. Assembled as he wished, and bound together in this "community of inquirers," we have here a Peircean pluralism realized. The cross-fertilization of ideas gathered here will predictably generate new intellectual energies. Such is the spirit and vitality of Jay Knaack to those of us who knew him and miss him.

I give special thanks to Ralph Lindgren for his generosity and patience, and for this significant fellowship which his editorship provides. The book itself becomes a "rite of passage."

* Director, Center for Semiotic Research in Law, Government and Economics and Distinguished Professor of Philosophy, Penn State University

Chapter One
The Ritual of the Judicial Opinion

Denis J. Brion*

Introduction

A recurring phenomenon in academic commentary has been the often breathless discovery that the law is indeterminant. This strain of commentary, however, is not simply an exercise in description. In addition, it has embodied a strong element of criticism.

As description, this commentary is accurate. Taking "the law" to be the sum of judicial doctrine, it is beyond cavil that judicial doctrine is not telic—it has stubbornly refused to evolve toward a coherent and complete rational structure of rules that was the end-state hope of the late nineteenth century founders of the school of scientific jurisprudence. Instead, law as judicial doctrine has simply "developed". Because, however, it has not developed in any particular coherent direction, then a reversal of the formal conception of law is a phenomenal fact—rather than doctrine being the determinant of the results of disputes, doctrine seems forever to be chasing after the judiciary as they resolve disputes.

The consequence of this phenomenon—particularly in the political dimension—is not trivial. The salient fact is that the judiciary can be quite accurately described as carrying out an ongoing enterprise of making law. And this fact violates the popular understanding of a core element of our political order, the Rule of Law, which holds that the function of the judiciary is to find and apply the law and not to make it.

My purpose is to account for this indeterminacy and to demonstrate that it is not "bad" of itself. Instead, as I will argue, it is a necessary consequence of the very nature of the law in our system.

The Nature of Indeterminacy

Critique

Within a generation of the late nineteenth century rise of the school of scientific jurisprudence, a loosely allied group of critics, who came to be called Legal Realists, began to point out that there was a glaring inconsistency between the formalist conceptualization of the law[1] and reality. Karl Llewellyn's famous *mot* captured the essence of this critique—"What these officials do about disputes is, to my mind, the law itself."[2] The legal realist reaction to legal formalism was not, however, merely descriptive in nature. Its normative dimension advocated that law was not a formalistic structure but instead was, and ought to be, a functionalist process, the purpose of which is to serve the ongoing development of the social and economic order.[3]

Little more than a generation after the heyday of the Legal Realists, the Critical Legal Studies movement has again raised the charge of indeterminacy. The Crits, however, clearly are not the heirs of the Progressivist traditions of the Legal Realists. Their criticism is not directed toward the target of the Realists, a misconceived formalism. Instead, it is directed toward the fact of indeterminacy itself, which is a demonstration that the law is simply the instrument of those who occupy the positions of power in society—the law, rather than providing a determinant matrix of rules that shape the actions of individuals, instead is itself continually reshaped in order that the changing needs of the powerful will be accommodated.[4]

The considerable substantive bite of CLS criticism can be understood in terms of a core element in the American political Myth, the Rule of Law. In the popular understanding, the Rule of Law embodies two commitments. Citizens are committed to bringing their disputes to the judicial process for resolution rather than resorting to violence. In response, the judiciary is committed to resolving disputes based on a law that "stands outside" of themselves—an *autonomous* law—rather than on the basis of whim, or self interest, or political favoritism.[5] If, however, the law, as judicial doctrine, does not constrain the actions of officials, then the Rule of Law as it is commonly understood is violated. Rather than functioning autonomously of those who wield power in society, it is subject to capture by them.

The CLS charge can be restated in terms of modes of reasoning. The standard formulation of the Rule of Law implicitly embodies two classic modes of reasoning. The first mode, *deduction*, is commonly considered to be the "judicial paradigm"; this mode of reasoning proceeds from the General Rule to the Particular Case to the Result. The Rule, that is, determines the Result. If the legal process proceeds deductively, then the decisions of officials are constrained and the integrity of the Rule of Law is maintained.

The second mode, *induction*, captures the enterprise of the legal academician—if it is for the judges to settle disputes by applying rule-based doctrine to facts, then it is for the academicians to describe the substance of doctrine. This mode of reasoning proceeds from the Result to the Particular Case at hand to the General Rule. The Rule, that is, is inferred from the Result.

As every first year law student quickly discovers, however, judicial opinions read as if their authors had started with the Result and then constructed a chain of reasoning that supports this Result. And their insight is accurate—in the 1930s, two prominent members of the federal judiciary, Jerome Frank and Joseph C. Hutcheson, Jr., cheerfully admitted as much. According to Judge Frank, "whatever is said in opinions, the judge often arrives at his decision before he tries to explain it."[6] Judge Hutcheson describes the judicial act of deciding as the "hunch", or, more elegantly, the "judgment intuitive".[7]

Although this approach to decision making assuredly departs from the deductive and inductive modes of reasoning that are consistent with the formal requisites of the Rule of Law, it is not, of itself, logically invalid. Rather, this is a recognized form of reasoning, alternative to the more familiar modes of deduction and induction, that logicians term *abduction*.[8] The process of abduction proceeds from the Result to the General Rule that is necessitated by that Result to the Particular Case. In a reversal of the process of deduction, under abduction the Result determines the Rule.

In formal terms, then, Llewellyn's Legal Realist assertion, that the law functionally is what officials of the judicial process do about disputes, and the CLS charge, that judicial doctrine is not determinative of the outcomes to disputes in a predictive sense, come down to the same point—that the reality of the judicial function is that the reasoning process is fraught with abduction. More particularly, the conclusion seems to be inescapable that the judicial opinion, the vehicle by which courts set out the rationale for their decisions, is substantively empty. And, because it is empty, of course a law built up from the accumulation of judicial doctrine will not be determinant. We well could describe this as "the scandal of abduction"—a captured judiciary making law at the behest of the powerful.

The Genesis of Indeterminacy

What I propose to do is attempt to break the nexus between the understanding that judicial doctrine is not an autonomous, determinant body of rules and principles and the conclusion that the judicial commitment to the concept of the Rule of Law is irretrievably violated. That is, in terms of the standard formulation of The Rule of Law, I would like to suggest a way in which we can "learn to love abduction." I want to do this through two concepts advanced by Charles Sanders Peirce—the triadic nature of our World, and the ground of the linguistic sign.

Rene Descartes got it wrong by placing reason at the pinnacle of what it is to be human. A world of reason is dyadic in nature. That is, it is rule-based, proceeding in the mode of "If ... then ..." Descartes's view of the world does no more than replicate the sterile dyadic environment of the non-human organism.

By contrast, Peirce understood that our World, the milieu in which we exist as human beings, is not the simple Cartesian world of given fact and given rule. Rather, it is a World in which we create the rules that provide the starting point of the dyadic process of reason. Rule-creation is a process by which meaning is ascribed to facts. It is thus a World that is *about* facts—a *triadic* World of meaning in which truth is a matter of belief and meaning is the connection between fact and truth. What is distinctive about us as humans is that we construct our Worlds of meaning, and the vehicle by which we do this is the triadic sign-system of language.

In the dyadic semiotic theory of Ferdinand de Saussure,[9] meaning is negative in nature. The meaning of any one sign in a sign-system is what all the other signs in that system, taken together, do not mean. Jacques Derrida correctly has understood that, under a description of language as a dyadic system, meaning is "endlessly deferred."[10]

> Peirce's semiotic theory is based on his rich notion of the triadic sign:A sign ... is something which stands to somebody for something in some respect or capacity ....[11]

An integral aspect of Peirce's triadic sign is his concept of the *ground*:

> The sign stands for something, its *object* ... not in all respects, but in reference to a sort of idea, ... the *ground* .... .[12]

We can take Peirce's concept of the ground—this "sort of idea"—as an attribute of the individual user of the sign–system of language. More specifically, the ground is a locus of values. It is the values embedded in the ground that determine for the language-user the meaning of the signs in the system. Under Peirce's more complex concepts, the sterile dyadic structure of endlessly deferred meaning disappears and meaning itself becomes positive in nature.

Although the concept of the triadic sign accounts for the way in which meaning comes about, it does not posit that meaning is a stable attribute of language. The meaning of texts, for example, as the deconstructionists have abundantly demonstrated, is neither fixed nor homogeneous among all users of a particular language. Instead, it can be a highly contested matter, the consequence of particular interpretive practices.

The explanation for this chaotic phenomenon lies in the nature of the values that come to be embedded in the language-user's ground. Consider two propositions about the nature of the reality that we experience. The first is derived from Peirce's semiotic theory:

> The sign-user has a world.
>
> The world is segmented and named by language. All perceived objects and actions and qualities are named. Even the gaps are named—by the word *gaps*.[13]

The second is the anthropologist's concept of the sociology of perception:

> Anything whatsoever that is perceived at all must pass by perceptual controls. In the sifting process, something is admitted, something rejected and something supplemented to make the event cognizable. The process is largely cultural. A cultural bias puts moral problems under a particular light. Once shaped, the individual choices come catalogued according to the structuring of consciousness, which is far from being a private affair.[14]

The crucial concept is this matter of "the structuring of consciousness". The conscious reality that we experience derives from a selecting from and organization of the totality of sensory interaction with the cosmos that is available. And the perceptual controls that determine this selection and organization derive from a cosmology—which is a set of "fundamental assumptions about the universe",[15] held by the individual, "which generates necessarily its own self-sustaining perceptual blinders."[16] The cosmology provides the particular values that are embedded in the Peircean ground, which determine for the language-user the meaning of the signs in the system.

We thus can describe the process by which the structuring of consciousness comes about. The particular value-content of the ground determines the meaning that comes about within the language system. This, in turn, provides the perceptual controls by which we have a reality that takes the form of a coherent World. The cosmology thereby is the activating force in the inescapably abductive process by which we make our Worlds—we adopt a cosmology, and we thereby construct a language-generated World of meaning. Although the cosmology is held by the individual, it comes to be adopted within a process of social interaction—"the structuring of consciousness ... is far from being a private affair."[17]

Meaning is a seemingly chaotic arena of contest because of the heterogeneous nature of cosmology. Although an unlimited range of cosmologies is not available, cosmology is also not a unitary matter. All that we have available is a limited number of alternatives, which may be described as Individualism, Hierarchy, and Communitarianism, and the "default" cosmology of Atomized Subordination.[18] As the values-foundation for generating a World of meaning, these cosmologies have no inherent characteristics by which one can be deemed to be better or worse than another. Each has its strengths and weaknesses, and the choice to be made among them depends on, and is an interaction with, the social circumstances in which the individual is immersed.

An individual holds a cosmology; as a consequence, language takes on meaning and the individual experiences a meaning-charged reality. Thus, a "way of life ... is ... inevitably a way of thought."[19] As a consequence, "[t]here is nothing natural about the perception of nature; nature is heavily loaded with political bias."[20] At a rudimentary level, where one person might see a weed, another might see a valuable medicinal plant.[21]

Nor is the meaning of a text natural. Where one person might see a list, another might see a poem.[22] And, because the process is social in nature, we can well describe textual meaning as arising within "interpretive communities".[23]

Finally, because each cosmology possesses its strengths and weaknesses—each, that is, is incomplete—then, were all members of a particular society to adopt a particular cosmology exclusively, as the consequent World became implemented more fully, social breakdown and dysfunction would begin and become endemic, making necessary a turn to another cosmology.[24]

Perhaps paradoxically, over the long term, a society, and, in particular a relatively large society, in order to maintain an adequate level of functionality, must be made up of individuals holding a shifting mix of cosmologies. We have already seen how, synchronically, meaning is not necessarily homogeneous across a society that has a particular language. In addition, because the adoption and implementation of a particular cosmology cannot endure, then meaning, which is cosmology-consequent, will not be stable diachronically.[25]

We do not lack values. They are available to us, however, only in rationally incomplete and mutually exclusive sets. Each of us inevitably must choose one set or another, already knowing that any choice that we make will yield a World that will ultimately break down, requiring that we yield to another value set.

To be human is to have a World—a triadic milieu of meaning. But there is no *the* World; there are only alternative Worlds. And, our Worlds are not given; we must create them. But the process of creation is a process of ongoing paradox because we cannot have a World that will endure. Our World inescapably is the World of Sisyphus.

Indeterminacy in the Judicial Process

The purpose of the judicial process is to resolve disputes. Functionally, the judicial process is in its essence an exercise in language. As such, it necessarily is an integral part of our always contingent and conventional World—or, perhaps better, of our always ongoing process of Worldmaking.

Earlier, I described the process by which judges decide how a dispute is to be resolved in terms of "the scandal of abduction." If, however, I have described with any degree of accuracy the necessity that humans engage in Worldmaking, the process by which we engage in Worldmaking, and the role of the judicial process in the Worldmaking function, then, whether or not the abductive nature of judicial decision making is scandalous, it is unavoidable. And it is unavoidable because Worldmaking itself, particularly in a political milieu that honors a pluralism of values, is necessarily abductive.

Consider how Judges Frank and Hutcheson described the act of deciding. What did Judge Hutcheson mean by "the judicial hunch"? To decide abductively is to adopt and implement an ideology.[26] If what is being decided is the outcome of a dispute, then Judge Hutcheson's terminology is apt—the Result intuitively does "feel right" and it does so because it is consistent with a compelling implicit ideology. The abductive process thereby unfolds: the ideology determines the Result; the Result entails a Rule; and deduction consequently follows—the [abduced] Rule, applied to the Case, determines the Result.

If the act of deciding—the abductive process of determining a Result—functionally amounts to adopting and implementing an ideology, and if the "adoption of an ideology" proceeds on some level of the ineffable—it is compelling because the Result that it determines "just feels right"—then what is it that makes an ideology compelling?

I can comfortably assume that nearly all judges, nearly all of the time, are conscientious. That is, a judge does not—consciously—adopt an ideology just because this is the ideology that she happens to hold. The judge's "own, personal" ideology, however, derives from the cosmology that generates her World. Necessarily, then, her ideology can, and often enough will, act powerfully on the level of the subconscious.

Moreover, there is the mix of ideologies "at work" in society generally. There will be, of course, the ideology entailed by the cosmology embedded in our cultural Myth. This is the cosmology of Individualism, as represented by the image of the Yankee Trader or the Marlboro Cowboy. As well, there will be the ideologies held by the political and economic elite, which tend to be the ideologies of Individualism and Hierarchy.[27] The ideologies of our Myth and of the power elite will tend to dominate the values embedded in the ground of the language of public discourse.[28] Finally, there will be what might be termed an emergent ideology, based on the values held by the large majority of the non-elite, of "the rest of us".

Because the mix of cosmologies across society will be synchronically heterogeneous and diachronically shifting, the consequent ideologies will have the same characteristics. In the ground of the language of public discourse, the cosmology of the power elite will be made up of a pragmatically shifting mix of Individualism and Hierarchy. In addition, as opportunities for living out a cosmology of Individualism periodically wane, those who consequentially fall into a growing milieu of Atomized Subordination will tend to appeal to Communalism, which will then exhibit an increasing presence in public discourse.[29]

The judicial process subsumes the judge in a milieu of rhetoric. Moreover, the thrust of this rhetoric will carry a particular bias. Because the judicial process is an institution of power, then it will be embedded in the dominant public discourse, which will tend to reflect the values of the power elite. Moreover, because participation in the judicial process is costly, then the dominant voice in argumentation will tend to be that of the power elite. In consequence, as the process exerts its rhetorical power on the judge, the Result that "feels right" will tend to reflect the values of the power elite.

And this is entirely to be expected. The structuring of the consciousness of the judge "is not a private affair." She will have substantial economic and social status, and she will be likely to socialize with people of similar status; as a powerful individual, she will tend to participate in the dominant public discourse; and the cosmologies that underlie the dominant voice in argumentation will carry the same bias as that of her social milieu and of general public discourse.

"A cultural bias puts moral problems under a particular light."[30] The Result that is intuitively correct appears to be correct because it is consistent with a compelling implicit ideology. And the judge will tend to derive that ideology from the milieu in which she is subsumed.

We can now see why the CLS critique carries such considerable plausibility. Because the Results that seem to be intuitively correct derive from a non-homogeneous mix of values that shifts over time, then judicial doctrine—the body of Rules entailed by the ongoing course of Results—will necessarily reflect this same heterogeneity. As a consequence, judicial doctrine will not be determinant—it will not be possible to predict future Results from the Rules entailed by past Results. And, because the judge is socialized in a milieu that carries a strong cosmological bias in favor of the power elite, then the thrust of the ongoing course of Results will inevitably tend to be instrumental to the needs of the powerful. The process cannot help but appear to be captured by them.[31] It must be understood, however, that it is possible to accept the CLS critique that judicial doctrine is indeterminate and that the judicial process tends to function in a way that is instrumental to the needs of the powerful, and, further, to understand how this comes about, without having to conclude that judges are engaged *en masse* in a knowing and intentional violation of the judicial commitment to the Rule of Law. Rather, these circumstances come about by inadvertency, the consequences of a larger process that lies at the core of what it means to be human.

Ritual

Turn now from the act of deciding to the opinion. As we have seen, the opinion appears to be an after the fact rationalization of the Result that the court has determined. That is, rather than explaining *why* the court decided as it did, it seems instead to be an exercise in justifying what the court did. In terms of a portrayal of the *act of deciding*, the opinion is hollow.[32]

The ready term for a hollow act of this sort is "mere ritual"—which would suggest that the court is "just going through the motions" in offering the opinion. Consider, however, this definition of ritual. In terms of form, ritual is "symbolic behavior that is socially standardized and repetitive."[33] It is "action wrapped in a web of symbolism."[34] In terms of function, ritual is "a form of rhetoric, the propagation of a message through a complex symbolic performance."[35] That is, there is always an efficacious process with considerable substantive consequences occurring on the occasion of the performance of "mere ritual". Neither a court, nor anyone else, is "just going through the motions" in performing a ritual.

The Problem of Judicial Authority

Why is the judiciary routinely engaged in this particular ritual? And what is the message being propagated by this complex symbolic performance? By way of understanding the nature of this ritualistic performance, consider another aspect of the judicial process, the constraints that come to bear upon it.

The first we have already considered—the Rule of Law with its two core commitments. A second constraint is institutional in nature. In an important sense, our judicial process began to take form in eleventh century England as the Angevin monarchy sought to free the realm from the formalized violence of the feudal order literally by offering "better justice"—a way of resolving disputes that yielded outcomes that were, to the disputants, preferable to the results of interpersonal violence. The judicial officers who carried out this process of dispute resolution functioned explicitly as, and were understood to be, the representatives of the King in giving this better justice.

Because, however, of the separation of power among three coordinate branches of government in our constitutional structure, the role of our judiciary is considerably complex. Unlike the eleventh century judiciary, our judiciary is formally independent—judges are not the personal representatives of the executive, or of the legislature. Thus, the authority of the judiciary is not formally backed up by the other branches.

Moreover, a considerable aspect of the judicial role—the power of judicial review over the actions of the other two branches—is not expressly textually based; instead, it grew consequentially out of a course of judicial decision making.[36] Thus, this power is in effect bootstrapped;[37] there are no constitutive justifications for it independent of the justifications that the judiciary itself offers.

In addition, there is the political dimension of the judicial role. As a consequence of the assumed power of review, the nature of the questions that come before the judiciary takes on a particular, and particularly intensive, character—as Alexis de Tocqueville incisively observed, "There is hardly a political question in the United States which does not sooner or later turn into a judicial one."[38]

There is another facet to this political dimension—judges come to office by appointment or election in the political process. Thus, judges are a product of the political process, and they are intensively involved with the great political issues of the day. Yet, there is little in terms of their formal constitutive authority to distinguish the judiciary from the partisan political actors in our public processes.

Finally, in a very real sense, the judiciary has neither the resources nor the practical power to enforce its decisions. Instead, judges must, for the enforcement of their decisions, look to independent officials who come to office either by standing for election or by appointment within another branch of government. That is, they must depend on independent officials—over whose actions they have assumed the power of review—who have a political constituency and, immediately or ultimately, a political agenda.

In a very substantial sense, then, even within a political system founded on the concept of "the consent of the governed", what the judiciary does is not authoritative of itself; the judiciary does not have authority simply by virtue of holding office. Rather, the judiciary must continually earn authority. Just like its medieval counterpart, it must generate citizen commitment to the Rule of Law by offering a preferable process of dispute resolution. The citizenry must come to see that what they do is authoritative.

How does the judiciary earn authority? In a practical sense, this can be defined in terms of the judicial audience and its understanding of the Rule of Law. If citizen commitment is to be generated and maintained, then the losing party must still be able to see that the process is nevertheless preferable to self-help. That is, the court must not send the losing party away demoralized. It can hardly be avoided that the losing party will be disappointed—"I am sorry that I lost, but I can understand why." The authority of the court is undermined, however, if the losing party reacts, "I am sorry that I lost, and I was done an injustice."

Similarly, the general audience of the judiciary must see that the judiciary is living up to its commitment to settle disputes by appealing to an autonomous law. At the level of the common understanding of the Rule of Law, the court must engage in justice as regularity—following precedent rather than "making the law."

It is not difficult to describe what earning authority amounts to in practice. Carrying this out, also as a matter of practicalities, however, is far more complex. First, the two criteria can conflict. Assume that a judge faithfully reflects the current mix of values in society—Mythic values and emergent values as well as elite values. By doing so, often enough she will be able to avoid having a demoralized losing party only if the values implicit in the Result depart from the values embedded in precedent. In such instances, she can satisfy one criterion of the task of earning authority only by violating the other.

Second, as we have seen, the very embeddedness of the judiciary in the ongoing process of public discourse works powerfully to prevent the judge from reflecting this mix of values faithfully—the judicial hunch will tend to reflect only elite values. In these instances, she will consequently run a very substantial risk of demoralizing the losing party, and thereby violate one criterion of earning authority. If, in addition, elite values themselves are in a state of flux, she might well also depart from the tenor of the values embedded in precedent, and thereby violate the other criterion as well.

When we saw earlier that the judicial opinion appeared to be the enactment of a ritual, this raised two questions—why does the judiciary use the opinion as a ritual? and, what is the message that the judiciary is thereby seeking to propagate? We can now see what the answers to these questions might be. As we have just seen, the judiciary clearly will have considerable difficulty in earning authority by what they do—that is, by their act of deciding.

The occasion of the opinion, however, the purported explanation of the act of deciding, offers the opportunity for the judiciary to seek to earn authority by what they say. That is, the opinion, which is ritualistic in form, takes on the function of ritual if it rhetorically propagates a message. It must function as an argument—to convince its audience that its decision is authoritative.

In order to be efficacious, the argument must address two matters—that the losing party ought not be demoralized by the outcome, and that the general audience ought to understand that the court, by way of reaching the outcome, was faithful to the judiciary's Rule of Law commitment. Clearly, the occasion of the opinion does provide the opportunity to make those arguments.

The court can conform the Result to the Rule of Law criterion of justice as regularity by constructing a rationale that weaves it into the fabric of precedent. This is not a difficult task. Judicial doctrine is not deterministic of Results. And, it reflects a shifting mix of values. Thus, the appropriate principles can almost always be found in the body of precedent.

The court can conform the Result to the criterion of avoiding demoralization by seeking to sway the beliefs of the losing party. The outcome might indeed be contrary to the losing party's interests. The opinion, however, provides the court with the rhetorical opportunity to blind the losing party to the fact that the decision is contrary to her interests, or to convince her that her interests, and the values underlying them, are not substantial enough to deserve protection, or to demonstrate to her that other interests, and their underlying values, are more deserving of protection.[39] If the court succeeds in any of these ways, the losing party will not be demoralized, and the opinion will be successful in conveying its message.

The Power of Ritual

What of ritual of itself? How does it achieve its purposes? What *are* its purposes? And why are those purposes important?

Because the judicial opinion is a ritual, it has considerably greater importance than it would have if it were simply an exposition of the judicial act of deciding, for the reason that ritual is a central function of all political societies. It is indispensable to the creation of social solidarity.[40] "If symbols and rituals are used to build political reality, it is because, as humans, we can do it no other way."[41]

All societies "feel the need of upholding and reaffirming at regular intervals the collective sentiments and the collective ideas which make its unity and its personality."[42] And the fact of the judicial process—the fact, that is, that people do bring their disputes to it—is an important indicator that there is social solidarity. At a most basic level, there is no solidarity if people do not disavow violence as a means of settling disputes.

The efficacy of ritual derives from its combining of the realm of the emotional with the realm of the cognitive. "The 'ultimate force of symbols ... depends at least as much on their power to stir the emotions' as on their cognitive content."[43] Rituals do not, however, "simply excite, they also instruct. But the potency of that instruction depends heavily on the power of ritual to place the individual in a receptive frame of mind."[44] Ritual accomplishes its purposes because of the emotional dimension—"an exchange takes place between the emotional and the cognitive, and the emotions aroused in ritual infuse the cognitive view fostered by the rite, rendering it compelling."[45]

The ritual of the judicial process in general, and of the judicial opinion in particular, does not, of course, provide the overt emotional punch of, say, a parade, or a political rally. Nor, in the typical case, does it carry the immediacy of the parade or the rally for the overwhelming majority of the judicial audience. The emotional dimension, however, is nevertheless abundantly present. The judicial opinion is an integral element of a larger process that is packed with formalized elements that come to bear upon all immediate participants—costume, architecture, procedure, oath, stylized locution in both form and substance—all bespeaking the solemnity and seriousness of what is occurring, all demanding the submission of the participants, and all designed to generate respectful awe on the part of the participants and observers.

The court does not render its decision at the conclusion of the process of argumentation; instead, it defers the act of deciding, allowing for the opportunity for calm, reasoned deliberation. The opinion itself typically follows a particular structured sequence of elements. Certain kinds of stylized locution dominate.[46] And, once the decision is made, the opinion does not simply issue from the court; rather, it is typically announced, in the formal setting and with the formal procedures of the larger process, and, often enough, to the breathless attention of the news media.

Although, for most ritual, the venue, the trappings, and the actions of the principals dominate the sensory impact on the observer as much as what is said, ritual is a form of rhetoric.[47] Successful ritual "creates an emotional state that makes the message uncontestable because it is framed in such a way as to be seen as inherent in the way things are. It presents a picture of the world that is so emotionally compelling that it is beyond debate."[48]

In the judicial process, where what is said is more overtly present than what is acted out and with what trappings it is acted out, emotional framing is still strongly present and functionally important. Whether the event is a parade along Main Street or a parade of witnesses before a jury, the substance of ritual's message is conveyed as much by the techniques of emotional framing as by the syntax of what is said. Thus, ritual is "a potent means of legitimation because it offers a way to unite a particular image of the universe with a strong emotional attachment to that image."[49] Through that emotional attachment, ritual "converts the obligatory into the desirable."[50]

In the judicial process, whether by ritual act or by word, the core message is, "We are rendering justice by what we say and do here today." Most importantly of all, then, ritual does not simply enact reality; rather, it creates reality—ritual "not only gives meaning to the universe, it becomes part of the universe."[51] Ritual thus is the performance by which we create, or sustain, our Worlds. "Men possess thoughts, but symbols possess men."[52] Ideas create Worlds—our Worlds, as systems of meaning, are conceptual rather than physical. But, as well, Worlds create ideas—the act of ritual, the acting out of a World, creates the ideas that generate our Worlds.

And the centrality of ritual to Worldmaking is crucially relevant to the purpose of the ritualization of the judicial opinion—creating and sustaining judicial authority—because the connection between ritual and authority is so strong. "[T]he hallmark of power is the construction of reality."[53] To perform a ritual is to exercise a World-making rhetorical power.

And the ritualistic exercise of power thereby creates authority in the performer, because authority is "the belief that a person has the right to exercise influence over others' behavior."[54] Because authority is itself an abstraction[55]—it is a belief by one person about another, and thus is an element of our World of meaning—"people can conceive of who has authority and who does not only through symbols and rituals."[56] And the judiciary, because it is obliged always to earn authority, must turn to ritual in order to insure that it will be treated as authoritative, as the giver of justice. "A man becomes a king because he comes to be treated as a king."[57]

Conclusion

We began with the "scandal of abduction" raised by the CLS critique of the law, which holds that judicial doctrine is indeterminant and that the judicial process is captured—it works to serve the interests of the economic and social elite. This is not a trivial charge, because it amounts to the conclusion that the judiciary is engaged in a systematic and wholesale violation of the general understanding of the Rule of Law. Our analysis of the nature of the judicial process concluded, however, that, because of the human condition—in particular, the necessity of, the constraints on, and the consequences of, the endeavor of Worldmaking—judicial reasoning is unavoidably abductive rather than deductively formal, then, necessarily, the nature of dispute resolution consequentially amounts to an ongoing process of law-making, and any statement of the law as judicial doctrine will necessarily be indeterminant. Thus, the first element of the CLS critique does no more than describe a necessary consequence of the judicial process.

Our analysis also shows, however, that, because of the non-foundational nature of values, and because of the way in which values come to bear in the judicial process, there will be a tendency for the course of dispute resolution to reflect more strongly the values of the economic and political elite. To the extent that this tendency occurs, the course of dispute resolution will tend to be functionalist in terms of the needs of the power elite. Thus, the second element of the critique—the charge that the law is captured—carries a substantial degree of plausibility. This capture, however, is more likely the result of judicial inadvertence than it is of intentional judicial participation.

Finally, our analysis reveals that, because of the structure of our public institutions, the judiciary is obliged to engage in an ongoing process of earning authority. The constraints of the popular understanding of the Rule of Law demand of the judiciary that it resolve disputes by the dictates of an autonomous law. The reality of the process of dispute resolution, however, necessitates that the judiciary function as law-makers rather than as law-followers. As a consequence, the judicial opinion functions not as an explanation of the act of deciding but instead as the principal tool available to the judiciary for meeting its obligation to earn authority. The opinion thereby functions as a powerful ritual, a rhetorical exercise designed to convince the judicial audience of the authoritativeness of what the judiciary does.

Thus, it is possible to see that the workings of the judicial process are not unjust by the fact that a judge's act of deciding is abductive in nature. It is also possible to see, however, that the process can accomplish considerable injustice behind the authority-generating ritual of the judicial opinion. To the extent that the CLS charge of capture is accurate, then the extent to which the judiciary nevertheless retains authority attests to the power of ritual.

What, then, of the problem of capture? My argument comes down to the proposition that the judicial process will not, because it cannot, generate doctrine that will converge on a determinant and controlling law. Moreover, the same factors that prevent this convergence also disable us from constructing *a priori* a coherent and rationally complete body of law. Thus, the legal science movement that began in the late nineteenth century must finally be understood to have been an exercise in futility. More importantly, the problem of injustice engendered by the phenomenon of capture cannot be solved by an autonomous law because such a law simply is not available.

The problem of capture is a matter of the utmost gravity—it must be addressed. Its solution, which I can describe here only suggestively, derives from the understanding that law is not some mysterious entity that lies outside of us; rather, it *is* us—a principled way of acting, of having a World. The concept of "a government of laws and not of men" is an empty shibboleth because it is incapable of realization. Ironically, we truly do have a democracy—we rule ourselves, and only we can. There is no "the law", as some reified thing, outside of us that can rule us. Thus, the solution lies in the direction of performance—all those who participate in, and make up the audience of, the rituals of the judicial process must perform their roles with greater sophistication.

My argument has presented a definition of justice in terms of how well judicial Results reflect faithfully the continually developing mix of societal values. To state the matter succinctly, the participants in the judicial process—the judiciary and counsel—must perform with greater awareness of the way in which values come to bear. And the general audience must come to a more sophisticated understanding of the concept of the Rule of Law; the audience must understand and accept what cannot be changed in the judicial process, and it must demand that the process yield justice rather than rhetoric.[58]

* Professor of Law, Washington & Lee University.

Notes

1. Because of the broad power of judicial review that developed early in the nineteenth century, it is not inaccurate to define "the law" as being the body of rules and principles that may be induced from the opinions of the various courts as they go about their function of resolving disputes. This essay proceeds on the basis of such a definition.

2. Karl N. Llewellyn, *The Bramble Bush: On Our Law and Its Study* 12 (1960).

3. Laura J. Kalman, *Legal Realism at Yale*, 1927–1960 14–20 (1986).

4. *E.g.*, Mark V. Tushnet, "A Marxist Analysis of American Law", 1 *Marxist Perspectives* 96 (1978).

5. In terms that are unavoidably non-gender-neutral, the old aphorism holds that we have "a government of laws and not of men."

6. Jerome Frank, "What Courts Do In Fact" (pt. 1), 26 *Ill. L. Rev.* 645, 653 (1931).

7. Joseph C. Hutcheson, Jr., "The Judgment Intuitive: The Function of the 'Hunch' in Judicial Decision", 14 *Cornell L. Q.* 274 (1929).

8. For a succinct description of abduction, see Umberto Eco, *Semiotics and the Philosophy of Language* 39–43 (1986); Charles Sanders Peirce, "Abduction and Induction", in *Philosophical Writings of Peirce* 150–156 (Justus Buchler ed., 1955).

9. *See* Ferdinand de Saussure, *Course in General Linguistics* (Charles Bally & Albert Sechehaye eds., 1966).

10. Jacques Derrida, *Of Grammatology* (1976).

11. Charles Sanders Peirce, "Division of Signs", in 2 *The Collected papers of Charles Sanders Peirce* ¶228, at 135 (Charles Hartshorne & Paul Weiss eds., 1931–1935).

12. *Id.*

13. Walker Percy, *Lost in the Cosmos: The Last Self-Help Book* 100 (1983). Percy's proposition is based on a substantial exploration and development of Peirce's semiotic theory.

14. Mary Douglas, "Introduction to Grid/Group Analysis" in *Essays in the Sociology of Perception* 1 (Mary Douglas ed. 1982) [hereinafter cited as "*Introduction*"].

15. *Id.*

16. *Id.* at 2.

17. *Id.* at 1.

18. For a general treatment, see Michael Thompson *et al.*, *Cultural Theory* (1990) [hereinafter cited as "*Cultural Theory*"].

19. *Introduction*, *supra* note 14, at 5.

20. *Id.* at 7.

21. Shelby M. Givens, "The Walk that Wasn't Pedestrian", *The Washington Post*, July 12, 1992, at C8.

22. Stanley Fish, *Is There A Text in this Class? The Authority of Interpretive Communities* 322–337 (1980).

23. See generally, *id.*

24. This is treated at some length in *Cultural Theory*, *supra* note 18. The process echoes Thomas S. Kuhn's conceptualization of scientific paradigms that he developed in *The Structure of Scientific Revolutions* (2d ed. 1970).

25. Relatively [but not ultimately], stable societies are more likely to form when they are dominated by either Hierarchy or Individualism. David Ostrander, "One- and Two-Dimensional Models of the Distribution of Beliefs", in *Essays in the Sociology of Perception* 14 (Mary Douglas ed., 1982). In a large, cosmologically heterogeneous society, the power elite will tend to be made up of individuals who hold either of these cosmologies. As a result, there will be a tendency for the ranks of Atomized Subordination to grow:

> The groups [Communal and Hierarchical] . . . expel and downgrade dissenters; the competition of individualists . . . pushes those who are weak into the more regulated areas where their options are restricted and they end by doing what they are told.

Introduction, *supra* note 14, at 6. As this proceeds, there will be further tendency for this growing segment of society to be attracted to Communalism as the best alternative to improving their powerless condition.

26. Because the judicial process is an integral part of our political system, it might be more apt to use the term *ideologies* rather than cosmologies. The theme, however, remains the same—values; and the ideologies of Conservatism, Libertarianism, and Liberalism more than roughly correspond to the cosmologies of Hierarchy, Individualism, and Communalism.

27. See *supra* note 25.

28. Indeed, a consequentialist way of defining power is in terms of the capacity to exert an efficacious presence in the process of public discourse, which, in a practical sense, amounts to the capacity to imbue the ground of the language of public discourse with a particular cosmology. This is "power in the third dimension" in Steven Lukes's taxonomy of power—shaping the "perceptions, cognitions and preferences" of others. Steven Lukes, *Power: A Radical View* 24 (1974) [hereinafter cited as "*Power*"].

29. The dynamic is described briefly in note 25. As this occurs, the values embedded in the ground of the language of public discourse will change. Daniel T. Rodgers, *Contested Truths: Keywords in American Politics since Independence* (1987) insightfully traces the constantly and radically shifting meanings of the principal terms of our "textually stable" Cultural Myth [the words remain the same, but the meanings do not].

30. *Introduction*, *supra* note 14, at 1.

31. For an incisive and extended description of this tendency toward instrumentalism, see Morton J. Horwitz, *The Transformation of American Law* 1780–1860 (1977).

32. A ready parallel is provided by the typical run of speeches delivered on the floor of each of the two houses of the United States Congress; the business—the actual decision making—goes on elsewhere.

33. David I. Kertzer, *Ritual, Politics, and Power* 9 (1988) [hereinafter cited as "*Ritual*"].

34. *Id.*

35. *Id.* at 101.

36. *Marbury v. Madison*, 5 U.S. 137 (1803).

37. This term is not being used in a pejorative sense. Worldmaking itself is a process of bootstrapping; and the judicial process is an integral part of the process of Worldmaking.

38. Alexis de Tocqueville, *Democracy in America* 270 (J.P. Mayer ed., 12th ed. 1988).

39. *Power*, *supra* note 28, at 24.

40. *Ritual*, *supra* note 33, at 62.

41. *Id.* at 95.

42. *Id.* at 62, quoting Emile Durkheim, *The Elementary Forms of the Religious Life* 427 (1915).

43. *Ritual*, *supra* note 33, at 99.

44. *Id.*

45. *Id.* at 100.

46. Some styles of locution are just not acceptable to the judicial audience. Recall the indignant response that met Justice Harry Blackmun's emotional statement that began, "Poor Joshua!" in his dissenting opinion in *DeShaney v. Winnebago County Dept. of Soc. Servs.*, 489 U.S. 189, 213 (1989), in which he decried the decision of the majority to deny a remedy against a social services agency that had knowingly and recklessly stood by while an extended course of physical abuse caused severe harm to a young boy, leaving him profoundly retarded for life.

47. *Ritual*, *supra* note 33, at 101.

48. *Id.*

49. *Id.* at 40.

50. *Id.*

51. *Id.* at 9.

52. *Id.* at 5, quoting Max Lerner, *Ideas for the Ice Age* 235 (1941).

53. *Ritual*, *supra* note 33, at 5.

54. *Id.* at 24.

55. *Id.*

56. *Id.* And this is a two-edged sword. Consider that judges are subject to disciplinary measures as much for acting, in court or out, with a lack of decorum as for corruption.

57. *Id.* at 25.

58. This essay is a substantially revised version of a paper delivered at the Annual Meeting of the Society for the Advancement of American Philosophy, March 1995, Waltham, Massachusetts. The author gratefully acknowledges the support of the Frances Lewis Law Center of Washington & Lee University for its generous support in the preparation of this essay.

Chapter Two
What Should One Think of Judicial Ritual in Law?

byAntoine Garapon

Summary and Translation

by Vivian Grosswald Curran*

The goal of legal anthropology is not just to seek the law of the other, i. e., the juridical phenomena in societies that are non-western, historical or distant. It is also to question the other in our law, i. e., the role of the symbolic in our juridical life. When western anthropologists study a non-western society, they instinctively are suspicious of the intentions expressed by its members Thus, for example, if they attend a ritual whose purpose is to assure fertility and make rain come, they will focus on the dances, costumes, songs, etc. Why not apply the same method to our own societies? What would a researcher see who "disembarked" at a trial? He would notice the robes, the *décor* of the room, the superannuated language.

Great scholars, such as Durkheim or Bourdieu, all advise us to beware of the illusion of instantaneous knowledge or understanding, i. e., of common sense. Of which spontaneous interpretations should one be wary? Should one guard against seeing in the legal ritual only folklore, unworthy of interest in comparison to law? Others see in the rituals of law only a wish to intimidate those subject to justice, and, thus, to reinforce domination. Those two attitudes are too conclusory, for they seek the function of rituals before having studied it!

Using as my point of departure Durkheim's view that "the conventional nature of a practice or of an institution never should be assumed," I have wagered that rituals had a meaning that can, in addition, rival that of law. I shall define the ritual in law restrictively, as the collection of rules of time, space, language, clothing and bodily postures that give trials their symbolic framework. Legal rites are inextricably linked to myth. Accordingly, the myth of origin in Æschylus will be examined first; and then the myth of man's fall in Kafka. It will be shown that attempts to distance the symbolic framework are negative and that, ultimately, justice must be conceived in combination with, rather than against, ritual.

Æschylus: The Birth of the Debate and Framework

The dilemma in Greek mythology of Orestes, raised by Apollo and the Furies, is whether, as the latter declare, Orestes owes obedience to Clytemnestra, his mother, or, as Apollo maintains, to Agamemnon, his murdered father. Orestes' acquittal inaugurates a new social order. The defeated Furies, representing matriarchy, are finally appeased by Athena and agree to a pact pursuant to which they will watch over and protect the city's fecundity and renounce revenge. They then become stable.

Judicial Ritual and Original Violence

The classic transition is from an old ritual that mechanically and cruelly applied revenge to a new conception of ritual that distributes speech and organizes the debate such that its foundational cruelty is not eliminated, but domesticated, stabilized. Significantly, the old, far from being extinguished, becomes integrated into the new. Tragedy teaches us to consider the old foundation on which the new edifice of a political community rests, an edifice formed of fears and anguish that subsequently are overcome and displaced, but also preserved.

This paradigm of tragedy illustrates the birth of trial as both debate and framework The meaning and economy of the trial's ritualistic character is to be found in the obscure connections between judicial debate, violence and tradition. As René Girard has shown, symbolic representations of violence allow society to eschew violence with trials linked to the sacrificial.

Power and Authority

Authority is the energy extricated from the foundation. The function of the rite is to repeat the foundational experience, to reproduce each time a distancing of revenge and of violence. The more society innovates and distances itself from tradition, the greater it needs to recall the event forcefully.

Tradition and Argument

In the relation between foundation and innovation lies an enigma far greater than that of the relation between power and violence. The idea of law as a threat, symbolized by the Furies, remains operative. The Furies, being *shown*, having become a spectacle, are stronger, but they also have become silenced in the process, and no longer participate in or interfere with the public discussion of norms.

Tragedy illuminates that the modern trial does not have its origin in a repression of tradition, but rather in the incorporation of tradition into the debate. Law and justice are not, respectively, simply matters of normative discourse and debate. Both need to have social roots, which means integration into a context, without which they cannot subsist. The symbol, then, is the link between text and context.

The framework is perception: its action is not immediately comprehensible to reason. It is presence, all-encompassing, the symbolic universe that is itself a representation of the universe. By contrast, language is linear, that which permits arguments to proceed in logical fashion and to exclude possible meanings in order to reach a solution. It contrasts in this with the symbol, which, by definition, has multiple meanings. The framework is immobile; it is repetitious, sensitive to political regimes, to time and to history. Not being a process, it does not evolve. It is a non-event, necessary for an event to be produced, and that event is the trial.

Like the United States Supreme Court, France' s courthouses are replete with the busts of great jurists, of terrifying images, of national emblems and of historical frescoes. In reminding us of the past, of tradition, they open for us the doors to eternity.

The framework takes the place of tradition in societies that have gone beyond tradition. No collective space is conceivable without a culture that procures a symbolic expression of identity for it. The Furies are there, ever-present, steadily contemplating man's debates with their eyes of stone.

Kafka: Ritual Without Debate

Kafka's is the tale of the fall-the final blurring between the individual event and the collective story that gives it meaning. With the disappearance of meaning, only the obsessive framework is left, crazy images, unable to be the foundation for debate. The Kafkaesque experience is that of a justice which is no longer anything but a context, a context without law or deliberation, which exists on its own and no longer elicits horror, as it did for Orestes, but, rather, anguish.

In *The Trial,* space itself is without structure. It answers to no law. Law has no space of its own. It is devoid of interiority. In Kafka's work, power no longer is in the form of a pyramid, as the law would have us think, but, rather, fragmented and linear, proceeding by contiguity and not by height or distance; hence, the importance of the inferior official.

The "outside" is no longer distinguishable from the "inside." It is not space that is problematic with Kafka, but, rather, the Law, and the absence of language of separation. In *The Trial*, Kafka invites us to reflect on the symbolic function of trials, on the need to establish distinctions, starting with those of a special nature.

We do not look at Kafka's images of justice; they look at us. Kafka is not able to mourn the tradition that modernity has silenced. Kafka lies in the interstices of a world that is ending, based on the transcendence of God, and an autonomous world about to be born.

Justices Without Ritual?

The 20th century has been marked by an insane framework that harbors sinister parodies in lieu of true debate, and that has been deserted by democratic law.

Denunciation of an Oppressive Framework

The question which arises is whether the symbolic framework does not ultimately harm and detract from justice. Rituals answer to a logic that reveals the true nature of the trial. It is not the search for responsibility that gives trials social justification, but, rather, the need to purge the social emotion born of crime. As Durkheim said, an act does not shock the common conscience because it is a crime; it is a crime because it shocks the common conscience.

René Girard points out that the judicial system removes its function from sight as soon as it is the only one to reign. Just like ritual sacrifice, it hides, despite its simultaneously revealing that which makes it equatable with revenge. The only difference between revenge by the judicial system and all others is that this one is the last-it will not itself be avenged.

Judicial ritual assigns a space to each participant and thus allows each discourse to be situated. It is essential for each participant in a trial to have his/her assigned, clearly identifiable, space: the perspective of the dissent, of the prosecution, etc.

The media represents itself as a more accessible and expressive means of representation, more faithful to the reality and diversity of opinions; in short, it is more democratic that the procedural framework of the courtroom. But a trial is a very complex and sophisticated mixture that allows the combination in a unity of time, place and action of a language and performance meaning on the one hand, and of a theatrical production on the other; in other words, an intellectual and logical operation, a social ceremony designed to purge collective emotion. In a trial, everyone must hear the same thing, and nothing else, about the case. The jurors must see everything which is proffered in evidence, and hear everything to make up their minds and render a fair decision. The performance is possible thanks to the selection of what is to be represented. This is the difference between a public and a mob: the former watch a spectacle from beginning to end, while the latter do not compose a group; nor is there any in what is represented.

Therein lies all the difference between the contradictory and the right of response. What is the value of a right to respond via the media a few days after the damage has been done, usually followed by a few lines of disclaimers? There is no equality of weapons in a controversy; even worse, the media might, on the contrary, merely reproduce the inequities of fact and the relation of force. Controversy is reduced to a spectacle closer to bullfighting than to reasonable discussion. The goal of communication becomes communication itself, the distraction it offers, the noise it makes, the money and power it obtains, rather than linking subjectivities by means of a code. Contradiction is distinguishable from controversy and cannot be satisfied by exercising a right to respond. Let there be no mistake about it: the concept of a superior truth which would not need to be established through contradiction, the will to know everything, justifies the most barbaric inquisitorial means, those which our law has spent so much time getting rid of. Regulated exchange of arguments is the very contrary to justice.

To Think Justices With Ritual

The media will never be able to replace justice for lack of an appropriate framework. We can see a link between ritual and the construction of meaning and thus judicial truth. We understand—a *contrario*—how justice derives from this framework. Trials are, in reality, co-constructions of meaning. Procedure and contradiction are only a certain ethic of storytelling. Trials are *a priori* no more protected than is the press from the danger of constructing such imaginary stories, but, paradoxically, its framework protects the trial more than does that of the press. The guarantee that the judiciary offers is the ability to name and to reflect the telling of the tale and thus to master it a little, which is never the case with television. The central problem with justice is that the trial controls the telling of the tale, i.e., the way the facts are presented, proved and interpreted. On television the construction of reality is implicit and is never raised for discussion. The presence or the absence of contradiction depends upon the possibility of discussing the construction of reality made by others.

Justice in our democratic societies is threatened less by interference from political power, which concerns only a small number of cases, than by the sacrificial mechanism from which no institution can rid us completely, because it lies at the very heart of the judicial right. The illusion of direct democracy, the fantasy of a democracy without a stage, announces the populism flourishing in Europe today. The liberal ideology of a spontaneous harmonization of the interests of each individual under the gaze of the best arbitrator that exists in a democracy, i.e., public opinion, forgets the wisdom of the Greeks which reminds us that the more numerous the crowd, the blinder it is. The institution of a place of decision making is not the same as the smaller places of negotiation, nor even as the larger place that is the whole of public space. The State must guarantee the proper functioning of justice in a protected space, defined within the public space. Macchiavelli said it was important in a republic to have institutions that furnish the mass of citizens the means to express their aversion towards another citizen, for, if there are no legal means, they will use illegal ones. A democracy that would not represent itself on the stage of its institutions not only would not be the carrier of an ideal, but would be threatened by a regressive violence.

The tragedy of our era is that the disappearance of the judicial ritual brings us back to the state of nature. As Montesquieu said, the democratic principle becomes corrupt, not only when one loses the spirit of equality, but also when one has an extreme spirit of equality, and when each person wants to be equal to those whom he has chosen to lead him. For then the people want to do everything on its own, no longer to tolerate the power which it itself has conferred. An in-depth analysis of the judicial ritual leads us to revise our initial condemnation of it. The struggle for democracy insidiously has changes sides, such that, after years of considering institutions as being against democracy, we now must learn to preserve institutions from the extreme equality of which Montesquieu spoke.

All of this leads to the reconsideration and rehabilitation of rituals in trials. The question of rituals spans the entire history of humanity. We must rethink justice, not against ritual, but with it. What ritual reminds us of is the fundamental ambivalence in trials, for trials are composed of the best forms of justice and the worst forms of injustice.

There is no justice without adjustment to a public space that allows a public view of justice, but the public view, even while it guarantees the judge's neutrality, is impregnated simultaneously with hatred and irrationality. The paradox of justice is its publicity, without which there can be no justice worthy of the name, but which also is the realm of the sacrificial phenomenon. It is the irreducible ambivalence of the public gaze, at once a guarantee and a threat, both the condition for justice and the bearer of injustice, both antidote and poison. It is the paradox of the rite in that its denunciation in the name of a quest for greater authenticity allows for the individual's will to reform, but its suppression in the name of direct democracy destroys democracy. It is the paradox of the rule itself, of which our century, above all others, has been able to gauge the full danger. As Gilles Deleuze and Guattan Félix have put it, while nepotism has been identified since Montesquieu with power unfettered by laws, totalitarianism operates by hyperbolic affirmation of law.

How judge with ritual? Perhaps by becoming aware of its necessity rather than naively believing that breaking the thermometer will make the fever go down, and that negating the ritualistic of trials will make violence disappear from their origins. As Bourdieu has said, liberty does not reside in a magical negation of determinism, but in understanding the laws of reality. Prudence may lie in awareness of that prejudgment of the Furies, immobilized by a ritual that already had rendered its verdict before people began to deliberate.

* Visiting Assistant Professor of Law at the University of Pittsburgh.

Quefaut-il Penser du Rituel Judiciaire?

Antoine Garapon*

Le projet de l'anthropologie du droit n'est pas seulement de rechercher 1e droit chez l'autre, c'est-à-dire le phénomène juridique dans les sociétes non-occidentales, historiques ou éloignées mais c'est aussi questionner *l'autre dans notre droit,* c'est-à-dire la part du symbolique dans notre vie juridique. Quand des anthropologues occidentaux étudient une société non-occidentale, ils se méfient spontanément de l'intention exprimée par ses membres. Ainsi par exemple, s'ils assistent à une cérémonie rituelle destinée à s'assurer de la fécondité et faire venir la pluie, ils vont se concentrer sur les danses, les costumes, les chants, etc. Pourquoi ne pas appliquer la même méthode à nos propres sociétés? Que verrait d'abord un chercheur qui "débarquerait" dans un procès d'assises? Il remarquerait les robes, le décor de la salle d'audience, le langage suranné, etc.

Les grands auteurs, comme Durkheim ou Bourdieu, conseillent tous de se méfier *de l'illusion du savoir immédiat*, c'est-à-dire du sens commun.[1] En l'espèce de quelles interprétations spontanées faut-il se garder? De ne voir dans le rituel judiciaire que du folklore, peu digne d'intérêt comparé au droit. D'autres n'y voient que de la "poudre aux yeux", une volonté d'impressionner les justiciables et donc de renforcer la domination. Ces deux attitudes brûlent les étapes en cherchant une fonction au rituel avant même de l'avoir étudié! Méditant cette phrase de Durkheim: "*le caractère conventionnel d'une pratique ou d'une institution ne doit jamais être présumé*"[2], j'ai fait le pari que ces rites avaient un sens qui pouvait, de surcroît rivaliser avec le droit. Je donnerai au mot rituel judiciaire un sens restrictif, en le limitant à l'ensemble des règles de temps, de lieu, de langage, aux vêtements, aux postures corporelles qui donnent au procès son cadre symbolique. Participer à un rituel, c'est rentrer dans une communication non verbale dont le sens n'est pas maîtrisé par l'acteur; le rituel réalise ainsi "une solidarité sans consensus."[3] Entendu ainsi, il a été très peu étudié en tant que tel, si on fait abstraction du livre de Pat Carlen intitulé *Magistrate's Justice* et de quelques autres.[4] C'est unc notion plus restreinte du sous-ensemble des rites juridiques[5]: le paiement, la vente, etc. Il y a un rituel officiel du procès mais il y a maintenant beaucoup de rituels de la médiation, de la négociation. Autrement dit, l'opposition entre justice formelle rituelle et justice informelle non-rituelle ne résiste pas à l'analyse. Il y a du rituel partout, plus ou moins reconnaissable.

Alors que faut-il penser du rituel judiciaire? Quelle est sa signification et sa fonction? Le rite est indissociable du mythe: voilà pourquoi on commencera par remonter au *mythe de l origine* chez Eschyle (I) avant celui de la *chute* (II)que l'on trouvera cette fois chez Kafka (I). Nous verrons ensuite que les tentatives d'émancipation du cadre symbolique s'étant révélées négatives (III), on en est réduit à penser la justice *avec* et non plus *contre* le rituel (IV).

Eschyle: La Naissance du Debat et Cadre

Rappelons brièvement l'intrigue et l'enjeu de la tragédie. Oreste a tué sa mère Clytemnestre pour venger le meurtre par elle de son père Agamemnon Il est poursuivi par les Erinyes qui représentaient l'ancienne société tribale dans laquelle la filiation se faisait par la mère. Il trouve un défenseur dans la personne d'Apollon qui est traditionnellement l'interprète de Zeus. Le dilemme soulevé par Apollon et les Erinyes est donc le suivant: auquel de ses parents Oreste devait-il obéissance? A la mère disent les Erinyes; au père déclare Apollon. Le destin d'Oreste se trouve lié à cette confrontation entre la matriarcat et le patriarcat auquel il se substitue. Athéna institue un tribunal pour trancher; les voix sont égales et elle tranche en faveur d'Oreste parce que, dit-elle, "je n'ai pas eu de mère pour me mettre au monde... Sans réserve je suis pour le père. Dès lors je n'aurai pas d'égard particulier pour la mort d'une femme qui avait tué l'époux, gardien du foyer." Ce qu'inaugure l'acquittement d'Oreste, c'est la naissance d'un ordre social nouveau. Mais le récit ne s'arrête pas là et ce qui suit sera du plus grand intérêt pour le sens du rituel. Furieuses de leur défaite, les Erinyes promettent vengeance et en appellent à leur mère la nuit; Athena leur propose alors de devenir les gardiennes bienveillantes de la cité. A force de persuasion, Athéna finit par les convaincre et un pacte est conclu au terme duquel elles auront en charge la protection de la fécondité de la cité à condition d'abandonner l'antique Loi du talion: "que la poussière abreuvée de sang noir ne se paye pas en sa colère du sang de ses représailles qui font la ruine des cités! Que tous entre eux n'échangent que des joies remplies d'un mutuel amour" s'exclament-elles. Et Athéna de leur répondre: "Zeus, le dieu de la parole l'a emporté et mon obstination bienfaisante triomphe pour l'éternité." Les Erinyes se voient alors conférer le nom d'Eumenides, c'est-à-dire de "bienveillantes" et errantes qu'elles étaient elles deviennent stables.

Rituel Judiciaire et Violence Originaire

On relève classiquement l'opposition entre deux séries d'équations: spirituel-masculin-nouveau-olympien, d'une part et d'autre féminin-originel-instinctuel-ancien-démoniaque.[6] Ce récit met en scène le passage d'un vieux rituel qui appliquait mécaniquement et cruellement la vengeance dans une sorte de corps-à-corps sanguinaire à une nouvelle conception du rituel qui distribue la parole et organise le débat sur fond de cruauté non pas chassée mais domestiquée, stabilisée. Mais l'ancien loin d'être anéanti par le nouveau au contraire s'y intègre. Un des enseignements majeurs de la tragédie est donc la considération de ce "fonds ancien sur lequel repose le nouvel édifice d'une communauté politique [qui] est formé de craintes, d'angoisses natives, qui ont ensuite été surmontées, déplacées, et aussi préservées."[7] Cette tragédie met en récit la naissance du procès ou plus exactement la naissance conjointe du procès comme *débat* et comme *cadre.* C'est cette complémentarité qu'il faut approfondir. La tragédie nous livre en effet un enseignement sur les relations obscures qu'entretient le débat judiciaire avec la violence et la tradition. C'est dans ce rapport que l'on va chercher le sens et l'économie du rituel du procès.

La psychanalyse s'est interéssée à cette tragédiè à plus d'un titre. Pour saluer tout d'abord cette victoire du débat, du dieu de la parole contre le lien maternel et charnel, et donc la primauté de l'intellectualité sur les sens, de la présomption de paternité sur l'évidence du lien maternel. La psychanalyse permet d'expliquer ensuite la mutation de l'horreur et sa symbolisation dans le rituel. Le procès serait une répétition du crime par le truchement de la parole et de la procédure, une mise à mort symbolique de l'accusé qui ne seraient possible que grâce à l'effet d'occultation qu'opère le rituel. D'où la prolifération dans le rituel d'une symbolique cruelle souvent présente: qu'il s'agisse de l'aigle aux serres acérées, des gueules de lions, de l'épee et de toute la symbolique de nos salles d'audience. Peut-être que cette violence enfermée dans le rituel et dont les images arrivent à peine à notre conscience, remplissent un rôle de dédommagement. Ces vengeances terribles, ces gueules de lion, ces lances tranchantes non seulement nous inspirent le respect mais nous libèrent de notre agressivité en nous la restituant sous forme symbolisée, euphemisée. Ces représentations cruelles et terrible nous permettent de ne pas l'être a notre tour, elles désintéressent notre violence en nous offrant le spectacle terrifiant mais libérateur de la violence comme le soutient René Girard. Elles témoignent de la parenté du procès avec le sacrifice qu'il a si bien mis en lumière, nous rappellent de manière sensible la présence souterraine des Erinyes qui veillent toutes proches et rappellent la loi ancienne sur laquelle repose le pacte de notre justice.

Pouvoir et Autorité

Peut-être que les Erinyes cachées, les Eumenides dans leur grotte qui inspirent crainte et nous rappellent la violence originaire de la vengeance qui sommeille dans tout procès nous renseigne sur le fondement anthropologique de *l 'autorité.* Qu'est-ce que l'autorité? C'est plus, nous dit Hannah Arendt dans *La crise de la culture,* "qu'un 'indice', qu'une 'trace', qu'un 'écran' ou une 'dissimulation,' mais [c'est] un *complément* devenu pour nous un manque-bref un relais à la fois indispensable et impossible."[8] L'autorité est l'énergie tirée de la *fondation.* Répéter l'expérience de fondation, voilà la fonction du rituel, la repéter indéfiniment autant de fois que les Erinyes auront poussé leurs grognements infâmes, c'est-à-dire a chaque fois que la foule aura été échauffée, la haine raciale aiguisée, la passion sacrificielle reveillée. Ecoutons ce qu'en dit un jeune avocat que la politique n'avait pas encore rendu célèbre, Francois Mitterrand: "cette premiére tentative où les dieux se mêlent encore au jeu et aux passions des hommes, mais seulement pour leur apprendre à se passer d'eux, garde sa force et résonne au-delà du temps d'Eschyle. Elle demeure un point de repère que l'Histoire a préservé de l'oubli en signe de respect sans doute et peut-être d'amour, pour les vrais commencements."[9]

"C'est l'énergie perdurante de l'acte de fondation, l'énergie des commencements" pour reprendre la belle expression de Paul Ricœur. Voilà le sens de la *répétition* qui est le propre de tout rite: il répète inlassablement le moment de la fondation du procès et reproduit à chaque fois ce travail sans fin de mise à distance de la vengeance et de la violence fondatrice. Il répète dans l'atemporalité du symbole la fondation que personne mieux qu'Eschyle a mis en recit. Il n'est pas surprenant que plus une société innove et se détache de la tradition plus elle ait besoin de rappeler avec force cet événement. L'autorité est indispensable en raison du caractère "évasif" du pouvoir. "Le pouvoir est volatil, la fondation est ce qui le rend durable; parce que l'action est plus fragile que l'œuvre, le pouvoir dont elle émane a toujours besoin d'être augmenté par quelques équivalents de l'expérience romaine de la fondation."[10]

Tradition et Argumentation

Ce récit de la fondation n'est pas la simple émergence du débat public, la victoire éclatante de la raison sur la tradition mais une mise en scène de la réconciliation entre raison et tradition, du rapport nécessaire entre autorité et pouvoir délibératif. "Dans ce rapport entre fondation et innovation réside une énigme bien plus grande que celle du rapport entre pouvoir et violence."[11] Les Euménides continuent de terrifier une fois sous terre: "L'idée du droit comme menace qu'elles incarnent reste opérante... En les accueillant, Athéna, loin de disqualifier l'interprétation du droit par les Erinyes, en fait, avec le culte qu'elle instaure, l'objet d'une représentation publique et permanente. L'Erinye est d'autant plus puissante qu'elle est montrée; mais, de manière complémentaire, parce qu'elle est montrée, devenue spectacle, elle n'interfére plus dans la discussion publique des normes."[12]

Dans les Euménides, les divinités que les humains invoquaient pour justifier leurs droits rentrent elles-mêmes dans un débat juridique argumenté: elles se soumettent délibérément aux règles de la discussion publique. La solution juste ne peut plus être simplement déduite: elle "se constitue de manière pratique au sein d'une activité intersubjective," c'est-à-dire le débat. L'Aréopage est une instance où l'égalité abstraite inhérente au concept de justice se manifeste directement dans le compte des votes. .. La justice résultera de la combinaison des décisions partielles. L'idée de droit s'est transformée en procédure."[13] "Dans les débats publics, le droit pour être efficace doit aussi satisfaire une exigence de sens; il sera alors toujours réinvesti de contenus sémantiques d'expériences vécues, exprimées au moyen de symboles traditionnels... Il n'y a donc pas de contradiction, pour le débat démocratique institué avec la réforme, entre la nouveauté de la procédure —où, pour le mode de décision, il n'est plus fait appel à la tradition — et l'utilisation massive, dans les argumentations, de symboles ou de représentations de type mythique."[14]

Retenons de la tragédie que la naissance du procès modene tel que nous le connaissons encore aujourd'hui ne procède pas d'un refoulement de la tradition mais de son *incorporation* dans le débat. Il faut se garder d'opposer naïvement le débat et le cadre rituel. Limiter le droit à un simple discours normatif, la justice à un pur débat, c'est oublier qu'ils ne peuvent vivre en état d'apesanteur sociale et qu'ils ont besoin de s'enraciner socialement, ce qui ne signifie pas s'aliéner à un contenu mais s'intégrer dans un cadre sans lequel tout simplement ils ne peuvent exister. Le symbole sera le lien entre le texte et le contexte.

Le cadre est perception: son action n'est pas immédiatement intelligible pour la raison. Il est présence; c'est l'englobant, l'univers symbolique qui est d'ailleurs lui-même une represéntation de l'univers[15] le lieu qui abrite le déroulement de l'instance. Le langage, à l'inverse est linéaire; il permet d'enchaîner de manière logique les arguments et d'exclure les sens possibles pour mener à solution. Il contraste en cela avec le symbole qui est, par définition, polysémique. Le cadre est immobile, il est répétition: il est insensible aux régimes politiques, au temps, à l'histoire. Il n'évolue pas, c'est un non processus. C'est un non événement indispensable à ce qu'un événement se produise: celui du procès. Il donne aux arguments une situation, un point fixe: il n'a pas de mobilité sans sa fixité. Nos bâtiments parlementaires et judiciaires sont pleins de ces bustes de grands légistes, de ces images terrifiantes, d'emblèmes nationaux, de fresques historiques comme à la Cour suprême des Etats-Unis: en nous rappelant le passé, la tradition, ils nous ouvrent l'éternité. La statue de Lincoln ne demande pas que l'on vote comme lui mais permet par sa présence, au contraire, à ses piètres successeurs de bénéficier de son autorité. Ils nous permettent peut-être d'être résolument modernes, de nous libérer du sacré religieux. La justice religieuse n'a pas autant de symboles, c'est que la loi est dictée. Ce n'est plus le cas dans une société moderne. Le cadre est alors ce qui tient lieu de tradition dans une société qui l'a dépassée. Aucun espace collectif n'est concevable sans une culture qui lui procure une expression symbolique identitaire, qui exprime dans un langage de pierre à la fois ses valeurs et ses pères fondateurs. Pour reprendre l'excellente expression de Paul Ricœur, le débat ou l'échange réglé d'arguments n'est que la *"partie vive"* du procès, le "software"qui ne peut être compris que dans un "espace protégé."[16]

Les Erinyes sont là, toujours présentes, qui contemplent fixement dans leurs yeux de pierre les débats des hommes.

Kafka: Le Rituel *sans* Debat

Si la tragédie d'Eschyle met en scène la naissance de la justice avec son cadre, Kafka va mettre en récit sa chute, c'est-à-dire la disjonction entre la tradition, les éléments du rituel et le sens, la brouille définitive entre l'événement individuel et le récit collectif qui lui donne sens. Le sens ayant disparu, il ne reste plus que ce cadre obsédant, ces images folles incapables de fonder le débat. L'expérience kafkaïenne est celle d'une justice qui n'est plus que cadre, cadre sans loi ni délibération, un cadre qui existe par lui-même et qui suscite non plus épouvante comme pour Oreste mais angoisse.

Des Images Rituelles Obsédantes

Le fait que Le procès soit une confrontation de Joseph K. avec les images de la Loi, du Tribunal, du Juge, se trouve confirmé de façon saisissante par les nombreux tableaux, photographies, reproductions qu'il rencontre partout.[17] Est-ce un hasard si c'est le peintre Titorelli qui renseigne le plus Joseph K. sur la justice? Ne lui dit-il pas d'ailleurs: "Si je peignais là sur une toile tous les juges, les uns à côté des autres, et que vous présentiez votre défense devant cette toile, vous auriez plus de succès que devant le vrai tribunal."[18] C'est par la petite représentation de la justice qui se trouve à l'intérieur de l'écusson qui rehausse le dossier du siège du juge dont le peintre est en train de faire le portrait que nous approcherons le plus la Justice: image dans l'image, mise en abîme, image à la puissance deux. N'y a-t-il pas une sorte de correspondance entre le portrait, la représentation et l'acte de juger: "Pour portraiturer les différents échelons de la hiérarchie, déciare Titorelii, il faut respecter des règles si diverses, si nombreuses et surtout si secrètes qu'elles ne sauraient sortir de certaines familles."[19]

Dans Le procès, l'espace lui-même, n'est pas structuré, il ne répond à aucune loi: il se trouve, pour reprendre l'expression de Deleuze, "déterritorialisé", la justice devient atopique. L'espace de la loi n'est pas reconnaissable: se rendant à son premier interrogatoire, Josept K... "avait pensé qu'il reconnaîtrait de loin la maison à quelque signe dont il n'avait encore aucune idée, ou à un certain mouvement devant ses portes. Mais la rue Saint-Jules où le bâtiment devait se trouver, et à l'entrée de laquelle il s'arrête un instant, ne présentait de chaque côté qu'une longue série de hautes maisons grises et uniformes, grandes casernes de rapport qu'on louait à de pauvres gens."[20] Ainsi, la loi n'a pas de lieu propre, elle est dépourvue de toute intériorité: elle est toujours dans le bureau d'à côté ou derrière la porte. Dans le premier chapitre, lors de l'arrestation, tout se passe dans la "pièce voisine." A la hiérarchisation d'un espace séparé autour d'un centre s'oppose une sorte de contiguïté de la loi, d'architecturé élastique qui permet à la loi d'être partout; K..., ouvrant la porte d'un cagibi tout proche de son bureau à la Banque, se trouve dans un lieu de justice où l'on châtie les deux inspecteurs. Allant voir Titorelli "dans un faubourg diamétralement opposé à celui du tribunal"[21], il s'aperçoit que la porte du fond de la chambre du peintre donne précisément dans les mêmes locaux de justice. Cette justice atopique n'a pas, bien sûr, de centre: "Le pouvoir n'est plus pyramidal, comme la loi voudrait nous le faire croire, il est segmentaire et linéaire, il procède par contiguïté et non par hauteur et lointain (d'où l'importance des subalternes)."[22]

K. doit surveiller son comportement incessamment ne sachant pas s'il est dans le territoire de la justice ou non. De surcroît, la topographie n'est jamais fixe ni stable, les barrières se déplacent sans arrêt. "Dans la première représentation du tribunal on a encore affaire à un triangle bien déterminé avec le juge et deux côtés, droite et gauche. Mais, ultérieurement, on assiste à une prolifération interne, comme à une invasion cancéreuse, enchevêtrement inextricable de bureaux et de bureaucrates, hiérarchie insaisissable, contamination d'espaces louches."[23] Le tribunal va perdre sa géométrie triangulaire pour s'aligner sur une même ligne continue qui ne "réunit" pas seulement les deux parties, mais, qui se prolonge en faisant voisiner "des inspecteurs venaux, des brigadiers et des juges d'instruction stupides, et encore des juges de haut rang avec leur indispensable et nombreuse suite de valets, de scribes, de gendarmes et autres auxiliaires, peut-être même de bourreaux."[24]

Le "dehors" n'est plus distinguable du "dedans": les personnages entrent en scène subrepticement; ils sont déjà là et K. ne le découvre qu'ensuite (dans la scène de l'arrestation, deux employés de la banque sont présents, comme le commerçant dans le dialogue avec l'avocat). Cette entrée en scène renforce la structure onirique du récit et contraste avec le cérémonial de l'entrée des personnages dans le rituel judiciaire (l'annonce par l'huissier de l'entrée de la cour ou des témoins, etc.): comme si une telle dramatisation de l'entrée en scène des protagonistes du procès, qui n'a de sens que par rapport à un espace et un temps délimité, cachait une sorte d'inquiétude propre devant être surmontée.

Il en va ainsi également des personnages parmi lesquels il n'est pas possible d'identifier ceux qui appartiennent à la justice des autres: tout le monde est auxiliaire de la justice: les juges, les avocats, les huissiers, les policiers, mais aussi, les femmes, les petites filles, les servantes, le peintre Titorelli, K... lui-même!

L'espace n'est jamais libre, les rues sont encombrées d'immeubles, "mystérieux acteurs immobiles"; il y a partout des obstacles à vaincre, des portes à franchir, des couloirs interminables, "des escaliers simstres et des chambres trop étroites" où "l'âme étouffe". Joseph K..., pour son premier interrogatoire, doit aussi monter —à travers des haltes et des hésitations infinies— jusqu'aux étages supérieurs d'une étrange bâtisse, en passant par un escalier sur lequel "toutes les portes étaient ouvertes pour permettre aux enfants d'aller et venir. Elles laissaient voir en géneral de petites pièces à une fenêtre qui servaient de cuisine et de chambre à coucher...."[25] Kafka signifie cet encombrement en donnant une réalité physique à cet étouffement; il prend au mot le langage en donnant une épaisseur réelle à l'air (cf. l 'expression française "l'atmosphère lourde "). Pour Joseph K. en effet, l'air est lourd et il est pris d'étouffement dans les locaux de la justice; il asphyxie littéralement alors qu'aucune cause ne le justifie ("...Le petit poêle de fonte n'était certainement pas allumé: cette touffeur était inexplicable.")[26] Dans les préparatifs pour une noce il la campagne, Kafka confesse cette vérité qui éclaire singulièrement notre sujet: "Ce n'est pas l'inertie, la maladresse qui me fait échouer, ou pas même échouer en tout: vie de famille, amitié, mariage, profession, littérature, c'est le manque d'air, de sol, de loi. Les créer est ma tâche." Tâche dont il s'acquittera en expérimentant jusqu'à l'extrême leur absence. Kafka établit une sorte de transitivité entre ces trois termes (air, sol, loi): la première manifestation de cette absence de loi, c'est la déstructuration de l'espace. Ce n'est pas l'espace qui est problématique chez Kafka, mais la Loi, l'absence de parole séparatrice. Kafka nous invite dans Le procès à une meditation sur la fonction symbolique du procès, sur la nécessité d'établir des distinctions à commencer dans l'espace.

Aucune séparation ne vient délimiter un espace d'un autre, une intériorité d'une extériorité, une catégorie d'une autre: tout est contigu, illimité, immanent. Faut-il voir en opposition à cet espace encombré, obstrué, oppressant, la signification de la *distance* qui caractérise l'espace judiciaire qui s'organise tout entier autour d'un vide et qui place ses acteurs de manière quasi-obsessionnelle?[27] Sans scène pas de sens possible, mais s'il n'y qu'une scène immense qui correspond aux dimensions du monde réel, ni l'undividu, ni le sens ne peuvent émerger et se différencier.

Désintégrées D'un Cadre Qui Produise du Sens

Les images rituelles sont devenues comme folles n'étant plus integrées à un ensemble, n'étant plus réferées à un débat qui leur donne sens, dans la double acception de direction et de signification. Ce que l'on a vu pour l'espace va, bien entendu, se vérifier pour le temps. L'ordre chronologique est inversé. Chacun se souvient de l'alternative infernale que le peintre propose à Joseph K.: ou bien l'atermoiement illimité ou l'acquittement apparent.[28] En réalité, plus qu'une procédure absurde et totalitaire, il s'agit d'une non procédure dans le sens ou elle s'avère impuissante à produire une quelconque decision. Elle se borne à tourmenter ou, paradoxalement, à distraire le sujet pendant que s'applique une sorte de châiment nécessaire contre lequel, non seulement ni lui, mais ni elle non plus, ne peuvent rien! L'absence de règle se manifeste par l'impossibilité absolue d'obtenir un résultat; incapacité d'une quelconque emprise sur les événements: incapacité d'un quelconque effet de sens. Cette inversion du temps donne à l'action cette circularité, si typique de l'œuvre de Kafka, qui empêche toute action de prospérer. Par exemple, seules comptent les relations personnelles et sincères avec des fonctionnaires importants (dans les échelons subalternes, s'entend). "A tous autres égards la procédure se poursuit. On continue à la diriger vers les instances supérieures et à la ramener dans les petits secrétariats comme l'exige la continuité de la circulation des pièces dans les bureaux, elle ne cesse ainsi de passer par toutes sortes de hauts et de bas avec des oscillations plus ou moins amples et des arrêts plus ou moins grands...."[29]

L'absence de règle donne aux rapports entre les personnages un caractère de fusion ou de corruption: tout passe par le sang (comme Titorelli qui reçoit la connaissance par héritage), par contact[30] ou par seduction ("C'est pour vous mettre dans mes bonnes grâces que vous avez commencé par me parler de vos tableaux" dit le peintre à Joseph K.[31] Ce qui compte ce n'est pas les compétences professionnelles, techniques de l'avocat mais ses : "relations personmelles"; aucune triangulation des relations sociales n'est concevable.

Comme dans les Euménides, Joseph K. ne peut supporter la vue des images: le rapport entre le regard et l'objet contemplé *s'inverse* totalement. "Le masque de la Gorgone est, originairement, le contraire parfait d'un objet de contemplation: elle-même est 'regard', c'est-à-dire "mauvais-œil"-fait pour et destiné à forcer le contemplateur à détouner la vue, ou à le paralyser complètement. Ainsi, des images de la justice chez Kafka: ce n'est pas nous qui les regardons, ce sont elles qui nous fixent. Ainsi, dans le récit devant les portes de la Loi, la sentinelle dit-elle au paysan: "Tu trouveras à l'entrée de chaque salle des sentinelles de plus en plus puissantes; dès la troisième, même moi, je ne peux plus supporter leur vue."[32] A la fin du chapitre, K. ne supporte plus la vue de l'huissier: "Il lui tardait de se débarrasser de l'huissier, dont le bouton doré ne cessait d'attirer désagréablement son regard, bien que sans doute personne d'autre ne le remarquât"[33] c'est nous qui soulignons.

Kafka n'arrive pas à faire le deuil de cette tradition devenue muette dans la modernité: il est à l'affût de son message qui ne vient pas. Dans ce sens—là il est fin ou début. Fin d'un monde hétéronome, centré sur la transcendance de Dieu, début d'un monde autonome dont l'avénement se fait attendre. Kafka est à l'intersection de ces deux mondes dont il ressent —mais n'est-ce pas le rôle du poete?— plus que quiconque les contradictions: il se retrouve abandonné par ces temps qui loin de se chevaucher se dérobent en même temps. "Je n'ai pas été, comme Kierkegaard, guidé dans la vie par la main, déjà affaiblie du christianisme, et je n'ai pas comme les sionistes saisi tout juste la derniérè frange du châle de prières juif qui s'envole. Je suis une fin ou un commencement."[34]

Justices sans Rituel?

Ce savant de la chose humaine et bureaucratique qu'est Kafka ne se doutait probablement pas que dans un avenir très proche l'histoire de l'humanité allait offrir au monde de sinistres applications de ce qu'il n'avait imaginé que pour le conjurer dans le laboratoire de son imagination. L'obsession d'un cadre fou qui n'abrite plus de vrais débats mais que de sinistres parodies, déserté par la véritable loi démocratique a secoué tout notre XX ème siècle. La scène judiciaire et les détournements dont elle a été l'objet par les différents totalitarismes nous ont fait nous retourner vers d'autres scènes dont deux principalement: la scène thérapeutique et la scène médiatique. On a attendu d'elles qu'elles nous libèrent de ce rituel oppressif. Y ont-elles réussi?

La Dénonciation D'un Cadre Oppressif

Tout cet encadrement symbolique du procès ne nuit-il pas finalement à la justice? Beaucoup d'auteurs ont montré comment ce rituel avait pour but de distinguer entre ceux qui possèdent ce langage symbolique, les professionnels, les juges, les avocats et ceux qui ne le possèdent pas, l'accusé. Cette inégalité n'est-elle pas scandaleuse? Le rituel répondrait à une logique enfouie qui nous révèlerait la véritable nature du procès. La critique n'est plus polémique mais redoutablement construite. Voyons-en rapidement la teneur.

Paul Fauconnet, proche disciple de Durkheim, tout d'abord, inverse notre perception: ce n'est pas la recherche de la responsabilité qui justifie socialement le procès mais la nécessité de purger l'émotion sociale née du crime.[35] Il se fait l'écho de la célèbre phrase du maître: "Il ne faut pas dire qu'un acte froisse la conscience commune parce qu'il est criminel mais qu'il est criminel parce qu'il froisse la conscience commune."[36] Un soupçon pèse alors sur le rituel qui ne serait là que pour maquiller cette fonction sacrificielle dont parlera plus tard René Girard dans *La violence et le sacré*. "Le système [judiciaire], estime ce dernier, fonctionnera d'autant mieux qu'on aura moins conscience de sa fonction. [...] A partir du moment où il est seul à régner, le système judiciaire soustrait sa fonction aux regards. De même que le sacrifice, il dissimule—même si en même temps il révèle—ce qui fait de lui la même chose que la vengeance, une vengeance semblable à toutes les autres, différente seulement en ceci qu'elle n'aura pas de suites, qu'elle-même ne sera pas vengée."[37] Même sentiment chez Christian Nils Robert dans un livre au titre parlant: *L'impératif sacrificiel:* "La crise toujours prétendue de la justice fait illusion, au moins autant que les réformes continuelles qu'elle subit. Ces dysfonctionnements, auxquels certains tentent de remédier depuis des générations, ne sont que les principes mêmes de son fonctionnement. Il n'y a jamais eu crise de l'institution, *mais constante ignorance ou inconscience de sa fonction véritable.*"[38]

Une justice moins formelle et plus réparatrice, voire thérapeutique, en matière familiale ou pénale, ne serait-elle pas moins mutilante et surtout moins archaïque. Le rituel paraît un vestige inutile et handicapant du passé: le temps n'est-il pas venu de chasser définitivement les Erinyes de l'horizon la cite? La critique de M. Foucault ne s'est pas faite attendre: le rituel est très oppressif quand il est présent mais quand il disparaît, le contrôle social des sujets est encore pire. Le procès se transforme en un contrôle de l'intériorité, en une sorte de thérapie sociale qui n'a plus aucur respect pour les individus. Quand la barrière rituelle ne contient plus les symboles terrifiants de la Loi, ce n'est pas le citoyen qui rentre dans la loi, mais ce sont d'autres rites, en apparence plus doux comme les usages sociaux, qui envahissent silencieusement l'espace social pour mieux le contrôler! Comment rendre une justice dont les formes symboliques —dont on s'est rangé a la nécessité— ne soient pas pour autant oppressives?

Avant de répondre à cette question, remarquons que la concurrence a pris ces dernières années un tour nouveau dans nos démocraties: ce n'est plus la *déformalisation* qui guette les institutions mais une *délocalisation* dans les médias, qui semblent affranchir la justice d'un espace physique déterminé. Le *lieu d'où parle le journaliste* n'est, en effet, jamais précisé. Peut-être même s'agit-il d'un lieu qui n'existe pas? D'un lieu où l'on prétend dire la vérité sans la traiter, où l'information passe sans jamais être fixée. Les médias sont tantôt du côté de l'accusation, tantôt du côté de la défense, tantôt du côté de la morale, tantôt de celui de sa subversion: ils occupent toutes les places de manière *insidieuse* et *insaisissable.* Ce qu'illustre de manière exemplaire les rapports entre la justice et les médias aujourd'hui, c'est l'illusion contemporaine d'une *democratie directe* qui pourrait se passer de formes et donc de rituel.

L'illusion De La Démocratie Directe

On passe subrepticement de la *dénonciation* d'un dysfonctionnement à une *disqualification* des institutions et, enfin, à une *substition* ponctuelle au travail de l'institution mais suffisante pour montrer que les médias peuvent mieux faire, qu'ils sont devenus le véritable lieu de la vérité démocratique parce que le plus apte à représenter les attentes sociales et à faire communiquer les citoyens entre eux.

Il s'agit de la disparition progressive et silencieuse non pas des dispositions positives du droit mais des mécanismes concrets qui en fonde le *lieu.* Comme si le débat pouvait se passer de cadre: nous voilà revenus à la problématique eschylienne. Peut-on, en effet, qualifier de "débat" cette suite ininterrompue de prises de position versatiles, sans mémoire ni souci de cohérence: un journaliste dit le contraire de ce quil a dit la veille, fait le contraire de ce qu'il a annoncé, et ce en toute impunité. Il est grand inquisiteur et en même temps le dernier recours, il dénonce et répare, dit le juste et l'injuste, attise les braises et demande quon les recouvre de cendres. D'un journalisme situé par rapport à l'institution, pour en rendre compte et au besoin la dénoncer, on est passé à un journalisme de *surplomb*. Mais cette ubiquité n'est-elle pas le contraire de l'espace public? Le principe du contradictoire est-il aussi facilement délocalisable? C'est peut-être faire beau jeu dc l'expérience de nos démocraties qui ont défini au fil des affaires et au prix de tant de déchirements, les règles les plus aptes, si ce n'est a réaliser la justice, au moins à limiter les injustices?

Le rituel judiciaire assigne à chacun sa place et donc il permet que chaque discours soit *situé:* on n'a pas trouvé meilleur antidote contre la manipulation que de la postuler, ce que fait le procès en rendant visible la place de chacun. Partant, il est essentiel que chaque intervenant dans le procès ait une place assignée, clairemant identifiable: le point de vue de la défense, de l'accusation, etc. Vouloir donner à un seul acteur deux places est illusoire. La télévision ne se contente pas de mettre en scène: elle a la prétention de jouer tous les rôles (position totalisante et totalitaire par excellence). Elle se substitue à toutes les fonctions du cadre symbolique comme celle d'attribuer à chacun sa place. Lorsque l'on rentre dans une salle d'audience, on identifie chacun sans difficulté: le procureur, le juge, l'accusé, etc.

Les médias se présentent comme des moyens de représentation plus accessibles, plus expressifs, plus fidèles à la réalité et à la diversité des opinions, bref plus démocratiques que le cadre procédural de la salle d'audience. Il suffirait d'instiller un peu plus de contradictoire dans les médias pour se protéger de certains dérapages; c'est oublier qu'un procès est un ensemble très complexe et très sophistiqué, *tributaire d'un espace —physique et procédural— homogène qui* permet de combiner en une unité de temps, de lieu et d'action, une mise en langage et une mise en sens d'une part et une mise en scène d'autre part, en d'autres termes une opération intellectuelle et logique, et une cérémonie sociale destinée a purger l'émotion collective, d'autre part. C'est cette unité de temps, de lieu et d'action que precisément la presse fait voler en éclats. Or, elle est capitale: dans un procès, il faut que tous entendent la même chose et rien d'autre sur l'affaire. Les jurés doivent tout voir de ce qui est représenté dans le prétoire, tout entendre pour se faire une idée et rendre une décision juste: cette performance n'est possible que grâce à la délimitation et à la sélection de ce qu'il y a à représenter. C'est la différence entre un public et la foule: les premiers voient de bout en bout un spectacle, les autres ne forment pas un groupe; il n'y a pas d'unité non plus dans ce qui est répresenté. C'est toute la différence entre le contradictoire et le droit de réponse. Que vaut un droit de réponse quelques jours après que le dommage soit fait, le plus souvent suivi de quelques lignes qui le contredisent? Il n'y a pas d'egalité des armes dans la controverse; pire, il se pourrait que les médias, au contraire, ne fassent que reproduire les inégalités de fait et le rapport de force. "La controverse est réduite à un spectacle plus proche de la tauromachie que de la discussion raisonnable. La finalité de la communication est devenue la communication elle-même, le divertissement qu'elle apporte, le bruit qu'elle fait, l'argent et le pouvoir qu'elle procure, et non point la mise en rapport de deux subjectivités à travers un code."[39] La contradiction se distingue de la simple controverse et ne peut se satisfaire de l'exercice d'un droit de réponse. Ne nous y trompons pas, cette conception d'une verite supérieure qui n'aurait plus besoin d'être établie contradictoirement, cette volonté de tout savoir justifie les methodes inquisitoires les plus barbares, celles dont notre droit a mis tant de temps à se defaire. C'est le contraire même de la justice qui est un échange réglé d'arguments.

Penser La Justice *Avec* Le Rituel

Les médias ne pourront jamais se substituer à la justice faute de cadre approprié. Voilà la question du rituel une nouvelle fois posée! On voit donc le lien entre le rituel et la construction du sens et donc de la vérité judiciaire. On comprend —a contrario— en quoi la justice est tributaire de ce cadre. Le procès est, en réalité, une *co-construction de sens;* la procédure et le contradictoire ne sont qu'une certaine *éthique de la mise en récit.* Le procès n'est *a priori* pas plus à l'abri que la presse du danger de construire de tels récits imaginaires mais son cadre paradoxalement l'en protège plus que celui de la presse. La garantie qu'offre le judiciaire, c'est la capacité de nommer et de *réfléchir* cette mise en récit et donc de la maîtriser un peu, ce qui n'est jamais le cas de la télévision. Ce problème au centre de la justice: le procès contrôle la mise en récit, c'est-à-dire la manière dont les faits sont présentés, prouvés et interprétés; à la télévision, la construction de la réalité est implicite et n'est jamais soumise à discussion. La présence ou l'absence du contradictoire, on le voit, dépend de la possibilité de discuter la construction de la réalité faite par les autres.

Ce qui menace le plus la justice dans nos sociétés démocratiques, c'est moins les interventions du pouvoir politique qui ne concernent qu'un nombre infime d'affaires mais bien plutôt le mécanisme sacrificiel dont aucune institution ne nous débarrassera complètement parce qu'il est au coeur même du rituel judiciaire comme le rappelle René Girard. L'illusion de la démocratie directe, le fantasme d'une démocratie sans scène n'offre aucune résistance à cette dérive bureaucratique, plus encore, elle annonce tous les populismes sécuritaires qui fleurissent en Europe aujourd'hui.

L'idéologie libérale d'une *harmonisation spontanée* des intérêts de chacun sous le regard du meilleur arbitre qui soit dans une démocratie, l'opinion publique, oublie une fois encore la sagesse grecque qui nous rappelle que "plus la foule est nombreuse, plus elle est aveugle."[40] L'institution d'un lieu de déliberation ne se confond ni avec le lieu plus petit de la négociation ou de la thérapie, ni encore avec le lieu plus grand, c'est-à-dire l'espace public tout entier. L'Etat doit garantir "le bon fonctionnement de la justice dans un *espace protégé,* délimité à l'intérieur de l'espace public."[41]

"Il est utile, important dans une république, dit Machiavel, d'avoir des institutions qui fournissent à la masse des citoyens des moyens d'exhaler leur aversion contre un autre citoyen. A défaut de ces moyens autorisés par la loi, on en emploie d'illégaux. qui sans contredit produisent des effets bien plus funestes."[42] Une démocratie qui ne se représenterait plus sur la scène de ses institutions, non seulement ne serait plus porteuse d'aucun ideal mais risquerait de sombrer dans une violence régressive. Le tragique de notre époque ne serait-il pas que la disparition du rituel judiciaire nous ramène à l'état de nature? "Le principe de la démocratie se corrompt, dit Montesquieu, non seulement lorsqu'on perd l'esprit d'égalité, mais encore quand on prend l'esprit d'égalité extrême, et que chacun veut être égal à ceux qu'il choisit pour lui commander. Pour lors, le peuple, ne pouvant plus souffrir le pouvoir même qu'il confie, veut tout faire par lui-même, délibérer pour le sénat, exécuter pour les magistrats, et dépouiller tous les juges."[43] Et si une analyse un peu approfondie du rituel judiciaire nous invitait à réviser sa condamnation spontanée? Et si le combat pour la démocratie avait insidieusement changé de camp, et que, après des années où on le concevait *contre* les institutions, les fronts s'étaient renversés et qu'il nous fallait apprendre à les préserver contre "l'égalité extrême" dont parle Montesquieu?

Tout cela amène à reconsidérer —voire réhabiliter— le rituel du procès. La question du rituel traverse toute l'histoire de notre humanité comme nous l'avons rapidement vu en posant obstinément une même lancinante question: arrivera-t-on un jour à libérer le procès de sa gangue imaginaire, de sa violence fondatrice, de son lien avec les commencements? La sagesse d'Eschyle nous dit que non et nous voilà amenés à repenser la justice non pas *contre* le rituel mais *avec* le rituel. Ce que nous rappelle le rituel, c'est l'ambivalence fondamentale, constitutive du procès qui porte en lui-même les meilleures formes de la justice et les pires formes de l'injustice.

Il n'y a pas de justice sans aménagement d'un espace public qui permette un regard public sur la justice mais ce regard public, en même temps qu'il garantit la neutralité du juge, est chargé de haine et d'irrationnel. On est donc confronté à une sorte *d'indépassable de la forme rituelle du procès* en même temps que l'on bute sur ses paradoxes. Paradoxe de la *publicité* tout d'abord sans laquelle il n'y a pas de justice digne de ce nom mais qui fait le lit du phénomène sacrificiel. C'est "l'ambivalence irréductible du regard public, à la fois garantie et menace, condition de la justice et porteur d'injustice, antidote et poison."[44] Paradoxe du *rite*, ensuite, dont la dénonciation au nom de la recherche d'une plus grande authenticité laisse libre cours à une volonté de réforme intérieure de l'individu, que personne n'a mieux mis à jour que Michel Foucault, et dont la suppression au nom de la démocratie directe détruit la démocratie. Paradoxe de la *règle* elle-même enfin, dont notre siecle a pu, plus que n'importe quel autre, mesurer les dangers. "Lors même que ce dernier [le despotisme] s'identifiait depuis Montesquieu au pouvoir affranchi des lois, le totalitarisme fonctionne à l'affirmation hyperbolique de la Loi."[45]

Comment juger avec le rituel? Peut-être en commençant par prendre conscience de sa nécessité plutôt que de croire naïvement que de casser le thermomètre fera baisser la température et que la négation du rituel du procès fera disparaître la violence de ses commencements. Nous voilà renvoyé à la conscience des acteurs, c'est-à-dire des citoyens, des avocats et des juges, à leur éthique. "Ce n'est pas en effet, dit Bourdieu, en refusant arbitrairement la pesanteur physique qu'on a réussi à vaincre et à conquérir l'espace... Il peut en aller de même pour la pesanteur sociale. La liberté n'est pas dans la négation magique du déterminisme mais dans la compréhension des lois du réel."[46] Le praticien de l'audience ne peut faire fi de son environnement en estimant que ce monde de l'audience est comme en état d'"apesanteur sociale" comme le mythe du droit voudrait le faire croire. C'est peut-être le sens de la prudence, c'est-à-dire de l'éthique du juge comme meilleure —et seule— antidote contre ces dérives toujours possibles, comme complément indispensable de toute procédure démocratique. La prudence ne serait autre que la conscience de ce pré-jugement des Erinyes, figé dans le rituel qui a déjà rendu son verdict avant que les hommes n'aient commencé à délibérer.

* Secrétaire Général de l'Institut des Hautes Etudes sur la Justice, Paris (France)

Notes

1. Bourdieu P.,(1973) (en collaboration avec J. C. Chamboredon et J. C. Passeron) *Le métier de sociologue*, Mouton, Paris, p.27.

2. Durkheim E.(1901), *Les règles de la méthode sociologique*, 15 ème édition, Paris, PUF, 1963, p.XII.

3. Femandez J. W. (1965), Symbolic Consensus in a Fang Reformative Cult, *American Anthropologist,* 67: 902–929.

4. Carlen P. (1976) *Magistrate's Justice,* Londres, Martin Robinson.

5. Winn P. (1991), Legal ritual, *Law and critique,* Charles and Deborah publications, Liverpool, Vol. 1, No. 2.

6. Reinhardt K. (1991) *Eschyle, Euripide*, trad. Emmanuel Martineau, Paris, Gallimard, p 155.

7. Ibidem, p. 154.

8. Ricœur P. (1992) *Lecture I*, Paris, Le seuil, p 36.

9. Le pacte des Euménides, in Cahiers de la compagnie Madeleine Renaud, Jean-Louis Barrault, Eschyle et l'Orestie, Paris, Julliard, 1955, p. 13.

10. Ricœur, Op. Cit., p. 40.

11. Ibidem, p. 42.

12. Judet de la Combe P. (1990) Rationalisation du droit et fiction tragique: les Eménides, in *La naissance de la raison en Grèce,* PUF, p. 270.

13. Ibidem, p. 269.

14. Ibidem, p. 274.

15. Garapon A. (1985), *L'âne portant des reliques, essai sur le rituel judiciaire,* Le centurion.

16. Ricœur, Op. Cit., p. 191.

17. Marthe Robert, Op. Cit., p. 108.

18. Franz Kafka, *Le procès,* traduction d'Alexandre Vialatte et préface de Bernard Groethuysen, Paris, Gallimard, p. 222.

19. Ibidem.

20. *Le procès,* traduction Vialatte, Op. Cit., p. 85.

21. Ibidem, p. 244.

22. Deleuze Gilles; Guattan Felix, *Kafka, pour une littérature mineure,* Paris, Editions de Minuit, p. 103.

23. Ibidem, p. 22.

24. Ibidem, p. 101.

25. Starobinski Jean, Op. Cit.

26. *Le procès,* traduction Lortholary, Editions Grands Ecrivains, Paris, 1985, p. 244.

27. Garapon A. (1985) *L'âne portant des reliques, essai sur le rituel judiciaire,* Le centurion, Paris, p. 34.

28. Kafka, *Le procès,* traduction Vialatte, Op. Cit., p. 230.

29. Ibidem, p. 237.

30. "N'etes vous pas frappé de voir que je parle presque comme un juriste!" dit le peintre à K., "C'est le résultat de mon contact constant avec ces messieurs de la justice." *Le procès,* traduction Vialatte, Op. Cit., p. 228.

31. *Le procès*, traduction Lortholary, Op. Cit., p. 223.

32. Ibidem, p. 308.

33. *Le procès,* traduction Vialatte, p. 245.

34. Kafka, *Les préparatifs d'une noce à la campagne*, p. 136.

35. Fauconnet P. (1928), *Essai sur la responsabilité,* Paris, Alcan.

36. Durkheim E. (1978), *De la division du travail social,* Paris, PUF, 10 eme edition, p. 48.

37. Girard R. (1973), *La violence et le sacré,* Paris, Grasset, pp. 39–40.

38. Robert C.N. (1986), *L'impératif sacrificiel*, Lausanne, Editions d'en bas, p. 7, c'est nous qui soulignons.

39. Domenach J. M. (1992), *Morale sans moralisme,* Paris, Flammarion, p. 83.

40. Pindarre, *Néméene* VII, 24.

41. Ricœur, Op. Cit. p. 191.

42. Machiavel (1952), *Discours sur la première Decade de Tite-Live,* Paris, Galimard, Pléiade, p. 400.

43. Montesquieu, *L'esprit des lois, VII,* Chap.II.

44. Garapon A. (1991), *Les paradoxes de l'image de la justice, Les Cahiers Français,* La Documentation Française, p. 109.

45. Bouretz P. (1991), *La force du droit, Panorama des débats contemporains,* Paris, Editions Esprit, p. 12.

46. Bourdieu P. (1973), Op. Cit., p. 27.

Chapter Three
The Hammer and Sickle in Court Symbolic Struggle in the Italian Communist Party

David I. Kertzer*

"Power comes through becoming authorized to provide a name for a thing, and thus to make it experienced in a new way" (Bourdieu 1977:170–1).

Pierre Bourdieu has entreated us to pay more attention to the role played by words in the construction of social reality. Indeed, he argues that the social sciences "must take as their object of study the social operations of *naming* and the rites of institution through which they are accomplished" (1991:105). The emergence of these objectifications comes, in Bourdieu's view, not through an anonymous social process, but rather through competition among elites, struggling over the ultimate power, the power to name.

Such is the power entailed in naming that Bourdieu refers to the leader's ability to provide the group with a representation as "his truly magical power over the group" (1991:192). In this, he echoes Tambiah's (1968) famous discussion of the "magical power of words", and of course Tambiah was himself taking a theme developed earlier by Malinowski in his treatment of Trobriand magic. As Tambiah observes, the belief that the power of naming is a creative power, one that brings reality into being rather than simply provides a name for a thing, is found throughout the world and throughout history, often linked to supernatural beings who could, through uttering a name, bring the thing about. The word, in short, is the breath of God, the word creates the world.

"By structuring the perception which social agents have of the social world," writes Bourdieu, "the act of naming helps to establish the structure of this world." There is no more basic element, then, in the political struggle, than the struggle over control of naming: "There is no social agent who does not aspire, as far as his circumstances permit, to have the power to name and to create the world through naming..." (1991:105).

The case I investigate here offers a particularly rich field for examining these processes, focusing on the use of the judicial system in this symbolic battle. It is an examination into what Bourdieu (1991:106) refers to as "the alchemy of representation...through which the representative creates the group which creates him." The naming in question is of a particularly crucial kind, for it is the power of providing people with a name for themselves, with a symbolic identity that links them both to the leader and to one another.

The Italian Communist Party

The setting is Italy; the symbolic location is the fall of the Berlin Wall in late 1989; the focus: Italy's second biggest political party, the Italian Communist Party (or PCI, for Partito Comunista Italiano), the largest and most influential "Communist" party outside the Communist-governed world. Founded in 1921, and existing for its first two decades as a tiny, beleaguered organization persecuted by the Fascist government, the party mushroomed at the war's end, growing from a few thousand members to around two million. By the late 1980s, it was a party with nearly a million and a half dues-paying members, a prodigious professional bureaucracy, and tens of thousands of militants. It elected well over a quarter of the members of the two houses of the nation's parliament, and enjoyed tremendous influence in the social, economic, and intellectual life of the country. Thousands of local party sections dotted the landscape, each marked by the party symbol: a hammer and sickle with two superimposed flags: one red and the other the tricolored Italian flag, and the letters "PCI"[1]

The personal identity of being Communist had assumed great importance to the large numbers of people who identified with the party. "Sono comunista" (I am a Communist) became not only the answer to inquiries into a person's political allegiance, but also to such queries as "are you Catholic?" Identification as Communist, for many, achieved a salience that identification as Italian did not.

Providing people with such a unitary identity involved a tremendous amount of symbolic work. Political representation could not simply be left to Rome and to the mass media (which, in any case, were poorly developed in the immediate postwar period). The goal was to provide a party section in every community throughout the country, as well as in all major factories and places of employment. These sections sponsored a host of activities rich in the display of the Party's symbols, the telling of their sacred myths, and the performance of their sacred rites.[2] Through participation in this common symbolic system, people who otherwise had little in common—neither education, nor class, nor even language—would be made to feel as if they shared a common, and fundamental identity.

La Svolta: Going Nameless

Although unable to displace the Christian Democratic party electorally at the national level, and excluded by the stigma of their Communist identity from national government, the PCI remained a powerful political, social, and economic force in Italy throughout the postwar years. At the apex of its influence, in the mid-1970s, it counted a third of all members of parliament, within 3% of the Christian Democrats, and it headed the municipal governments of all of the nation's largest cities and a number of its regions.

The Party had long sought to fashion a double identity for itself, taking advantage of what the Communist symbolism offered—linking the party and its members to a complex panoply of myth, ritual, and historical representation—while seeking to distance itself from the repressive aspects of the governments identified as Communist. The symbolic space it occupied was one clearly involving opposition to the United States, which served as the major symbol of capitalism and imperialism. However, as the years wore on, close identification with the east bloc became more costly and efforts were made to provide some symbolic distance. Hence, while the Hungarian invasion of 1956 had been applauded, the 1968 Czechoslovakian invasion was condemned.

Throughout the 1980s, the party's share of the national vote, and especially its appeal to young voters, began to decline. By the late 1980s, a sense of panic began to creep into segments of the party leadership, as events in the Soviet Union and eastern Europe seemed to undermine the allure of the party's Communist identity and make the party's traditional "fraternal" relations with the governments of the Communist countries and their ruling party apparatuses seem like an insufferable burden.

As the Berlin wall began to come down, and with Communist regimes throughout Europe crumbling, the party head, Achille Occhetto, after consulting only with his closest allies in the party leadership, announced that the time had come to create a new party, with a new name. His announcement—branded the *svolta* (turnabout)—came as a bombshell, enraging his opponents in the party leadership—who branded the move dictatorial and shameful—while leaving the mass of committed members in shock, their identity cast out.

Indeed, for several months after making the announcement of the impending change, Occhetto provided no name for the new party, which he simply referred to as the "new political formation." Journalists soon took to referring to the nameless entity as the "thing" (*cosa*). It was practically a year after Occhetto's initial announcement of the *svolta* that he finally unveiled the new party name (Partido Democratic della Sinistra, the Democratic Party of the Left) and symbol (an imposing oak tree, with the old party emblem at the roots).

Occhetto's opponents within the party meanwhile organized a group opposed to the abandonment of the Communist name. Rallying around the emotional cry that they would never renounce their identity as "Communist," the group, which initially took the name Rifondazione Comunista (Communist Refoundation), ultimately petitioned the court to adopt the old party name—Partido Comunista Italiano. In justifying their right to do so, and their claim that the new party, the PDS, had given up its right to the old name, they argued: "In fact for a long time the new political formation was officially called "the Thing," whereby the vagueness of the name itself served to indicate the broad universe of names possible, excluding only that of *Communist*."[3] We will return to this legal battle over the name a little later.

Although ironically helped by the PCI's tradition of endowing charisma on its party leader, and by the concomitant tendency to see the leader as the embodiment of the party, Occhetto faced heavy opposition from both party members and segments of the party leadership. What the party provided many was, above all, an identity. The proposal to do away with the party's name threatened at the same time to do away with this personal identity. Occhetto implicitly recognized this in the gradual manner in which he moved away from the communist identification. Asked, for example, in December 1989, how he would define himself after the new party was formed, he responded: "I am and I remain an Italian communist." In this he allied himself with the tens of thousands who in section meetings and in letters to the editor of the PCI press, proudly and firmly stated they would call themselves "Communist" until the day they died (and indeed, even after, given the tradition of draping the flag of the Party section over the casket of deceased militants!).[4] He continued to sprinkle his speeches to party members with the phrase, "we communists" (*noi comunisti*), a practice, however, that would not last long.

The line used at this point by Occhetto was that, in giving up the Communist name, and in giving birth to a new political entity in which other forces would join them, the Communists would be enlarging and strengthening their political base. Yet, in fact his ambitions were quite different: the renaming of the party was a means of providing it with a new representation, enabling it to abandon symbolism that had been tarnished. The adoption of a new set of symbolism would not only cause others to view the "Communists" differently, but also get the old party members to view themselves differently as well. It was a move that had the additional virtue of marginalizing his opponents within the party leadership, as they would inevitably rally around the (suddenly oppositional) Communist symbolism.

Yet these goals could not be directly expressed; indeed they had to be repudiated. The identity of the members could not be directly attacked; their self-conception could only be changed gradually.

At the heart of the matter was, again, the relation of the name to the thing. The opposition never tired of denouncing Occhetto for proposing the "scioglimento"—the dissolution— or the "liquidazione" of the party, a charge the Party secretary angrily and repeatedly rebuffed. Such dissolution or liquidation would mean, of course, the liquidation of the identity of the huge number of people who identified with the PCI. This struck a nerve.

The New Name

As the time for the 20th national congress of the PCI approached (it would be held at the end of January, 1991)—the congress which was designed to give birth to the new party's name (not, that is, to the party's new name)—Occhetto announced that the name would be the Democratic Party of the Left (PDS). Around the same time, Occhetto's most implacable foes in the party began to plan a secessionist movement, arguing that they would only be part of a party in which they could continue, with pride, to call themselves Communist.

This prospect, which Occhetto had foreseen from the beginning, haunted the PCI leader, who feared losing a significant portion of the party membership. Occhetto recognized that the opposition drew a good part of its strength from the symbolic potency of the Communist name and the emotions produced both by the name and its accompanying symbolism for many of the party members. What he particularly wished to head off was any attempt by his opponents to claim the old party name as their own, that is, to steal the symbolic capital of the PCI. This is exactly what happened.

The leaders of this secessionist movement sought to create the new party through naming. In doing so, though, they presented themselves not as the creators of a new "Communist" party, but rather as participants in what might best be conceived as a process of nature, a process dictated by history.

In his harshly worded speech at the 20th PCI Congress, the godfather of the secessionist Communist party, Armando Cossutta, proclaimed: "The need for us to feel ourselves to be and in fact to be communists cannot be dissolved or annulled by force. The communist question exists. You must not, you cannot cancel it. Driven from its names and its symbols, repudiated in its behavior, it would nevertheless arise again." It was not he, said Cossutta, who wanted a split in the party, but rather the others: "But you cannot stop me from remaining a communist, from thinking and acting as a communist. Nor can you stop our children from doing so."[5]

"In the symbolic domain," writes Bourdieu (1991:213), "takeovers by force appear as *takeovers of form*...." The minority struggled against the imposition of a new name and, with it, a new system of power. What remained crucial for them was to remain Communist, but what did this mean? By most traditional measures, there was little Communist ideological content to the PCI already. The party embraced multiparty parliamentary government, and opposed both nationalization of the nation's economy and democratic centralism. Indeed, it even championed Italy's membership in NATO. What was "Communist" about the party was in fact its name and a variety of symbols, myths, and rites that went with it. This is what the party members had in common.

Occhetto and his allies had to do everything possible to prevent the opposition from being able to claim the old party name and symbolism for themselves. Yet this presented them with problems. If the new party, the PDS, were no longer to be Communist, if it was going to be something entirely new, how could it claim symbolic continuity with its past? On what grounds could it prevent others from adopting that name and the symbolism that went with it? Combating the attempts of others to take up the old symbolic space of the PCI would undermine claims that the new party was in fact new, not the same "thing" but some*thing* new.

Interestingly, and tellingly, what mattered above all for Occhetto was changing the name of the party, the key symbol of "Communist" itself. By contrast, he was willing to compromise in other aspects of the symbolic domain, retaining much of the old party symbolism, such as the red flags, the old party songs, the incessant use of "comrade" (*compagno*) in ritualized speech, and the party festivals, still called *Feste dell'Unità*.'[6] Only the hammer-and-sickle, though never directly spurned, came to be seen as too closely allied with the Communist identity to be displayed any more than necessary. The other symbols were slowly redefined to be interpreted not as "Communist" but rather as part of a more generic socialist heritage.

Much drama attended the wait for Occhetto to announce what the new party name and emblem would be. The scene was reminiscent of the selection of the new pope, replete with the highly secret deliberations of the powerful, and the impatient and emotionally charged vigil of the represented. For Occhetto, what was crucial was to overcome the strident denunciations of the competing party elite and, at the same time, to overcome the anguished calls of the tens of thousands of members whose identity was so emotionally bound up in the Communist name. The new name, the new representation, must excise the Communist name. Yet, at the same time, Occhetto had to defend against the appropriation of the party symbolism, its identity, by opposition groups.

The solution Occhetto came up with, announced in October of 1990, was to combine an entirely new name with a composite symbol. The name, Partito Democratico della Sinistra, could hardly be more generic, not only rejecting the Communist name, but also the obvious alternatives of Socialist and Social Democratic as well.[7] The name in fact merely provided a symbolic place-marker, locating the party on the left. Indeed, the relational value of the new name was such that one member indignantly replied to the announcement by muttering, "as if the PCI weren't democratic!"

The new symbol was dominated by a powerful oak tree, composed of a sturdy trunk and abundant green leaves. Although attempts were made to portray the tree as a traditional symbol of the left (much being made of the symbolic use of the tree in the French Revolution), it lacked any such emotional or cognitive resonance for most people. The symbol could hardly have been more different from the old, dominated as it was by the red flag and hammer-and-sickle. Yet, cleverly, a small addition was made to the design: at the base of the tree, where the roots lay, was the old symbol of the party, complete with flags, hammer-and-sickle, and the letters "PCI".[8]

Communists in Court—Suing over a Name

The importance of this political maneuver would soon become clear, although the setting—a Roman court—may seem an ironic source of authority for determining who could legitimately call themselves "Communist". Indeed, within days of the majority vote at the twentieth—and presumably last—congress of the PCI which gave rise to the PDS, the secessionist group submitted a formal petition to the Tribunale di Roma. The purpose of the petition was to receive court authorization for the group to use, as its name, Partito Comunista Italiano. The basis of the suit was the argument that there existed—in the political universe—a Communist ideology, formerly represented by the PCI but now repudiated by it with the formation of the PDS:

> ...if a party is formed to mold national politics in an openly communist direction, one cannot prevent such a party from identifying itself with the name and the symbols of the Communist tradition. Still less can the

> exercise of that right...be impeded by another political group which, like the current PDS, has voluntarily given up the signs which it had possessed, holding that they no longer correspond to its current political-ideological heritage and, indeed, do not at all identify its personal identity.[9]

The argument employed here is revealing in several ways, not least of which is its explicit confusion of "personal identity" with the identity of a political representation. It also, of course, is based on the theory of first the thing and then the name. The party, it is argued, deserves the name "Partito Comunista Italiano" because that is what it is.

In their heated reply to the court, lawyers for the PDS rejected the claims made by the secessionist group. They claimed the exclusive right to the symbolism of the "PCI" without going so far as to argue that the PDS was still a "Communist" party. Occhetto's agents contended that "The use of the name and of the symbols of the Italian Communist Party...clearly constitutes the main instrument and vehicle through which the newly constituted association plans to make known its existence and seeks to extend its influence...." In short, the threat represented by the nascent party lay not in its program, nor its ideology, nor its leadership, but in its attempt to appropriate the name and related symbols of the old PCI.[10]

At the heart of the PDS's defense was its claim to have symbolic continuity with the old PCI. The PDS lawyers stressed the fact that the PDS "retains the symbol and the initials [of the PCI] in its new emblem, and does so insofar as it constitutes the natural continuation of the experience of the PCI."[11] The argument was over symbolic representations, and in this context the PDS lawyers expressed their horror over the secessionist party's hastily announced membership card, which consisted of the name and symbol of the PCI, along with the dates 1921/1991. Clearly, the secessionist party sought to lay claim thereby to the symbolic identity of the old PCI, which had been founded in 1921.[12]

In responding to the petition of the secessionist party, the PDS referred to it as the "*autodenominatasi Partito Comunista Italiano*," that is, as the "self-named" PCI. This phrase infuriated the leaders of the latter. Their response bears directly on our theme, for they attacked the PDS brief in these terms:

> We do not, in particular, understand the reasons why they insist on the fact that this association is *self*-named the "Partito Comunista Italiano," as if that weren't in the nature of voluntary associations, and as if the name of the Partito Democratico della Sinistra were somehow, by contrast, imposed on it by a decree of the President of the Republic![13]

The battle, in short, was over what kind of assertion of authority could legitimize the secessionists use of the PCI name, and hence their seizure of the symbolic capital of the old Communist Party. The PDS sought to delegitimate that claim by stressing the volitional nature of the naming process itself, suggesting that the naming process lacked the necessary societal consensus to be considered valid.

In the end, the court sided with the PDS, specifically recollecting the significance of the PDS's decision to retain the old emblem and name in its new symbol. The secessionist party (which was forced to settle for the name Rifondazione Comunista—Communist Refoundation) was hence forbidden from using the name and emblem of the old party. In its decision, the court ruled that the neo-communists must refrain from "the use of the name 'Partito Comunista Italiano,' the use of the initials 'PCI,' and the use of the symbol constituted by the hammer, sickle, and star on the double flag."[14]

The Name's the Thing

In the years following the official foundation of the PDS, the battle over symbolism has continued. The PDS leadership continues to contest any reference to the events of 1990–91 as constituting the dissolution of the Italian Communist Party, preferring the murkiness of an apparent transsubtantiation to an admission that the birth of the new party required the death of the old.

One can, indeed, argue that the old party never did die, and here too one would point especially to the continuity of symbolism: virtually all of the leadership of the PDS consists of former leaders of the PCI, the symbolic center of the new party remains that of the old (the Roman headquarters referred to by the street it is on: Botteghe Oscure), and throughout the country members of the new party continue to meet on the premises of the old (though the level of popular participation has continued its long-term decline).[15]

Is it, then, "only" the name that has changed? While some in Italy take this view—especially those on the extreme right, who do so for their own reasons—in fact the change of name and accompanying symbolism meant a radical change in the Italian political world. The results of the "alchemy of representation" are there for all to see. Meanwhile, the even newer secessionist Rifondazione Comunista has occupied both the semantic and symbolic space previously belonging to the PCI.

The process of naming was a process of political creation. As should be evident from our account, it is a process that involves complex negotiations of meaning. These negotiations, in this case, not only involved contenders for power within the old PCI, but entailed struggles for recognition from outside sources of legitimation as well. The key role of state institutions in this case is clear in the role played by the courts in adjudicating contending systems of representation. Of equal importance was the fact that the power-holders in most of the other Italian political parties immediately seized on the new name (PDS) and hence gave it credibility. It was not sufficient for acceptance of the new symbolism to come from within the party; it had to come from outside as well.

The power to name—hotly contested, negotiated in a complex field of political relations—once again revealed its magical ability to transform the political world.

* *Dupee University Professor, Department of Anthropology, Brown University.*

References

Court documents

The following documents—connected with the civil suit filed by the "Partito Comunista Italiano" against the Partito Democratico della Sinistra—filed with the Tribunale di Roma were consulted:

1. February 8, 1991. Original brief by the "Partito Comunista Italiano" bringing suit against the Partito Democratico della Sinistra (19 pp.).

2. March 4, 1991. Original response by the Partito Democratico della Sinistra (11 pp.).

3. March 22, 1991. Reply by the "Partito Comunista Italiano" (39 pp.).

4. April 10, 1991. Reply by the Partito Democratico della Sinistra (20 pp.).

5. April 15, 1991. Supplement to oral arguments by the Partito Democratico della Sinistra ("Note per conto del PDS") (6 pp.).

6. April 26, 1991. Decision of the Tribunale di Roma (14 pp.).

References Cited

Bourdieu, Pierre. 1977, *Outline of a Theory of Practice.* Translated by Richard Nice. Cambridge: Cambridge University Press.

_____________. 1991. *Language and Symbolic Power.* Translated by Gino Raymond and Matthew Adamson. Cambridge: Harvard University Press.

De Grand, Alexander. 1989. *The Italian Left in the Twentieth Century.* Bloomington: Indiana University Press.

Kertzer, David I. 1980, *Comrades and Christians: Religion and Political Struggle in Communist Italy.* Cambridge:Cambridge University Press.

_______________. 1988. *Ritual, Politics, and Power.* New Haven: Yale University Press.

Spriano, Paolo. 1967–75. *Storia del Partito comunista italiano.* 5 vols. Turin: Einaudi.

Tambiah, Stanley. 1968. "The magical power of words." *Man* 3:175–208.

Tarrow, Sidney G. 1967. *Peasant Communism in Southern Italy.* New Haven: Yale University Press.

Notes

1. There is a huge literature on the history of the Italian Communist Party. Among the major Italian sources are Spriano's (1967–1975) five-volume work. Among the notable works in English, see Tarrow (1967), De Grand (1989), and Urban (1986).

2. The local-level symbolic activities of the PCI sections are the focus of a study by Kertzer (1980). For a more comprehensive statement of the theoretical underpinning of my analysis of political symbolism, see Kertzer (1988).

3. Suit, document 1, p. 4. See listing of sources for fuller information on the legal documents consulted.

4. Occhetto's comments are found in Fabrizio Rondolino's interview with Occhetto, *L'Unita* 3 dicembre 1989, p. 9.

5. "Gli interventi dalla tribuna di rimini," *L'Unita'* 3 febbraio 1991, p. 16.

6. *L'Unità* is the name of the PCI newspaper. The newspaper retained its name following the founding of the PDS, and the PDS also retained the annual round of summer festivals held to raise money for it.

7. Although this must be understood in semantic context. As there already existed both a Socialist party and a Social Democratic party in Italy, Occhetto was somewhat constrained in his choices.

8. Occhetto's interpretation of the new symbol is to be found in "La dichiarazione di intenti di Occhetto," *L'Unita'* 11 ottobre 1990, pp. 8–9

9. Suit document 1, p. 10.

10. Suit document 2, pp. 6–7.

11. Suit document 4, p. 5

12. Suit document 2, p. 6.

13. Suit document 3, pp. 1–2.

14. Suit document 6, p. 15.

15. The Rifondazione Comunista has in fact done rather well in the short run, becoming Italy's fifth largest party in the parliamentary election of 1994. The PDS retained its second-place status.

Chapter Four
Semiosis, Ritualization and Magic

J. Ralph Lindgren*

Discussions of both semiotics and ritual have undergone fundamental reorientation over the past several decades. Traditionally, both were approached exclusively from a cognitivist perspective. From that perspective what is known is regarded as primitive and what is done is treated as behavior scripted by knowledge. When approached from that perspective, semiotic relations appear as a matter of the coding and decoding of messages. Ritual approached from a cognitive perspective grants primacy to mythology and represent ritual as enacted belief.

The cognitive perspective has been increasingly abandoned in both ritual studies and semiotics. It is now widely allowed that the cognitivist approach does little to illuminate the significance of unusual rites and perhaps religious observances generally. The recent renewal of interest in the significance of the ancient mysteries results in large part from a change in the perspective from which they are viewed. Over the past two centuries the cognitive orientation has been increasingly displaced in religion studies by various forms of non-cognitivism, an approach that gives primacy to practice over knowledge, to ritual over mythology. (Burkert, 1983, 1987)

In semiotics, the limits of the cognitive perspective became plain when attention was devoted to the history of sign systems and in particular to the ways in which they emerge and dissolve. Kevelson, for one, argued that, contrary to the cognitive expectation, patterns of sign transformation need not always reduce to a function of the decaying sign systems. Indeed, she pointed out that when considered dynamically, sign systems always exhibit a considerable degree of "free play." (Kevelson, 1990)

Recent historical case studies in both semiotics and ritual studies flesh out an alternative perspective for both. According to this non-cognitive approach primacy is to be accorded to process over structure, to practice over knowledge, to ritual over ideology. Although the more exciting projects in both semiotics and ritual studies have shifted from a cognitive to a non-cognitive approach, they have developed at a different pace and in different directions. In this paper I will suggest several ways in which each of these discussions can benefit from developments in the other.

I.

From its first mention by John Locke ([1690] 1959: II, 461–2), through the classical theorists C. S. Peirce and Charles Morris, to the present day, semiotics has been understood as the study of signs. Just what signs are and how they function with one another, of course, has been a matter of great controversy. However, there is consensus on this much, viz., that signs are anything that can be taken by someone as standing for anything else.

Until very recently, the cognitive approach to semiotics dwelt almost exclusively on the synchronic relations of signs, usually within the same sign systems. An important transition was marked when Umberto Eco began to compare the functions of signs across sign systems. It was his venturing into that borderland of inquiry that opened the way for his discovery of the centrality of metaphor. (Eco, 1984: 43, 88)

The traditional view, until about fifty years ago, was that metaphor is elliptical simile, useful for stylistic, rhetorical, and didactic purposes, but which can be literally paraphrased without significant loss of cognitive content. Since then a small library of writings on the metaphorical process, rich in interdisciplinary research, has appeared. (Lindgren, 1989; Ortony, 1993) Several general themes are now well established. Metaphors are not completely paraphrasable, nor is their function limited to figurative speech. Metaphor pervades not only all discourse, but all thought and action as well. (Johnson, 1981: 42–4) Although at first regarded as a purely verbal transfer, the metaphorical process is now thought to be manifested wherever we conceptualize one domain in terms of another. (Lakoff and Turner, 1989; Lakoff, 1993)

On this new understanding, metaphor inevitably involves putting dedicated tokens to unconventional uses, e.g., 'Mary is a peach.' At the same time, the main use of metaphor is not to inform, but to urge hearers to regard its subject in other than conventional ways. Even so, metaphors must retain some linkage to a common ground if at least some hearers are to be able to distinguish them from lies. Accordingly, a certain tension between the metaphoric act and its context is a characteristic feature of metaphor. (Johnson, 1981: 23)

Consider one of Eco's examples, 'the tooth of the mountain.' There the nouns (tooth and peak) are substitutable because in this context they both express a common meaning (sharpened form). But there is more to it than that. Metaphor is not elliptical simile. Besides having something in common the substituted nouns also stand in opposition. The peak of the mountain is not part of a living organism. A tooth does not afford a habitat for alpine flora.

For metaphors to 'work' the unconventional usage must not be so pronounced as to overwhelm auditors, else they would have no way to distinguish them from falsehoods. As competent hearers regularly do make such distinctions, Eco reasoned, they must do so by calling upon their acquaintance with the way that terms in current usage are juxtaposed. Eco referred to this as a "cultural encyclopedia." Eco's image of an encyclopedia conveys one of his key premises, viz., that metaphor presupposes metonymy. The terms in a metaphor are not transferrable because one is included in the definition of the other. Metaphors are not grounded in a cultural dictionary. Rather, they are transferrable because the terms are already juxtaposed in a larger cultural context available to speaker and hearer alike. Where dedicated tokens are put to unconventional uses, the metaphorical usage can be recognized for what it is if the terms are familiar and the novel juxtaposition is not without precedent in the cultural encyclopedia of the participants. (Eco, 1984: 127)

In discussing these metonymic foundations of metaphor, Eco emphasizes the cognitive. The shared context in which the substitutable terms are already contiguous was discussed as an encyclopedia, as a set of information, beliefs and modes of inference. As speakers draw upon already juxtaposed terms in their cultural encyclopedia, interpreters require access to that same collection of lore if they are even to identify metaphorical utterances. (Eco, 1976: 82)

Others have argued that metaphor is also founded on shared affect. Ted Cohen observed that the use of metaphor has a bonding effect. The exchange between those who direct metaphors to others and those who respond to them, builds on and reinforces the intimacy of community. Both speaker and hearer share common attitudes and aptitudes, else they would not 'get it.' (Cohen, 1978: 6)

David Cooper took that proposal a step further. Interpretation of a metaphorical expression often, if not invariably, involves understanding why a more conventional utterance would have been less appropriate. Knowing why 'he didn't just come right out and say it' is part of appreciating a metaphorical performance. In addition to access to cultural lore, this dimension of appreciation of metaphor requires sympathy with the moods and attitudes, the affective orientation shared by the speaker and competent hearers. (Cooper, 1986: 163)

These contributions to discussions of metaphor were also central to the clarification of yet another central feature of semiotics, viz., semiosis. Semiosis is the process whereby signs systems are formed and transformed. It was but a short step from Lakoff and Johnson's insight that metaphor is ubiquitous to the discovery that semiosis is itself a metaphorical process. The process by which anything is taken as standing (in) for something else is the same process as puts a dedicated token to unconventional uses. Both involve establishing new associations of objects. (Lindgren, 1992)

II.

Ritual studies have traditionally focused rather narrowly on religious rites. Until the late nineteenth century they were undertaken solely from the perspective of ritual masters or priests. More recently, with the rise of scientific anthropology, ritual has been studied from more objective perspectives. Thus, Victor Turner defined ritual as "prescribed formal behavior for occasions not given over to technical routine, having reference to beliefs in invisible beings or powers regarded as the first and final causes of all effects." (Turner, 1982: 79) Other anthropologists urge that the religious reference be dropped. (Leach, 1968) That move has enabled ritual to be found at the core of most, if not all, cultural activities. Thus, Catherine Bell sees "ritual as a 'window' on the cultural dynamics by which people make and remake their world." (Bell, 1992: 3)

As indicated above, ritual, and especially religious ritual, was studied from a cognitive perspective until very recently. On that view, the cognitive content of ritual was of paramount importance. The ritual activities themselves were represented as simply a matter of enacting these beliefs. On this view, ritual is to be approached as a culturally produced text that is to be interpreted by participants, much as performers interpret scores or scripts and observers interpret spectacles presented to them.

The cognitive perspective has recently come under attack from within ritual studies. Bell rejects casting ritual "as action opposed to thought and theory." (Bell, 1992: ix) She cites several reasons for abandoning the cognitive perspective on the study of ritual. First, there is growing evidence that the interpretations given by participants in even the more central rituals of a culture are not unambiguously similar. One need not cite religious examples in support of this observation. Political examples abound. People who participate in the central rituals of democracy, e.g., voting, think of what they are doing in radically different ways. As ritual is riddled with ambiguity, its interpretation cannot be a reliable indicator of what it does and what it is. (Bell, 1992: 183)

A second reason that Bell gives for abandoning the cognitivist approach to ritual is that the interpretation given any ritual changes over the years. Not only do different generations see what they are doing when participating in a cultural ritual differently, but so do the accounts given by the same individuals at different points in their lives. Ritual is riddled not only with ambiguity, but also with instability. (Bell, 1992: 184–5)

Instead of continuing with the cognitive approach, Bell prefers to approach the study of ritual from a framework that emphasizes the centrality of the ritual as practice, or what she calls "the ritualization of activity." (Bell, 1992: 219) As a general matter, ritualization for Bell has two aspects. On the one hand, the regularization of particular forms of interaction differentiates what is being done from other forms of action. On the other hand, repetition presents what is being done as justified or the right thing to do. (Bell, 1992: 90) These "activities are performed in culturally relevant ways to generate the perception that these activities are both intrinsically different from other acts and privileged in their significance and ramifications." (Bell, 1992: 219) Beyond establishing what Bell calls a "privileged distinction," the practice of ritual also constructs the environment, identify, and orientations of participants. For her, ritualization "temporally structures a space-time environment through a series of physical movements ..., thereby producing an arena which, by its molding of the actors, both validates and extends the schemes they are internalizing." (Bell, 1992: 109–10)

III.

For all the advances signaled by Bell's new framework, it is still narrower than it might be. Ritualization, as she employs the term, is still restricted to conventional processes, i.e., those by which humanly contrived routines constitute our lifeworlds. But this is an overly narrow view of ritualization for it neglects the place of ritual in animal behavior. It is worth remembering that the concept of ritualization was first developed in the field of animal communication. (Huxley 1923) Some attention to the distinctive features of ritualization among other animals enriches discussions of both semiotics and ritual.

Serious discussions of such ceremonial patterns of animal behavior as courtship are by now familiar. The process by which those behavioral patterns evolved and are sustained is perhaps best understood as the evolutionary modification of behavior to serve communication.

To see how the evolutionary approach applies here, consider the following schema. Animal A engages in a fixed sequence of behavior beginning with (1) simultaneously opening its mouth and staring at animal B and ending with (2) biting animal B. Individual Bs may react in a variety of ways. Those that retreat in response to (1) have a clear survival advantage over and so are more likely to be represented in subsequent generations than are those that do so only in response to (2). In this way natural selection favors animals that respond to (1) as a threat. Similarly, individual A's that are more successful in bringing about the retreat of Bs without undertaking the risks associated with (2) have a survival advantage over their less successful counterparts. As embellishments that exaggerate threatening displays increase the likelihood of such success, natural selection favors exaggerated behavior such as prolonging the stare, exposing the teeth, and vocalizing loudly. (Barash, 1982: 206–7).

Discussions of both semiotics and ritualization are sharpened by broadening their focus to include animal communication. From that perspective it becomes clear that communication is not necessarily a matter of exchanging encoded messages. Instead, communication amounts simply to the coordination of stereotyped display and response patterns. (Lindgren, 1991)

The import of this clearer grasp of the basic characteristic of communication for semiotics is plain. Communication is the paradigm sign relationship. If communication can emerge if only stereotyped display and response patterns are coordinated, then the semantic dimension of much human communication is not a universal semiotic requirement. Instead the famous semiotic triad of syntax, semantics, and pragmatics, is applicable only to communication that are grounded on convention rather than natural selection.

The import of the clearer grasp of communication for ritual studies is also plain. It is certainly true that humanly contrived routines can and do stereotype and coordinate display and response patterns. However, as rituals among other animals show, these also result from natural selection of causally functional properties in optimal combination. That being the case, ritualization must be understood as the coordination of stereotyped interactive behavioral patterns, whether by natural selection or convention.

Several startling inferences issue from this broader approach. One is that ritualization and semiosis merge into the same process. Both embrace whatever sequences of events result in the coordination of stereotyped interactive behavioral patterns. (see: Lindgren, 1991) Another surprising result of adopting the broader focus is that ritualization/ semiosis is irreducibly dualistic. There are two sources of ritualization/semiosis, viz., natural selection and convention. (see: Lindgren, 1992)

The critical issue that distinguishes sign systems and rituals that result from natural selection and those that result from convention is whether the alternative patterns of coordination make any substantial causal difference to the survival of the populations involved. In the schematic example of threat and retreat developed above, the alternative patterns of coordination do make a causal difference. Animal B's that retreat from animal A's only after being bitten are less likely to turn up in the next generation than are those that do so after being threatened. For that reason the former are said to be selected against.

IV.

There are innumerable forms of coordination that are not a product of natural selection. Human language is the most obvious example. The accuracy of linguistic communications can make a big difference in our lives. Suppose that I paint your barn on the explicit understanding that when I finish you will give me one of your cows. Now, initially, it makes no difference whether the name for that animal is "cow" or "cat" or "car," so long as we agree of which it is. The coordination of one of these alternative names and the animal in our linguistic community, does not turn on the causal superiority of using one of these alternatives as opposed to the others. It doesn't matter to our survival which we use, just so we both use the same one. That we use "cow" to designate the animal, then, cannot be the result of natural selection. That is clear enough, but how is the selection made, if not by natural selection? To answer that question we consider an analogous conventional sign, viz., money.

The term "money" admits of a variety of definitions. Each has merit for one context or another. For the purposes of this discussion, the term "money" will be used as a synonym for currency. Whatever may serve as a medium of exchange and a measure of value in an economy, its purchasing power makes a difference in the lives of us all. However, there are many possible forms that money might take. Over the millennia many types of materials have served as the medium of exchange, e.g., glass beads, iron, gold, silver, paper, etc. Following the abandonment of the gold standard early in the twentieth century, few still believe that any particular commodity is causally superior to any other as a medium of exchange. Instead, the most common view is that green pieces of paper have purchasing power because people think they do and the extent of that value is worked out, just as is the exchange value of anything else, in a market consistently with factors affecting supply and demand. (Friedman, 1992: 10)

This admission introduces a puzzle. Exchange transactions do not occur unless merchants and potential customers are reasonably confident that each will be willing to accept the same money form in payment for their own goods and services. But, in the absence of a causally preferred money form, what sustains that confidence?

A simple schema lays out the elements of the problem. Everyone in a population can presumably benefit if trading can be fostered. That can be done only if almost everyone is willing to accept the same set of commodities in exchange for their goods and services. What stands in its way is a lack of coordination. Initially, different people are willing to accept only some items in payment for their goods and services, but those items differ from one group to another and even between individuals. I will accept only copper, you only gold, he only paper, she only glass, etc. Everyone presumably knows that it doesn't much matter which of these is ultimately accepted, only that almost everyone is willing to accept the same ones. But, initially, everyone is willing to accept a given commodity as a medium of exchange only if others do as well. And there's the rub. Unless each of us can be confident that almost everyone accepts the same commodity, hardly anyone will accept it as a store of value. How can such confidence arise? The standard answer, of course, is by convention.

David Lewis' analysis of convention shows how the confidence exhibited by a population in a standardized medium of exchange arises and is sustained. In this respect, Lewis followed David Hume. Convention in Lewis' and Hume's usage is an acquired motivation, something like an habitual expectation about the behavior of others. Two people who row the same boat fall into the habit of coordinating their strokes, not by any overt agreement, but by convention. As Hume put it, "the actions of each ... have a reference to those of the other, and are performed upon the supposition that something is to be performed upon the part of the other." (Hume, [1739]1958: 490) For Lewis, as for Friedman, money is a prime example of a convention. Thus, Lewis says that "A medium of exchange — say, coin of the realm — has it's special status by a convention among tradesmen to take it without question in return for goods and services." (Lewis, 1969: 48) Friedman makes that point as follows: "The abstract concept of money is clear: money is whatever is generally accepted in exchange for goods and services — accepted not as an object to be consumed but as an object that represents a temporary abode of purchasing power to be used for buying still other goods and services." (Friedman, 1992: 16)

There is little room for doubt that convention, and not either causal action or natural selection, founds the confidence that makes a common medium of exchange possible. What remains obscure is just how confidence results from convention. Lewis describes the mechanism by which that confidence typically arises as an accidental convergence of recognized need for more efficient interaction and some salient feature of the alternative selected. For him an alternative is salient just in case it "stands out from the rest by its uniqueness in some conspicuous respect." (Lewis, 1969: 35) In our examples, gold may be less easily counterfeited than glass; paper more portable than gold; glass less costly to supply than silver, etc. Any of these properties may recommend one of these commodities over the others for the purposes of traders in a given culture, climate, time, etc. But what isn't explained is the backdrop against which the selected alternative contrasts.

What makes the uniqueness of the one stand out more than does that of the others?

It is at this point that a non-cognitive approach once again proves useful. Conventions afford participants a motive to follow through on stereotyped sequences once they are initiated. That additional motivation is, as Lewis and Hume pointed out, what constitutes the core of convention. The known presence of that motivation is what affords all participants sufficient confidence to carry the sequence forward. What distinguishes convention from other forms of ritual is that the objects and behaviors that it coordinates are causally unrelated phenomenon.

V.

Two theses have been developed so far. One is that semiosis, the process by which sign systems emerge, transform and dissolve, and ritualization, the process by which privileged distinctions are established, altered and abandoned, are the same process. Both involve the coordination of stereotyped interactive behavioral patterns. Perhaps language best illustrates this thesis. The other thesis is that there are two sources of this process. One is natural selection by which the causally inferior alternative combinations are selected against. For example, communication patterns among animals. The other is convention by which the coordination among causally unrelated phenomena results from humanly contrived routines. The development of money is an example of that process.

In the remainder of this paper I will explore several ways in which the semiotic/ ritual processes resulting from these two sources have been melded. Roughly speaking, natural processes have often been represented as manifesting conventional features and conversely, conventional processes have often been represented as manifesting natural features. These moves have traditionally been criticized as unfounded superstitions. In a post-foundational era such objections carry little persuasive force. I will urge that such moves be regarded simply as other more manifestations of the basically metaphorical pattern of the semiotic/ ritual process. Like any other metaphor, these moves amount to partial mappings of one domain, nature or convention, on the other. Nothing more.

Throughout history people have attributed conventional patterns to natural processes. Pastoral poetry comes most easily to mind, as do religious stories purporting to account for the cosmos by indicating how it derived from the antics or choices of divine beings. These stories are often linked to ritual practices. Later Hinduism developed a philosophy of ritual called the Purva Mimamsa. According to this view the universe is constituted by an impersonal ritual process. In order that the ritual order of the universe be maintained, it is necessary that its ritual process be repeated and sustained, not only by Brahmanic ritual performances, but also by everyone's enactment of the duties *(dharma)* appropriate to their caste, sex, and age. (Zuese, 1987: 407–8)

Poets and religious seers are not the only ones to represent nature in conventional terms. Even such stalwart scientists as Newton and Einstein represented natural processes as expressions of divine influences. Beyond these extra-scientific pronouncements, however, the validity of scientific accounts are regularly represented as mirroring the patterns of nature. For example, Darwin represented biological processes as being governed by "natural selection." In doing so he was conscious that his own conception of "natural selection" was a metaphor, drawing upon the selection techniques developed by others who contrived to domesticate certain species of animal and to hybrid various strains of plant life. (Darwin [1863], n.d.: 15–50)

Our representations of nature, then, are rooted in metaphorical applications of features of our everyday conventional sign systems and rituals. This may well be inevitable. However, that does not indicate that convention is the foundation of our representations of nature. The same can be said of conventional practices as well. Our representations of conventions are rooted in metaphorical applications of features of nature.

One commonplace example of the ways that we represent the conventional as natural is the entire range of habits. During the initial phases of acquiring the ability to carry out a performance, whether it is toilet training, language learning or ciphering, the effort and concentration required is enormous. Even after some command over these skills is attained, monitoring and self-correction is frequently required. However, when these abilities are mastered, they are carried out flawlessly and effortlessly, without further deliberation or self-criticism. The virtuoso, whether at the violin or the fast ball, describes her performance quite simply as "doing what comes naturally." Nor is this torturing the language. Habits have been referred to as "second nature" from classical times. The point here is that the motivation and execution of well-entrenched ritual performances are indistinguishable to the actor from their reflex responses to causal cues. Both are spontaneous and unsupervised, in a word, natural.

Another example of treating the conventional as natural is mentioned by Bell. Repetition of formalized behavioral patterns in culturally relevant contexts results in drawing attention to those contexts and what is being done in them, as distinguished from what might alternatively be done. This is the process of ritualization which is the focus of Bell's study, the process of drawing privileged distinctions. Once accustomed to living within such ritualized contexts, participants come to see their ritualized activity as "responding to a place, event, force, problem, or tradition." They tend to see responding in that way "as the natural or appropriate thing to do in the circumstances." (Bell, 1992: 109) Patterns of activity that are ritualized, in other words, are self-justifying in the eyes of participants. They are natural in the sense that they stand in need of neither reasons nor arguments to warrant their execution. Once the ritually correct moment arrives, the proper response is simply carried out without further adieu.

VI.

In the last section, several examples were given of the processes by which causal domains are partially mapped onto conventional domains and vice versa. These examples show that the semiotic/ ritual process manifests itself principally in metaphorical patterns. In the concluding section one last example of mapping a conventional onto a natural domain is explored in somewhat greater detail. This example, magic, shows how useful these insights can be in comprehending otherwise puzzling phenomenon.

The term "magic" is used in a wide variety of ways. In general, magic can be considered to encompass all the arts that purports to control or forecast natural events, effects, or forces by invoking the supernatural or that purport to control supernatural forces by natural means. Examples of the former are medical magic wherein a medicine woman applies charms and amulets to ward off the wicked spirits that cause illness in a client, and conversely, black magic wherein a witch invokes the wrath of wicked spirits upon an enemy by means of spells and incantations. Examples of the latter are ceremonial magic wherein a priest encourages an abundant corn crop by spreading the hair of newt on the seed bed and a chieftain repeats highly formalized gestures in anticipation of the tribe's annual fishing expedition to gain favor with the spirits that look after the resources of the sea. (O'Keefe 1982: 2–19)

In this way magic bridges natural and conventional domains. Natural causation is central to magic. Magic, begins from the conviction at least some desired states can be brought about by deliberately performing certain well-defined behaviors. Plant a seed in fertile soil under appropriate climatic conditions and a plant will emerge from the soil within a specified span of time. These lessons may have been learned by mimicking the natural life cycle of native species of plants or by trial and error. However, magic is also firmly rooted in convention. Magic also recognizes that desired states can also be brought about by conventional gestures and rites. "Please pass the salt" results in the salt moving from where it was into my hand, at least in polite company. These lessons are certainly learned from those who have managed some mastery of the conventional arts.

Magic supplements the more mundane arts that are limited to natural or conventional causation. Although impressive, these arts are limited in what they can accomplish. The medical arts cannot cure some conditions or even alleviate some types of symptoms. Literacy can accomplish some, but not all, desired conditions. Magic is invoked to fill these voids. In this way, magical means supplement more ordinary means, and so are said to be extranatural or supernatural. The magician prepares a variety of special objects — spells, incantations, or potions — which are thought to bring about, in some mysterious way, real changes in a person, object, or event, that cannot be accomplished either by natural or conventional causation alone. Inserting pins in a voodoo doll or hanging a rabbit's foot over the door of a friend are examples of such magical practices, as are crossing one's fingers and avoiding walking under ladders. (Hill, 1987)

Traditionally, magic was used to bring about good effects for those who were favored and bad effects for those who were in disfavor. The curse invokes magical powers to rain down evil on one's enemies. A recent account of one type of ancient curse, the defixion, illustrates the general pattern.

> Overall, the language and structure of judicial *defixiones* follow the developmental pattern of curse tablets in general. The earliest examples name the opponents; they sometimes invoke local deities by their familiar names, though some examples omit both verbs of binding and the names of the deities; and they mention the physical and mental faculties, usually tongue and mind, to be bound or tied up so that the

> targets will be unable to pursue their case. Later examples, by contrast, tend to longer, to use secret names and mystical terms (the *voces mysticae),* to invoke spirits and deities from many traditions, and to provide specific details for every aspect of the binding process. (Gager, 1992;: 118)

Blessings, on the other hand, invoke magical powers to bestow needed assistance upon those in good standing in the community. Thus, we find magic at work not only in the darker regions of our heritage, but also in the central practices of main line religions.

> In his account of the Jewish uprising against the foreign dynasty of the Greek Seleucids, the pious author of 2 Maccabees relates the following episode (12:34–39): Judas, surnamed Maccabeus ("the hammerer") lost a number of his men in battle; on the following day, when Judas went out to recover their bodies, he discovered that every fallen soldier had been wearing an amulet ("sacred tokens of the idols of Jamnia"), which, the author notes in a sanctimonious aside, "the Law forbids Jews to wear " Whether Judas thought to check for similar amulets among the survivors, the author does not trouble to say, for the message is clear — the dead had fallen because of their forbidden compromise with heathen beliefs and practices. But the great likelihood is that the survivors, too, had fortified themselves against "anything harmful" by putting on their engraved stones or their inscribed sheets of metal or papyrus. To be sure, 2 Maccabees does not offer the sort of hard demographic data preferred by modern social scientists, but the fact remains that in this randomly chosen sample of ancient Jews, every one wore an amulet, as did virtually every sensible person of the time. (Gager, 1992: 218)

Beyond these speculations we also know that Moses and Elijah had magic wands. (*Exodus* 4:20, 17:8–13; II *Kings* 4:29–31) More important was the magic of the word, especially associated with the name of Yahweh. (*Exodus* 3:14; *Judges* 13:6–18) What have become the main rituals among Christians, baptism and the Eucharist, also bear the mark of mysterious practices. (I *Corinthians* 1:10–16, 8:1–11:34; *Romans* 6:3–10) (Worgul, 1980 and Betz, 1987) Indeed, at least in the Catholic tradition, sacraments are recognized as means of grace. Thus, in the thirteen century, Thomas Aquinas taught "we must say that in some way the sacraments of the New Law cause grace." (Aquinas, 1953: III, 62, 1) By the sixteenth century the Roman Church declared, in the Council of Trent, that it is heresy to say:

> that the sacraments of the New Law do not contain the grace which they signify, or that they do not confer that grace on those who place no obstacle in their way, as

> though they are only outward signs of grace or justice received through faith and are but certain marks of Christian profession whereby among men believers are distinguished.... (Quoted in Worgul, 1980: 164–5)

The magical has long played a central role in legal institutions as well. The role of the seal in law is but one example. The earliest practice of sealing, predating even the invention of writing, consisted in securing the contents of jars, baskets, caves, burial chambers and the like. Before the invention of locks, this was accomplished either by shaping clay over the stopper or lid or by fastening the opening with a cord and pressing clay around the knot. In each method the clay was then impressed with a distinctive mark. Cylinder seals, stamps and signets were commonly used for that purpose until Roman times. To the extent that sealing actually deterred unauthorized intrusions, it appears to have worked by means of a threat of magically induced consequences. This is particularly likely where religious symbols were impressed on the clay medium. These marks of divine authority are thought to have excited awe and reverence in the population generally.

Just as the motivation to honor a sealed container during ancient times was supplied by the fear of magical consequences suggested by the inscriptions on seals, so also in the middle ages, reverence for a seal fostered acceptance of sealed instruments at face value. Corbin observed that the awe inspired by the sheer formality of ceremonies surrounding the use of a seal was sufficient to motivate acceptance. (Corbin, 1952: Sec. 240) In remarking about the self-proving dimension of the seal in the common law of England, Pollock and Maitland echoed that sentiment and also remarked how strict sealed obligations were in medieval England. "[A] deep seated reverence for a seal served to adjourn some difficult questions which otherwise must have come before the king's courts. A natural person is bound by his seal; he has himself to blame if some one else, at all events some one whom he has trusted, puts his seal to a bad use." (Pollock and Maitland, 1899: I, 508)

Seals are still in use in our day. Public credit seals are kept and used by public officials to authenticate their official acts. These include the seals of states, the federal government, foreign and domestic courts and certain public officials, such as notaries public. Public credit seals prove themselves in the sense that the authenticity of documents that bear appropriate public seals is established without the need for witnesses. For example, the seal of a notary public, once shown to be genuine, is sufficient to establish that the signatures on a document. (Lindgren, 1994)

In all these manifestations, magic involves representing the conventional in terms of the natural. The special objects prepared by the magician, incantations, potions, etc., are represented as having causal powers which bring about a natural effect, e.g., the death of an enemy, the health of a friend, or the authenticity of a document. The practitioner's routine is presented as a cause in nature, although one of which only those with special "knowledge" are aware. For the same reason magic involves metaphorical usage. In the place of objects, events or expressions generally known to have causal influence over natural effects, the magicians invoke special objects, events or expressions from other domains. In this way, magicians, as well as other rhetors, traffic in putting dedicated tokens to unconventional uses.

* *Clara H. Stewardson Professor of Philosophy, Lehigh University.*

References

Aquinas, Thomas. 1953. *Summa Theologiae*. Ottawa: Commissio Piana.

Barash, David. 1982. *Sociobiology and Behavior.* 2d Ed. New York: Elsevier.

Bell, Catherine.1992. *Ritual Theory, Ritual Practice.* New York: Oxford University Press.

Betz, Hans Dieter. 1987. "Magic in Greco-Roman Antiquity." In *The Encyclopedia of Religion.* M. Eliade, ed. New York: Macmillian Publishing Co. vol. 9, pp. 93–97.

Burkert, Walter. 1983. *Homo Necans*. Berkeley, Calif.:University of California Press.

____. 1987. *Ancient Mystery Cults.* Cambridge, Mass.: Harvard University Press.

Cohen, Ted. 1978. "Metaphor and the Cultivation of Intimacy." In S. Sacks (ed.), *On Metaphor.* Chicago: University of Chicago Press.

Cooper, David. 1986. *Metaphor.* Oxford: Basil Blackwell.

Corbin, Arthur L. 1952. *Corbin on Contracts*. One Volume Edition. St. Paul, Minn.: West Publishing Co.

Darwin, Charles. [1863], n.d. *The Origin of the Species and the Descent of Man.* New York: The Modern Library.

Eco. Umberto. 1976 *A Theory of Semiotics.* Indiana University Press.

____. 1984 *Semiotics and the Philosophy of Language*. Indiana University Press.

Friedman, Milton. 1992. *Money Mischief.* New York: Harcourt Brace Javanovich, Publishers.

Gager, John G., ed. 1992. *Curse Tablets and Binding Spells from the Ancient World.* New York: Oxford University Press.

Hill, Donald R. 1987. "Magic in Primitive Societies." In *The Encyclopedia of Religion.* M. Eliade, ed. New York: Macmillian Publishing Co. vol. 9, pp. 89–92.

Hume, David. [1739] 1958. *A Treatise of Human Nature.* Oxford: Clarendon Press.

Huxley, Julian S. 1923 "Courtship Activities in the red-throated diver (Colymbus stellatus); together with a discussion of the evolution of courtship in birds." *Journal of the Linnaen Society of London* 35:253–92.

Kevelson, Roberta. 1990. *Peirce, Paradox, Praxis: The Image, the Conflict, and the Law.* New York: Mouton de Gruyer.

Johnson, Mark. 1981. *Philosophical Perspectives on Metaphor.* Minneapolis: University of Minnesota Press.

Lakoff, George. 1993. "The Contemporary Theory of Metaphor." In Ortony 1993, pp. 202–51.

Lakoff, George and Mark Turner, 1989 *More than Cool Reason.* University of Chicago Press.

Leach, Edmund R. 1968. "Ritual." In *International Encyclopedia of the Social Sciences.* D. Sills, ed. vol. 13. New York.

Lewis, David. 1969. *Convention: A Philosophical Study.* Cambridge, MA: Harvard University Press.

Lindgren, J. Ralph. 1989. "The Pervasiveness of Metaphor: Privacy and the Supposed Independence of Legislation and Adjudication." In R. Kevelson (ed.) *Law and Semiotics* Vol. 3. Plenum Press. Pp. 221–40.

____. 1991. "Semiosis as Ritual." In R. Kevelson, ed. *Law and the Human Sciences*. New York: Peter Lang. Pp. 233–54.

____. 1992. "The Emergence of Signs: The Seminal Convention of Money." In R. Kevelson, ed. *Flux, Complexity, and Illusion.* New York: Peter Lang. Pp. 283–98.

____. 1994. "Seals, Oaths and the Primacy of Ritual." In R. Kevelson, ed. (forthcoming).

Locke, John. [1690] 1959. *An Essay Concerning Human Understanding* 2 vols. New York: Dover Publications.

O'Keefe, Daniel L. 1982. *Stolen Lightning: The Social Theory of Magic.* New York: Continuum.

Ortony, Andrew, ed. *1993. Metaphor and Thought.* 2d ed. New York: Cambridge University Press.

Pollock, Frederick and Frederick W. Maitland. 1899. *The History of English Law Before the Time of Edward I.* 2d ed. 2 vols. Boston: Little, Brown and Co.

Turner, Victor. 1982. *From Ritual to Theatre: The Human Seriousness of Play.* New York: Performing Arts Journal Publications.

Worgul, George S. 1980. *From Magic to Metaphor: A Validation of the Christian Sacraments.* New York: Paulist Press.

Zuesse, Evan M. 1987."Ritual." In *The Encyclopedia of Religion.* M. Eliade, ed. New York: Macmillian Publishing Co. vol. 12, pp. 405–22.

Chapter Five
Aladdin and the Law

Emily W. Salus*

Although American idealism and the Federal Court House in New York state that everyone in the country has "Equal Justice Under Law," many do not believe that this ideal is met in any way. Orwell's view that "all animals are equal, but some animals are more equal than others" appears to be more often the case. That some face one justice under the law and others face a different justice is displayed in popular culture forms as well as in the courtroom. One recent Disney film demonstrates the way in which laws are used unevenly in populations. Although the film is fictional and was created primarily for children, it illustrates how prevalent these ideas are precisely because of the movie's mainstream audience.

Disney's movie *Aladdin* is a fairly basic boy meets girl, boy loses girl, boy gets girl back story. Jafar, the evil advisor to the Sultan, is in search of the Genie's lamp. He discovers that only Aladdin, a "street rat" who steals food in the marketplace of Agrabah, may enter the Cave of Wonders to retrieve the lamp.

In the meantime, Princess Jasmine is in the palace rebelling against the law that states that she must marry a prince before her next birthday. She runs away from the palace to experience life for herself, disguises herself, and goes to the marketplace. Because she is naive about the world, Jasmine gives some children an apple off a cart in the marketplace though she doesn't have any money. While the merchant tries to cut off her hand for the theft, Aladdin intervenes, takes Jasmine off to his home, and they fall in love.

Aladdin, who has been told Jasmine is the princess, is taken prisoner by the palace guards on Jafar's orders and Jasmine is told by Jafar that Aladdin has already been executed for kidnaping the princess. Jafar takes Aladdin to the magical Cave, Aladdin retrieves the lamp, and, when the Cave self-destructs, finds himself with the lamp thanks to his monkey friend Abu's crafty fingers.

After discovering the secret of the lamp and returning to Agrabah, Aladdin has the Genie give him the wealth and demeanor of a prince. Once again, Aladdin and Jasmine fall in love, only for Aladdin to lose faith in his abilities because he has not told Jasmine about his true identity. The Sultan, who has been hypnotized by Jafar, is delighted to hear that Jasmine has at last chosen a husband, because he was about to marry her off to Jafar. Jafar's tricks are discovered by Aladdin and Jafar barely escapes imprisonment.

The lamp is stolen from Aladdin by Iago, Jafar's sneaky parrot, and Jafar proceeds to use some of the Genie's three wishes to make him, first, Sultan and, second, the most powerful sorcerer in the world. Jafar keeps Jasmine and the Sultan as slaves while he hurtles Aladdin to snow-covered mountains. Aladdin escapes with the help of the magic carpet and goes rushing back to save Jasmine and Agrabah.

The battle ensues. Having remembered that a genie has great powers, but that they are confined to a lamp and a master's wishes, Aladdin tricks Jafar into using his third wish and Jafar insists, at Aladdin's suggestion, on becoming a genie. Jafar is thrown into his own Cave of Wonders, Aladdin makes good on his promise to free the Genie from his bondage to the lamp, and the Sultan, finally free of Jafar's spells, changes the law to allow the princess to marry whoever she deems worthy. Jasmine, of course, chooses Aladdin as her husband.

Despite the film's apparently simple narrative, there are some problematic ideas contained within the story that concern to whom law is administered and how law is altered. The overt tale shows that things are not always what they seem and that sometimes "street rats" are honorable. A more detailed look at the story, however, shows that the law is flexible, that it only pertains to certain individuals, and that it is the characters' moral qualities as defined by the good-bad dichotomy within the movie which determine how the laws are used.

In the first narrative scene, Jafar meets with a thief who has brought him the second half of a gold scarab which, when put together, flies away and leads Jafar and the thief to the Cave of Wonders. When they first meet, Jafar asks if the thief has the piece. The thief responds that he has it, but that he had to "slit a few throats" to get it.

When they arrive at the Cave, Jafar sends the "humble thief" into the Cave, which promptly eats the thief and declares that only one, a "diamond in the rough," may enter. Jafar, careless of the death of the thief, determines that he must find the "diamond in the rough" and send him in after the lamp. Jafar's only response to the Cave's eating of the thief is that the thief "must have been unworthy." There is no question that Jafar is unworthy, it is clear that he is; we know this from the fact that he doesn't care that people were killed in order for him to have the scarab piece or that his thief has been eaten.

Our first sight of Aladdin is less sinister, but still related to robbery. We see Aladdin, loaf of bread in hand, fleeing through the marketplace and hear someone yell, "Stop, thief!" The guard goes on, "I'll have your hands for a trophy, street rat!" Aladdin, deadpan, looks into the camera and asks, "All this for a loaf of bread?" Immediately, the audience is told that it should side with Aladdin, who is presented as young, attractive, and humorous. This is contributed to by three women standing at a window who say, rather fondly, "Getting into trouble a little early today, Aladdin, aren't you?" Aladdin, nonchalant, responds, "Trouble? No way! You're only in trouble if you get caught." He is promptly caught and states, "I'm in trouble." He is, of course, rescued by the monkey, Abu, as he launches into song.

The fact that Aladdin denies that he is in trouble unless he is caught displays his lack of respect for law and his view of how law works. Laws have not been broken, according to Aladdin, unless someone is caught for breaking the law. In the song, "One Jump Ahead," Aladdin explains why he is stealing and how he can justify his actions:

Gotta keep one jump ahead of the bread line
One swing ahead of the sword
I steal only what I can't afford
That's everything
One jump ahead of the lawmen
That's all and that's no joke
These guys don't appreciate I'm broke. . .
[harem girls singing] Oh, it's that Aladdin's hit bottom
He's become a one man rise in crime
[harem matron] I'd blame parents except he hasn't got 'em
[Aladdin again] Gotta eat to live, gotta steal to eat

Tell you all about it when I've got the time
One jump ahead of the slow pokes
One skip ahead of my doom
Next time gotta use a nom de plume. . .
One jump ahead of the hitmen
One hit ahead of the flock
I think I'll take a stroll around the block. . .
Gotta eat to live, gotta steal to eat
Otherwise we'd get along
One jump ahead of the hoofbeats
One hop ahead of the hump
One trick ahead of disaster
They're quick, but I'm much faster
Here goes, better throw my hand in
Wish me happy landin'
All I gotta do is jump!

From this we know that Aladdin is an orphan and that he only steals because he needs to sustain himself. The concept of working, however, is never addressed. Although Aladdin does take the bread and gets away with it, he ultimately is shown to be a "good guy." Unlike Jafar, Aladdin kills no one and, when he sits down to eat, he sees two children even hungrier than he is and gives them his bread. Even Abu, the greedy monkey who has been assisting Aladdin throughout, gives his bread to the children.

The third character who steals is Jasmine. Because she has never before been outside the palace grounds, she sees a hungry child, gives him an apple from a nearby cart, and begins to walk away from the cart. Until she is caught by the merchant, she has no concept of paying for the apple. Aladdin, through his trickery, saves the princess from "justice" and they escape from the marketplace.

Jasmine:	Oh, you must be hungry. Here you go. [gives the apple to the child]
Merchant:	You'd better be able to pay for that.
J:	Pay?
M:	No one steals from my cart!

J: I'm sorry, I don't have any money.

M: Thief!

J: Please, if you let me go to the palace, I can get some from the Sultan!

M: Do you know what the penalty is for stealing?! [grabs her hand and his sword]

J: No! No, please!

[Aladdin holds the Merchant's wrist before the merchant cuts Jasmine's hand off]

Aladdin: Thank you, kind sir! I'm so glad you've found her! [to Jasmine] I've been looking all over for you!

After convincing the Merchant that Jasmine is crazy and thinks that Abu is the Sultan, Abu is found to have stolen several apples and some gold from bystanders. The three flee the marketplace while being chased by the guards.

Jasmine's innocence about everything outside the palace is what make us excuse her for her theft. Although the merchant never gets his apple back (Aladdin palms one and gives it back to him), we excuse Jasmine's behavior because she simply did not know that she was robbing the merchant. The fact that the merchant is about to punish her for her very real, though inadvertent, crime makes us aware that she has, in fact, broken the law. But this is quickly forgotten as the child disappears immediately from the scene and Abu and Aladdin entertain us with their antics. Still, the merchant does not regain his property, nor is he, to the best of our knowledge, ever reimbursed for the loss of his produce.

Further thievery goes on as Aladdin and Abu try to retain and regain the Genie's lamp and Jafar and Iago try to take it from them and hold on to it. Jasmine is not seen to steal again, though she does deceive Jafar in order to assist Aladdin in regaining the lamp later on.

The differences between the "good guys" stealing and the "bad guys" stealing are judged as acceptable or unacceptable by the morality of the movie and by the audience in accord with the movie. Why the "good guys" are allowed the same behaviors without punishment or without as severe punishment is not overtly addressed.

One of the important differences between the "good" and the "bad" in *Aladdin* is that the "good" never kill or permanently harm anyone. Although Aladdin, Abu, and Jasmine may resort to trickery (Jasmine, after all, disguises herself in the marketplace to begin with), they never damage their opponents. Even when they dispose of Jafar, they only induce him to become a genie and then banish him (and it is the Genie who actually does this). In contrast, Jafar commends the killing of people in order for him to attain the half of the scarab and does not care when the thief is eaten by the Cave. All characters are expendable to Jafar, even, perhaps, his parrot Iago. Jafar also shows no sympathy for humans when he tells Jasmine that Aladdin has already been killed for kidnaping the princess, although it is not true and he is merely holding Aladdin for his own purposes. It is, however, the *theft* of the princess for which Aladdin is purportedly beheaded.

The law regarding theft appears to be fairly static. The guard yells at Aladdin that he will have Aladdin's hands for his robbing and the merchant attempts to cut off one of Jasmine's hands. This, however, is the punishment for overt robbery. Other kinds of theft, like the theft of the lamp from the cave, the theft of the lamp from Aladdin by Iago, the recapture of the lamp by Aladdin and the "theft" of the princess, and the imprisonment of Aladdin on Jafar's orders receive no immediate punishment, nor is dismemberment brought forward as an option. These are private robberies, not those of the public sphere, but those of private grudge. Only the so-called kidnaping of the princess is a public issue and the crime is fictional in any case. There are ethical, rather than legal, punishments for these types of behavior.

The repeated exchange of the lamp is a battle for power, not for property, and is therefore a battle played out in the world as the conflict between "good" and "bad." Because Jafar wants the Genie to grant him wishes that have to do with personal and private power, he is "bad." While Aladdin's wishes are also personal, making him into a prince and saving his life, they are done in the name of "love" so they are considered virtuous. The division between the two types of personal gain is difficult to discern. It is only because we already know that Aladdin is our hero, that we do not perceive his wishes to be as self-centered. Indeed, Aladdin only wants power so he individually can be happy, while Jafar wants power so he can make others miserable. It is Aladdin's claim that he will use his third wish to free the Genie that makes his other two wishes appear less egocentric.

When Aladdin does not immediately free the Genie with his third wish as he has promised, he loses the lamp. Because Aladdin puts his personal future ahead of the Genie's and because he has never disclosed his true identity to Jasmine, the lamp is vulnerable to theft by Iago. Aladdin has been dishonest and his punishments are the removal of his opportunity to be virtuous and the increase in power that his enemy receives. Aladdin's guilt regarding lying about his identity is intensified when the Sultan, delighted that his daughter has finally found someone to marry, declares that Aladdin is "a person of. . .unimpeachable moral character." The audience knows, of course, just how unimpeachable that character is: Aladdin has lied, stolen, misrepresented himself, and, in the next scene, will break his word to the Genie about freeing him from the lamp.

When Jafar gets the lamp, he has no thought for the Genie, or anyone but himself. He embarrasses and dishonors the Sultan and Jasmine and makes them slaves to wait on him and amuse him. Then he provides himself with the power to keep them in his control while continuing to boast about his power. It is this self-centeredness, as well as his treachery, which finally punishes Jafar. His greed for power allows Jafar to fall for Aladdin's trickery and Jafar eagerly demands that he be made into "an all powerful genie" without recognizing that genies do, in fact, live in lamps and must grant the wishes of the lamp's master. Contained in his lamp, it is easier for the heroes to dispense with Jafar.

In both cases, the lamp's masters are victims of their own greed and are punished for it. Aladdin, because he repents his greed (and does, eventually, free the Genie), is able to get the lamp back for his third wish. Because Jafar retains his gluttony for power, he loses control of that power and is confined. These punishments are not dictated by any human law, but rather by the law of morality and "fairness" that exists in the Disney world.

The Sultan's dispensation of law is different. Rather than making judgments immediately, the Sultan mulls things over. Although he is Sultan and can, as such, change laws, it take him a ninety minute movie to determine that he can, in fact, change the law that states that a princess must marry a prince. Of course, without his slow action, we would not have the premise of the movie. But even when Jafar is revealed as having repeatedly hypnotized the Sultan (which perhaps is a reason for the Sultan's sloth-like law making), the Sultan sends him to the dungeons, rather than determining the punishment for Jafar's treachery immediately. This is in direct contrast to Jafar's punishments which are carried out immediately. When Jasmine asks about the boy from the marketplace (Aladdin), Jafar informs her that he has already been punished by being beheaded. Although this sentence has not been carried out, it does imply the rapid methods with which Jafar is familiar. Indeed, Jafar is twitted by the Sultan for his hasty behavior and is told to consult with the Sultan on all subsequent punishments of criminals. The Sultan says:

S: Jafar, this is an outrage! If it weren't for all your years of loyal service! From now on you're to discuss all sentencing of prisoners with me *before* they are beheaded!

The Sultan does not reject the notion of beheading prisoners, but the fact that the beheadings occur quickly and without the Sultan's approval. Having changed Jafar's responsibilities, the Sultan believes all is well and demands that Jafar and Jasmine make up their differences.

The non-human characters in *Aladdin* are numerous. Jasmine has a companion tiger named Rajah, Aladdin has his monkey friend Abu, and Jafar has his Brooklynite parrot, Iago. Rajah is merely a loyal friend to his lady, but Abu and Iago are active participants in the machinations of their human comrades. Iago is the one who retrieves the lamp from Aladdin; Abu is the one who causes the Cave of Wonders to destroy itself and (almost) the creatures inside as well. While Iago merely obeys his "master," Abu has a mind of his own and is a better pickpocket than Aladdin.

Iago's grand theft is that of the lamp, but this involves little trickery. Iago disguises his voice to sound like Jasmine's and calls Aladdin out into the garden. Aladdin, miserable because he has not yet told Jasmine about his true identity as a peasant, rushes off to find Jasmine and confess himself. He leaves the lamp behind in his chambers. Iago then slips into the chamber and simply removes the lamp.

Abu, on the other hand, is full of greediness for himself, rather than for another. Although Abu is a loyal friend to Aladdin, he is an independent thief. It is clear that Abu would get along a lot better without Aladdin than Aladdin would without Abu, despite the fact that it is Abu who fouls up the escape of Jasmine, Aladdin, and himself from the marketplace, the merchant and the guards. His greed led him to take several apples from the cart and to pickpocket some of the bystanders and relieve them of their gold. When this is found out, the three are forced to flee the marketplace in a hurry. At the same time, Abu has proved himself a fantastic pickpocket. Even though much attention has been focused on him, he has managed to pilfer a great deal in a short time. It is only Abu's pride at being the center of attention that causes him to bend over and spill out the contents of his vest. Abu plays decoy in the market while Aladdin lifts a melon behind another merchant's back and he also makes a remarkable distraction while Aladdin proceeds with his stealing and/or sweet talking.

The largest flaw in Abu's greedy character manifests in the Cave of Wonders. After Abu rids himself of his fear, he notices the riches and wants to take them for himself. Aladdin restrains him and they go off in search of the lamp. When the lamp is found, Aladdin leaves the magic carpet and Abu behind to wait while he climbs the many steps up to get the lamp. He explicitly tells Abu to keep his hands to himself, a clear foreshadowing that the monkey will do nothing of the kind. Sure enough, Abu spots a huge red jewel in the hands of (strangely enough) a golden ape statue and goes after it. The carpet attempts to hold him back, but fails. As soon as Abu's hands touch the jewel, the Cave begins to destroy itself and all the wealth disappears.

Abu's redemption comes when Jafar, in disguise, tells Aladdin to hand him the lamp and then he will give Aladdin his "reward." Aladdin hands the lamp up and Jafar tries to stab Aladdin. Instead, Aladdin falls back into the Cave, only to be rescued by the carpet. Once Aladdin awakens, he curses the stranger who deceived him (Jafar), and then realizes that they are all trapped in the Cave and that the stranger has the lamp. Abu, however, produces the lamp, Aladdin rubs it, and the adventure begins. At this point, Abu has evened up his score, since, although he caused the destruction of the Cave and caused them to be trapped, he has also snatched the lamp from Jafar's pocket. Aladdin's statement to Abu is a display of this balance:

A: We're trapped. That two-faced son of a jackal! Whoever he was. . . He's long gone with that lamp. [Abu presents the lamp] Why you hairy, little thief!

That Aladdin admiringly calls Abu a thief is an indicator of the values by which Abu and Aladdin live.

When the Genie appears, Aladdin, ever streetwise, tricks the Genie into getting him, the carpet, and Abu out of the sealed Cave without using up one of his wishes. The Genie confesses that this is so, but tells Aladdin, "No more freebies." Through deception, Aladdin and Abu manage to escape without using up their resources once again.

The overt law in *Aladdin* displays a distinct hierarchy of power. The Sultan, as previously mentioned, demands that Jafar tell him of all sentencing before it is carried out. By doing this, the Sultan exerts his control over the law and makes both Jafar and Iago more resentful of his power. Jafar, however, has more power than Jasmine; he is the Sultan's chief advisor, she is merely the princess. When Aladdin is about to be taken from his home to the palace dungeon, Jasmine demands that the guards release the boy. The chief guard refuses:

Jasmine: Unhand him by order of the princess!
Guard: Princess Jasmine?
Aladdin: Princess?!
G: What are you doing outside of the palace? And with this street rat!
J: That's not your concern! Do as I command. Release him!
G: I would, princess, except my orders come from Jafar. You'll have to take it up with him.
J: Believe me, I will.

Of course, by the time Jasmine consults Jafar, he has hidden Aladdin in the dungeons and tells Jasmine that the boy has already been beheaded. She, naturally, blames herself because Jafar tells her that Aladdin's crime was kidnaping the princess, although she assures Jafar that she ran away on her own.

This scene displays that, at least for the guards, Jafar has more power over the law than Jasmine. Jasmine, nevertheless, has reason to believe this will not always be so. When the Sultan attempts to make peace between Jasmine and Jafar, she tells Jafar: "At least some good will come of my being forced to marry. When I am queen I will have the power to get rid of you!"

Although Jasmine does not hold power as an unmarried woman, even a royal one, she will hold power as the wife of the (next) sultan. The quantity of legal authority here is clear. The Sultan is the most powerful, he has endowed Jafar with jurisdiction over Agrabah's laws, and Jasmine has power by birth, but has not yet matured enough to assume that power (which is available to her only by becoming a wife which, though a discussion of gender in the film will not be included here, is an interesting concept in itself).

This hierarchy of power is commented upon indirectly by Jafar when he is in disguise in the dungeon, coercing Aladdin into going to the Cave of Wonders. Jafar, dressed as an old prisoner, tells Aladdin about the Cave and informs him that there is a way out of the dungeon. He tells Aladdin: "There is a Cave, a Cave of Wonders! Filled with treasures beyond your wildest dreams. Treasure enough to impress even your princess, I'd wager."

Streetwise, Aladdin asks the old prisoner why he would share this information with a stranger. Jafar responds: "I need a young pair of legs and a strong back to go in after it!" Apparently, Aladdin is not streetwise enough, since he accepts this explanation and does not expect Jafar's later attempt to kill him for the lamp and leave him in the Cave.

What Jafar really tempts Aladdin with, however, is a single statement he makes early on in his attempts to convince Aladdin to go with him to the Cave. Jafar says: "You've heard of the Golden Rule, haven't you? Whoever has the gold makes the rules!"

Since this has been Aladdin's experience and is exactly what Aladdin has sung about in his first song ("Gotta eat to live, gotta steal to eat, otherwise we'd get along"), Aladdin is intrigued by the idea of having wealth and, thereby, having the ability to make his own rules and escape the rules of others. This is partially what he does by insisting with his first wish that the Genie make him a prince. Of course, Aladdin also enters the competition to marry Jasmine when he becomes a prince. The fact that Aladdin, while in the Cave, tells Abu that "a handful of this would make me richer than the Sultan" is further evidence of the linking of law and wealth by Aladdin and by the culture of Agrabah as expressed in the film.

The written law comes into consideration in the context of Jasmine's marriage. The problem, throughout the movie, is that Jasmine must marry a prince by her next birthday (three days away at the beginning of the film) and that she has not met a prince who she feels she can love yet. Jasmine, a Disney ideal, wants to marry for love, not because of the law. This law is mentioned at different times by the Sultan, Jafar, Jasmine, and Aladdin. Each one maintains the power of the law in this context. While the Sultan, Jasmine, and Aladdin bemoan the fact that the law exists, Jafar, being the "bad guy" sets out to do something about that law.

The Sultan restates the law that his daughter knows so well because he is trying to convince her to choose a husband.

Sultan:	The law says you must be married to a prince by your next birthday.
Jasmine:	The law is wrong.
S:	You've only got three more days.
J:	Father, I hate being forced into this. If I do marry, I want it to be for love.
S:	Jasmine, it's not only the law. I'm not going to be around forever. I just want to make sure you're taken care of. Provided for.

Although it is the law that has instigated the arrival of the princess's suitors, it is the Sultan's wish for his daughter to be attached to a husband, because he, as a father, cannot always be her caretaker, that forces him to follow the law. To Jasmine, marriage is a possibility. To the law and to the Sultan, Jasmine's marriage is something definite and something that must occur within three days. Again, I will not discuss the gender implications of the Sultan's notion that his female child must be provided for by a male, but I will note that Jasmine's statement that "the law is wrong" provides us with the idea that it is "unfair" and therefore must be altered or removed.

The Sultan is the sole controller of all the laws. Although Jafar may administrate how they are followed, it is the Sultan himself who has the ability to create and change laws. The fact that he does not change the law regarding his daughter despite her protest indicates that the Sultan is under the influence of Jafar's hypnotic staff even when Jafar is not actively using it. The sense of Jasmine's statement regarding the fairness of the law contradicts the benevolent and somewhat flighty Sultan's unwillingness to remove the law.

Jafar is nowhere near as resistant to changing the law as the Sultan. When Iago suggests that Jafar himself could marry the princess and then quickly kill both father and daughter, Jafar takes action. Jafar approaches the Sultan in the throne room and presents him with a long scroll, which he does not allow the Sultan to gaze at for very long.

Jafar:	Sire! I have found a solution to the problem with your daughter!
Sultan:	Really?
J:	[reading the scroll] If the princess has not chosen an husband by the appointed time, then the Sultan shall choose a husband for her.
S:	But Jasmine hated all those suitors. How could I choose someone she hates?
J:	Not to worry, my liege, there is more. If, in the event that a suitable prince cannot be found, the princess must then be wed to. . . hmmmm, interesting.
S:	What? Who?
J:	The royal vizier. Why, that would be me.
S:	But I thought the law says that only a prince can marry a princess. I'm quite sure that. . .
J:	Desperate times call for desperate measures, my lord.

The Sultan's uncertainty is put to rest by Jafar's hypnotic staff and the Sultan only escapes making the decree that Jasmine will marry Jafar by the ostentatious arrival of Aladdin and his entourage. It is clear that Jafar has written in the portion of the law regarding the possibility of the marriage of the princess to the vizier.

Jafar is more than willing to change the law to suit his purposes. By marrying the (beautiful) princess, Jafar can become heir to the throne and then dispose of the Sultan. Unlike the Sultan, Jafar realizes the flexibility of the law and the fact that the law is created, not permanent. The concept of the ability to alter the law that Jafar recognizes so well is precisely what the Sultan needs to learn. He finally does learn it after Jafar has been disposed of and the Sultan is no longer under the influence of Jafar's staff.

When Jafar has been banished to his lamp, the "good guys" gather as Jasmine and Aladdin try to figure out what happens next.

Aladdin:	Jasmine, I'm sorry I lied to you about being a prince.
Jasmine:	I know why you did.
A:	Well, I guess this is goodbye.
J:	Oh, that stupid law! This isn't fair! I love you.

While the Genie offers to forfeit his ability to be free (which can only happen if the master of the lamp uses up a wish to wish him free) and make Aladdin into a prince again, Aladdin refuses and grants the Genie his freedom. Having proven his worth and the fact that he is good to his word (even if it takes battling an evil sorcerer to do it), Aladdin gains the admiration of the Genie and the Sultan:

Genie:	No matter what anybody says, you'll always be a prince to me.
Sultan:	That's right! You've certainly proven your worth as far as I'm concerned. It's that law that's the problem!
Jasmine:	Father?
S:	Well am I Sultan or am I Sultan? From this day forth, the princess shall marry whoever she deems worthy.

Finally, the Sultan realizes that he embodies the law and may change it at will. That he knows little of Aladdin's history is clear, but since Aladdin has saved Agrabah it does not appear to the Sultan that Aladdin is unworthy. The fact that his daughter loves the thief and is finally willing to marry someone must be a great relief to him, particularly since the princess's birthday has not yet arrived.

Importantly, the Sultan has the ability to change the law with his word, while Jafar was only able to change the law through written means. It is clear that the Sultan's words mean much more than Jafar's. A similar pattern is seen in the market when Jasmine insists that Aladdin be freed, but the guards refuse because of Jafar's words to them. Jafar's words, here, are more valuable than the princess's. Presumably, the Sultan's words will be later documented, but his act of speaking, stating that the law is changed, is enough to change the law immediately. Who will document the law now that Jafar is gone is a different problem.

Throughout *Aladdin*, we see that the law means different things when applied to different people and that the executors of the law have different abilities, even when the laws are the same. In addition, the ability to change law is specific to the person making the alterations, and the amount of power that the lawmaker holds is directly related to the way in which the law is changed.

In his "Letter from a Birmingham Jail," Martin Luther King, Jr. discusses Saint Augustine's concept that "an unjust law is no law at all" and divides laws into the just and the unjust. This is similar to what occurs in *Aladdin*. The unjust law that states that the princess must marry a prince is one of the main concerns in the movie and is the issue which creates many of the other conflicts. That this law is, by the end of the film, changed is evidence that the law was perceived as unjust by at least some of the characters.

King's statement, however, applies also to thefts throughout the movie. Within the film, it appears that it is just to steal if one is hungry and that it is unjust to steal if one's only reason is greed. That the "good" characters only steal to benefit others or to sustain themselves is an example of their righteousness despite the law. The "bad" characters' theft in order to achieve personal gain completes the dichotomy of good-bad that we see throughout popular forms, particularly in forms created for children. Frequently, there are no complexities in children's stories and characters and actions are either entirely "good" or entirely "bad."

In discussing unjust laws, it is important to consider the first scene in which we see Aladdin in *Return of Jafar*, the sequel to *Aladdin*. Aladdin and Abu, having snuck up on some thieves in their lair, take the loot that the thieves have just taken from others. Aladdin and Abu escape on the carpet, and fly over Agrabah dropping all the loot (save one piece that Aladdin saves for Jasmine) to the poor, who collect it with glee and thanks. When Aladdin presents Jasmine with the jeweled flower that he has saved for her, she comments that it must have cost a fortune. Aladdin responds, "No, it was a steal." Jasmine, of course, has no idea that Aladdin has continued his thieving ways despite their marriage. Deception plays a large role throughout *Return of Jafar*.

Aladdin does not display the morality of the "Arab world." It displays the values of contemporary America, with a fictitious, and often derogatory, stylized "Arab world" as a backdrop. America's view of "Arab" crime and punishment is what is displayed, not the actual diversity of law and culture within that region. Only glimpses of American opinions of corporal punishment (such as cutting off a hand for theft) and women's roles (such as the briefly seen harem and Jasmine's confinement to the palace grounds) are seen. Both the view of women and the view of "Arabs" in *Aladdin* are worthy of further study.

It is not "Arab" justice that is illustrated throughout *Aladdin*, it is American justice. The inequality of individuals before the law based on their power within the culture is one of the main issues within the film, and an issue that is always a concern in legal battles, both those we hear about through news media and those less publicized.

Finally, when looking at *Aladdin*, we must consider what the movie tells the children who watch it. In the realm of legal issues, the film tells children that it is acceptable to steal food if you are hungry and that is it okay to break the law if you are "good." What we must consider what the meaning of "hunger," "goodness," and other attributes mean to children (as opposed to their "meaning" to the adult "authors" and to the general community) and decide if these are the messages that we, as a culture, really want to communicate to our young people.

** 471 S. Summit # 93, Bowling Green, OH 43402*

References

Aladdin. Animated. Disney, 1992.

King, Jr., Martin Luther. *Letter from Birmingham City Jail*. Philadelphia: American Friends Service Committee, 1963.

Orwell, George. *Animal Farm*. New York: Signet, 1974 (1946).

The Return of Jafar. Animated. Disney, 1994.

Chapter Six
'Incest' in Babylonia, Anatolia and India

Peter H. Salus*

At the same time that we are decidedly opposed to and revolted by the notion of 'incest' in our contemporary society, just what we mean by this term is largely unclear and unspecified. We are not alone in forbidding certain sexual activities. Nor are we alone in legislating against the forbidden acts. In this paper, I propose an examination of the concept of forbidden sexuality and then analyze the instantiations of prohibitions in the very oldest legal codes.

In her excellent study over a decade ago, Judith Lewis Herman confined herself to sexual molestation by a father of a daughter, specifically a pre-pubescent or pubescent child. (Herman 1981) While it is obvious that this is harmful to the child, the question emerges as to whether the taboo is against sex with one's offspring or child abuse, which is repugnant under any circumstances. (We do not, apparently, recoil from Lot's inebriate seduction by his daughters [Gen . 19.30-38]; nor did the Mosaic God. Is this because the daughters were adult or because they initiated sex with their father?)

But, clearly, we consider other sexual acts incestuous, too. In the Oedipus myth, for instance, we have to come to grips with unwitting adult mother-son incest; among the dynastic kings, with brother-sister marriages; in Iris Murdoch's *A Severed Head* (1961) with adult consensual sister-brother intercourse; in Jeanette Winterson's *At & Lies* (1994) with violent rape of a sister by an older brother. And this is far from all. There are many, many variants. Ibsen employs two more: in *Ghosts* (1881) the lovers discover they are siblings; in *Little Eyolf* (1894) it is revealed to us that the siblings, passionately in love, are indeed unrelated. First cousins, uncles, aunts. Step-parents. Even confining ourselves to Western -- to Judaeo Christian -- literature and mores we find both great variety and great variance in degree of condemnation. One contemporary extreme may be found in the *Encyclopedia of Biblical and Christian Ethics* (1992; s.v. incest):

> Incest is an evil immoral act that flaunts human lust and defies God's commandments regarding appropriate sexual behavior.... The abhorrent crime of incest ... demands the full weight of legal, moral medical, and religious sanctions in order to secure the proper punishment of the offender and the rehabilitation of the victim.

The *Oxford English Dictionary* (OED) (s.v.) defines incest as

> The crime of sexual intercourse or cohabitation between persons related within the degrees within which marriage is prohibited; sexual commerce of near kindred.

The *Encyclopedia* (loc.cit.) states

> This term denotes sexual relations between persons who, because of family membership, are forbidden such indulgences by law.

But problems arise with most definitions. Robin Fox (1967) puts his finger on the basis of most of these when he notes that it is important to differentiate sexual relations and conjugal relations. Both the OED and the *Encyclopedia* blur this distinction. To be more explicit: there is a difference in most societies between those with whom one may enjoy sex and those whom one may marry. In our Judaeo-Christian culture this distinction has been blurred. (Though note the ease with which majority males in the US could enjoy sexual relations with women of color in the past, though these women were on the wrong side of the exogamy line.) Fox points out that there are cultures in which parents initiate children to sexual behavior, that males marrying mother and daughter is traditional in Tibet (where fraternal polyandry -- brothers sharing a wife -- also occurs); and that in a number of African societies "marriage with the wife's sister's daughters" is popular. Bringing this to a close, the very definition of family and relative is confused when we cross cultures: some American and Australian tribes bar conjugal and sexual relations with those who possess the same totem (much as though, say, Americans eliminated those born under the same zodiacal sign from sexual or conjugal partnerships). Fraternal polyandry must have a basis in early Hindu culture, too, otherwise the marriage of Draupadi to all five of the Pandavas, which is fundamental to most of the *Mahabharata*, would have been viewed unfavorably. There is also the apparent contradiction involved in the Levitical requirement that a younger brother marry his brother's widow while Canon law prohibited marriage of in-laws. Presumably, this was in Shakespeare's mind while writing *Hamlet*.

It is far from easy to understand exactly where incest taboos arise. There have been many theories, ranging from the psychological (Freud) to the need for the maintenance of authority to the genetic — as though, on the one hand, human breeding were very different from that of the other primates, or, on the other, we thought that "Lucy" and her kin actually comprehended the concept of genetic defect and heritable disease. Without going into a great deal of detail, it is clear that there is no theory that has not been shot full of holes in the literature.

All of this is, however, prologue to the topic I wish to discuss here: the treatment of incest in the earliest non-Mosaic laws that come down to us: Babylonian, Hittite, and Hindu. (There are fragmentary laws from Ur, about 200 years prior to those of Hammurabi, referred to as the "Laws of Eshunna" Though there are several dealing with sexual offences, incest of any kind is not among these.)

Hammurabi appears to have reigned from 1728-1686 B.C.E. The codification of traditional lore that became judicial statute in his reign is the oldest such document preserved. And it is preserved in several modes and several locations. Most salient is the presentation on both sides of a stela found in Susa, doubtless taken there from much further east as a trophy. Hammurabi's laws have given rise to a vast literature over the past century, and I will not attempt to review it. However, the actual form of the inscription is relevant. It is made up of a lengthy introduction by Hammurabi lauding himself and Ishtar and Marduk (occupying four columns) and then launches into the laws, which are of the form "If...then..." The final columns are an authorial explicit.

As an example, the first law is: "If a man has accused a man and has charged him with manslaughter and then has not proved it, his accuser shall be put to death." The first 126 laws are concerned with crimes, including murder, theft, and business contracts. The code then turns to social matters (though these are contractual, too): "If a man has taken a wife and has not drawn up a contract for her, that woman is not a wife" [§127]; and to unhappy marriages: "If a woman has procured the death of her husband on account of another man, they shall impale that woman" [§153]. (This is certainly something that Gertrude and Claudius would have had to worry about.) The next four laws are those which will concern us.

> §154. If a man carnally knows his daughter, they shall banish that man from the city.
>
> §155. If a man has chosen a bride for his son and his son has carnally known her, and if thereafter he himself lies in her bosom and they catch him, they shall bind that man and shall cast him into the water.
>
> §156. If the man has chosen a bride for his son and his son has not carnally known her, and he himself lies in her bosom, he shall pay her ½ maneh of silver and further shall make good to her anything that she has brought from the house of her father, and a husband after her heart may marry her.
>
> §157. If a man after the death of his father lies in his mother's bosom, they shall burn both of them.
>
> §158. If a man after the death of his father is caught in the bosom of his chief wife who is the mother of sons, that man shall be expelled from his paternal estate.

What do we learn about Babylonia from this? First, that father-daughter incest results in exile, while mother-son incest results in death. Second, that bridal virginity was prized, as the penalty for deflowering one's son's fiancee is greater if the son had not already "known" her. Third, that sex with one's father's wives was permissible if that wife was not one's mother nor had sons of her own. Women were clearly "property" to the Babylonians, but they were valuable property. Thus, mother-son incest (an abomination) is rewarded with death, but other offenses result in loss of property or position: exile from the city, actual payment to the affronted fiancee, loss of one's inheritance. The nature of the role of women might be studied, reading the myriad letters and legal documents leads me to think their lot was not at all as lowly as might be assumed. There are certainly evidences of strong, independent and highly-honored women among the Babylonians. (Gadd 1973: 190-220 is especially illuminating.) Of importance to me, however, is the simple fact that only mother-son and father-daughter sexual relations are itemized in the oldest legal corpus that comes down to us.

The Biblical parallels to §154 are in *Lev.* 18:6–18; 20:10-21; *Deut.* 27:20, 22-23. But they show a very different attitude. Leviticus condemns both partners in mother-son incest or father-daughter-in-law incest to death. Brother-sister incest (or half-brother-half-sister) is penalized with exile, however. The penalties for uncle-niece or aunt-nephew intercourse are unclear. the *Deuteronomy* verses "curse" those who have sex with "father's wife," sister or half-sister, or "mother-in-law." It is not clear what the results of being cursed by the congregation are (nor does the reference in *Jeremiah* 11:3 help).

Chronologically, the Hittite laws come next. There was an assembly convened by both Hattusilis and by Telipinus (1650–1525 B.C.E.), which appears to have been what we would call a constitutional body, and that the Hittite monarchy was originally elective (like that of the Anglo-Saxons), but just who could speak is unclear. It is clear that Hattusilis didn't care exactly what the "citizens" said and did not feel bound by such things. (Gurney 1973:252-255). Nonetheless, the Hittite laws we have are largely from two tablets (each of 100 clauses) from the time of Hattusilis. There are also are large number of fragments with one or two laws on them. Tablet 1 begins with "If a man.."; Tablet 2, with "If a vine..." The laws are not ordered as neatly as the Babylonian ones are. However, a few sections of Tablet 2 concern sexual offenses. These read: Column III.

(20) If a man sins with a steer, it is an abomination. He "dies." [he may be killed?]

(21) He is to be brought to the court; the King can have him killed,

(22) or the King can let him live. He may not come before the King again.

(23) - (25) If a man sins with a sheep ...

(26) If a man sins with his own mother,

(27) it is an abomination. If a man sins with his daughter,

(28) it is an abomination. If a man sins with his son, it is an abomination....

(30) If a man sins with his Step-mother,

(31) there is no offence. Only if his father is still alive it is an abomination.

(32) If a man has sex with a free woman

(33) and with her mother; but one is in one country

(34) and the other in another, there is no offence.

(35) If they are both in the same locale and he knows it, it is an abomination,

(36) but not an offence....

(50) ... If a man

(51) has a wife and also has sex with her daughter [his step-daughter]

(52) it is an abomination. If he is married to the daughter and has sex with her mother

(53) or sister, it is an abomination.

It is nowhere stated what the penalty for committing an abomination is. As other sentences are quite explicit; e.g.

(83) If a man rapes a woman, the man shall perish, he shall be killed;

or , Column 4

(16) If a man has sex with a pig or a dog, he shall be killed.

This is a genuine lacuna. Whether it means that social obloquy, rather than an actual penalty, is the sentence, is open to interpretation. It may mean that the offender is subject to the "King's justice" and that (depending on the judge) the sentence might be light or exile or death. (While it may be interesting to note that sex with a steer or a sheep is abominable, but sex with a dog or a pig is fatal, I will not attempt to interpret this.)

It is notable that the prohibitions on sex with one's brother's wife and the wives of one's father (other than one's own mother) are constrained to while they are alive. The laws regarding the marriage of the wives of the deceased to his brother or nephew are remarkably similar to the (later) Jewish laws of levirate (Judah and Er, *Gen*. 38; Ruth and Boaz; *Ruth* 4). However, the most notable item in these laws is the omission of any prohibition on brother-sister incest. While we have little evidence, it appears that the queen of Mursilis I (1620-1590 B.C.E) was succeeded by her sister-in-law (though we have now way of knowing whether this was Mursilis' sister) and King Arnuwandas I (1440-1420 B.C.E) was married to his sister (Gurney 1973: 659-683).

The Laws of Manu or the *Manusmirti* is made up of nearly 2700 verses of Sanskrit, written just before the begging of the Common Era. As *smirti* designates a traditional religious text, rather than an inspirational text (like *veda*), it was clearly seen by the ancient Hindus as a composed text, not a revelation. Over a period of centuries, it became the standard teaching, though *laws*, as Wendy Doniger and Brian Smith have pointed out (1991), is an invention of the Raj, attempting to sway the Hindu towards the Empire's concepts. Its discovery by the west was of tremendous importance, as I have written elsewhere (Salus 1993, Salus 1994). About a third of *Manusmirti* is in the *Mahabharata*, though it is opaque as to which is derived from which. In any event, it provides us with a coherent view of ancient India.

Before examining what Manu (the mythical progenitor of mankind -- a sort of Hindu Adam) has to say about incest, let me point out that traditional Hinduism is very hard on sexual misconduct in general. Thus "If men persist in seeking intimate contact with other men's wives, the king should brand them ... and banish them" [8.352]. "A man who Corrupts an unwilling virgin should instantly suffer corporal or capital punishment; but a man who corrupts a willing virgin when he is her equal should not undergo corporal or capital punishment" [8.364]. "If a woman who is proud ... deceives her husband, the king should have her eaten by dogs..:"[8.371]. But Manu is quite a sexist: "Men must make their women dependant day and night ... A woman is not fit for independence" [9.2-3]. And quite hard on adultery: "there is nothing whatsoever here on earth more conducive to shortening life than doting upon another man's wife" [4.134].

Another point of importance is the sanctity of the guru, the teacher. In Hinduism, the guru is not necessarily unmarried: he is wise and learned. Thus, the first place that the reader encounters the notion of incest relates to this:

> Discharging semen into women born of the same womb as oneself, virgins, women of the lowest castes, or the wife of one's friend or son, is regarded as equal to the violation of the guru's marriage-bed. [11:59]

Later, we are told:

> A man who has violated his guru's marriage-bed should declare his error and sleep on a heated iron bed or embrace a red-hot metal cylinder, and by his death he is cleaned. Or he himself may cut off his penis and testicles ... walking straight ahead till he dies. Or he may carry a club shaped like a bedpost, wear rags, grow a beard, concentrate his mind, and carry out the 'Painful' vow of the Lord of Creatures for a year.... [11 . 104-06]

This requires some explanation. The club in the shape of a bedpost is one of the weapons of Siva. Siva punished Prajâpati for committing incest with his daughter by beheading him. Prajâpati's skull flew up and stuck to Siva and thus the staff with a skull atop it is the bedpost club. As Prajâpati (another name for Brahma) was the "Lord of Creatures," this relates Siva, the club, and the cognomen. In 11.212 we are informed that the 'Painful' vow was to "eat in the morning for three days, then in the evening for three days; for three days he should eat food that he has not asked for, and for the next three days he should not eat."

All of this having been said, let me now go to what the *Manusmari* says about incest:

> If a man has shed his semen in a woman born of the same womb as himself, with the wife of his friend or his son, with virgins or women of the lowest castes, he should

> carry out the vow for violating the guru's marriage-bed. If he has sex with the 'sister' who is the daughter of his father's sister, or with the daughter of his mother's sister or of his mother's full brother his first-cousins] he should carry out the 'Moon-course' vow. [11.171-172]

The most interesting point here, I believe, is that father-daughter and mother-son incest are not explicitly barred. In fact, in a society where men had multiple wives, sons are not barred from intercourse with half-sisters nor sisters with half-brothers ("born of the same womb"). On the other hand, violations of one's guru's marriage-bed are quite serious. This is because to the disciple, the guru is the adopted father. Indeed, he is more than one's father, for one has consciously and explicitly chosen him. Betrayal of his (the guru's) trust is not merely adultery with another man's wife, it is a betrayal of one's self.

If we now look back at Robin Fox's distinction between those one may have sex wish as opposed to those whom one may marry, we can look at the very next verse of Manu:

> An intelligent man should not take any of these three for his wife; he should not have sex with them because they are relatives... [1 1.173]

The Hindus, then, make precisely the distinction that Fox does. But let us turn back to examining the meaning of these sets of restrictions. Hammurabi's statutes provide for banishment for father daughter incest; for "dunking" for sex with one's future daughter-in-law (if she is not a virgin) and substantial payment if she is a virgin; loss of inheritance for violating one's (deceased) father's wives (if she has borne sons); and death for both partners of mother-son incest.

The Hittite laws abominate mother-son incest, father-daughter incest, father-son sex, stepmother-stepson sex (if the father is alive), sex with both a woman and her daughter (if they are both in the same town), and sex with one's stepdaughter or sister-in-law.

The Hindu laws prohibit sex with one's siblings (though not half-siblings), with first cousins, with one's son's spouse, with a friend's spouse, and with a guru's spouse. As I have said, this last is a substitute for mother-son incest; betrayal of friends must have been as mean in ancient India as in Dante's *Commedia* (where such traitors are in a lake of frozen feces).

The Babylonian laws are the easiest to analyze: all the ancient near eastern empires were built on commercial law. Violating trust and contract was a terrible thing (in the eyes of the merchants and the priesthood). Mother-son incest was a truly awful thing, as was intercourse with one of your father's other wives (who had borne a son). This was because such activity (and the possible progeny) confused the line of inheritance — something of great importance to a merchant class. While father-daughter incest was treated seriously, it was treated with exile, a truly dreadful punishment at a time where cities in the near east must have been extremely xenophobic. In fact, it may be that this was a way to condemn to death without doing the dirty work. Some other group in some other area would kill the fellow. Finally, as I stated above, women were considered property: defacing your son's property (virgin bride) was punishable by a fine. Violating the bride your son had already deflowered was rude, but little more. In fact, the dunking might be seen as either cooling the father's hot passions or dunking him for dipping a portion of his person in a forbidden area. It was not serious. It had no commercial meaning. The "merchandise" was no longer intact.

The Hittites put mother-son intercourse, father-daughter sex, and father-son sex on the same level: they were abominations. Sex with one's stepmother was only "wrong" if the father were still alive — if the son was taking the father's property too early. Sex with both a mother and her daughter or with two sisters was wrong, too. But in varying degrees, depending on the geography. In my opinion, this had a pragmatic basis, too. Sex with mother and daughter (when they were both in the same household) or with two sisters would tend to raise tensions and rivalries and could well bear upon questions of precedence and inheritance. The Hittites were always conscious of the mercantile implications of their actions — perhaps too much so. Siblings and cousins aren't mentioned at all. The reason that sibling incest was excluded was because the kings — or at least one or two of them -had either taken their (deceased) wife's sister or their own sister as consort, if not queen. There may also have been an influence of the Pharaonic tradition of sibling marriages. The Hittites and the Egyptians had a long and largely unhappy relationship, with many wars and even more battles. What social influences there may have been will never be a completely elucidated issue.

In an excellent article, Russell Middleton pointed out:

> Although instances of Pharaohs who married their own sisters or half sisters have been reported from several of the dynasties, the greatest concentration of cases appears to be in the 18th and 19th Dynasties. Indeed, probably a majority of the 18th Dynasty kings (1570-1397 B.C.E.) married their sisters or half sisters ... Documented cases of father-daughter marriage among the Egyptian kings are less numerous and more controversial.... Rameses II married not only two of his sisters, but also at least two of his daughters [it may have been three -- PHS] ... A second example of father-daughter marriage ... involves Amenhotep III (13971360 B.C.E.), who was probably married to his daughter Satamon and possibly to another daughter as well. [Middleton 1962]

It is important to note that contrary to the common notion that sibling marriage was confined to the Pharoahs, Cerny [1954] and Fischer [1957] have demonstrated that the practice occurred among the commoners as well. As time went on, the Greek influence on Egypt became strong, and we are told by Philo Judaeus that when Ptolemy II married his full sister Arsinoe, in the 3rd century B.C.E, it was considered scandalous by the Hellenized populace. Ptolemy's descendants followed his example, Ptolemy VII was married to two of his sisters and both Ptolemy X1I and Ptolemy XIII were married to their sister, the notorious Cleopatra VI. Returning to Middleton [op.cit.],

> During the period of Roman rule in Egypt there is ... an abundance of papyrus documents and records which give evidence that commoners often practiced brother-sister marriage.

It is interesting to note that Philo (who lived in Alexandria from 127-151 C.E.) seems to have been more affronted by the age of the women involved: "not only if they were younger than their brothers but also if they were older or of the same age." [Philo (vol. 7) Book 3, §4]

I have gone into this at such length because I feel that it is necessary to document the refutation of notions that incest is a universal taboo. The best instance of this attitude is in a paper by Talcott Parsons [1954]:

> In recent years there has been a revival of interest in the problem of what features are common to human societies everywhere and what are the forces operating to maintain these common features. One reason for my present interest in the incest taboo is that it is one of the most notable of these common features. With all the

> variability of its incidence outside of the nuclear family, there is the common core of the prohibition of marriage and in general of sexual relationships between members of a nuclear family.... no society is known where incest between mother-son, father-daughter or full brother-sister is permitted except the few cases of brother-sister in royal families ...

This is, as has been shown, false. As there was sufficient anthropological, sociological and psychological evidence available in the literature for decades prior to this assertion, it is not merely idle speculation to inquire into the suppression of the data on the part of sociologists and social workers involved with "the family." (And I believe that in stating the question in this way, I have answered it.) The "welfare" industry, especially in the English-speaking countries, has a vested interest in making "our way" into "everyone's way." This is not at all out of line with the western notion of bringing democracy or its version of human rights to the world. But neither the ancient nor the modern data supports the opening paragraphs of Parsons' well-known paper.

But this is all digression: my focus should be on the actual texts of the Babylonians, the Hittites, and the Hindus. They do, indeed, appear to bar mother-son sexual relations as well as (to a milder extent) father-daughter intercourse. (This last is most likely because all three were patriarchal societies in which occasional strong women existed, but where most women were treated as chattels.) Sibling relations and sibling matrimony, on the other hand, were clearly acceptable in the near east, though they are barred in India.

Most of the psychiatric literature (Freud 1900; Freud 1913; Jung 1912; Rank 1912; Masson 1984) deals with incest as child abuse (as does Herman 1981). Though Rank goes on to discuss at great length the mythological and literary evidence, he is time-bound to considering the material in a Freudian way (the meat of his book was read at three meetings of the Psychological Wednesday Society in October 1906). The sociological literature (which Parsons exemplifies) suffers from Freudian denial. The western religious literature is exemplified by the intolerance shown in the Encyclopedia. In order to discuss what might best be termed co-sanguinous sexual behavior, we must turn to the law, the historians, and the anthropologists.

Fox's attitude is far more circumspect than Parsons':

> We want to know why it is that in most places and at most times there has been a ban on, of if not a positive ban on, at least, an avoidance of, sexual relationships between

primary kin. So unthinking is our acceptance of this situation that it is often difficult to drive home to people that there is anything to explain. [1967: 55f.]

He goes further, in fact:

There is not in fact a universal horror of incest, and many societies do not have severe penalties for it; others practice it, and in yet others there does seem to be a genuine indifference to it. [1967:63]

In this paper, I have attempted to limn the regulations on familial sexual acts in three ancient civilizations: Babylonian, Hittite, and Hindu. I have brought in data from two others: Biblical and Egyptian. The Judaeo Christian attitude exemplified by the *Bible* and the *Encyclopedia* entry, with which we are most familiar, is by far the most rigid. The Egyptian is the most "liberal," though we know more about conjugality than we do about sexual practice. The Hammurabic Code is interesting in that with the sole exception of mother-son incest, all other regulations appear to be governed by the concepts of property and value, certainly not by mentality. The Hittite laws reveal an interest in property rights and (indirectly) the laws of inheritance. The Hindu admonitions are those based (on the face of it) in loyalty and morality: Sibling sex is expressly banned, but the other injunctions are less direct. The *Manusmirti* bars sex with one's daughter-in-law or with the wife of a friend. These are both violations of trusts. So is the offense which carries the most serious penalty: that of violating one's guru's marriage bed. As I have said earlier, the guru occupies the post of spiritual father, the guru's spouse is the father's spouse and thus the acolyte's mother. Mother-son incest has thus been shunted to this offense.

Finally, only the *Manusmirti* draws the conclusion drawn by Fox: one should not have sexual relations with those whom one cannot marry.

The incest taboo is part of the western cultural heritage. But it is important for us to recognize that (despite claims) there is neither solid biological evidence to uphold it nor is there evidence for natural aversions nor inhibitory responses. It is another part of our elaborate cultural baggage, but it is demonstrably not part of everyone's.

* #3303, 4 Longfellow Place, Boston, MA 02114

References

Cerny, Jaroslav, 1954, "Consanguineous marriages in Pharaonic Egypt," *Egyptian Archaeology*, Vol. 40: 23-27, December.

Doniger, Wendy, and Brian K. Smith, 1991, *The Laws of Manu*, London: Penguin Books.

Driver, G.R., and John C. Mills, 1955, *The Babylonian Laws*, Oxford: University Press.

Encyclopedia of Biblical and Christian Ethics, Rev.Ed., 1992 [R.K. Harrison, general editor], Nashville, TN: Thomas Nelson.

Fisher, Henry George, 1957, "A God and a General of the Oasis on a Stela of the Late Middle Kingdom," *Journal of Near Eastern Studies*, Vol. 16: 231, October.

Fox, Robin, 1967, *Kinship and Marriage*, Harmondsworth: Penguin Books.

Freud, Sigmund, 1900, *Die Traumdeutung*, Wiesbaden: Bergmann.

____________, 1913, *Totem und Tabu*, Leipzig: H. Heller.

Friedrich, Johannes, 1959, *Die hethitischen Gesetze*, Leiden: E.J. Brill.

Gadd, C.J., 1973, "Hammurabi and the end of his dynasty," *The Cambridge Ancient History*, Vol. II, Part 1, I.E.S. Edwards, C.J. Gadd, N.G.L. Hammond, and E. Sollberger, Eds. Cambridge: University Press, 176–227.

Gurney, O.J., 1973, "Anatolia c. 1750–1600 B.C.," *The Cambridge Ancient History*, Vol. II, Part 1, I.E.S. Edwards, C.J. Gadd, N.G.L. Hammond, and E. Sollberger, Eds. Cambridge: University Press, 228-255.

____________, 1973, "Anatolia c. 1600-1380 B.C.," *The Cambridge Ancient History*, Vol. II, Part 1, I.E.S. Edwards, C.J. Gadd, N.G.L. Hammond, and E. Sollberger, Eds. Cambridge: University Press, 659-685.

Herman, Judith Lewis, 1981, *Father-Daughter Incest*, Cambridge, MA: Harvard University Press.

Jolly, J., 1887, Mânavadharmasâstra, London: Trübner.

Jung, Carl G., 1912, *Wandlungen und Symbole der Libido*, Leipzig: Deuticke.

Masson, Jeffrey M., 1984, *The Assault on Truth*, New York: Farrar, Strauss & Giroux.

Middleton, Russell, 1962, "A Deviant Case: Brother-Sister and Father-Daughter Marriage in Ancient Egypt," *American Sociological Review*, Vol. 27, No. 5: 603-611, October.

Parsons, Talcott, 1954, "The Incest Taboo in Relation to Social Structure," *British Journal of Sociology*, Vol. 5: 101-117.

Philo Judaeus [Philo of Alexandria], 1929-1962, *Works*, Transl. by F.H. Colson and G.H. Whitaker, 12 vols., Cambridge, MA: Harvard University Press.

Rank, Otto, 1912, *Das Incest-Motiv in Dichtung und Sage*, Leipzig: Deutiche.

Salus, Peter H., 1993, "Preface," *Sir William Jones: A Reader*, Satya S. Pachori, Ed., Delhi and Oxford: Oxford University Press, 3-11.

____________ , 1994, "Another Culture," *The Peirce Seminar Papers*, Vol. 2.

Chapter Seven

So, this is how it is done...

Agnes T.M. Schreiner*

I.

What should you do if you have bought something and the seller turns out not to be the owner, or if the purchase turns out not to be any good? Fortunately you can take the matter to court because the law provides for this kind of situation. Often it is not even necessary to take the matter so far. The rights and duties of purchasers are clearly codified and the same is true of those of the vendor. You have the law on your side. You can handle the situation without having to go to court.

What can you do if you have been given the keys to a house that you have bought (by deed) and paid for, and a conveyancing ritual turns out not to have been performed? In a situation like this, the answer is: nothing. You can, however, still perform the ritual. This would mean that the hearth must first be lit and the fire then put out, that a piece of turf or else a twig is handed over, and a pot of porridge will be cooked and eaten together — an example I took from ancient rites.[1] There is no law that obliges you to perform or not to perform rites like these; nor is there any law to state that you are not the new owner if the ritual was not performed. Performing this ritual does not disturb the social order. At most it may cause a bit of a stir because this ceremony costs time and money.

Moreover the occasion of the performance of the conveyancing ceremony bears no traces of a chaos that is to be exorcized. Why is it then that we often assume that ritual exists to create order in a chaotic world? Why do think that once we have said that we have stated the crux of ritual? How is it possible that sometimes simple, sometimes complicated, but almost — at first sight — odd sequences of ritual acts can be summed up as having such a straightforward function?[2]

It is a great deal easier to prove that *the law* has been brought into existence to create order. Unlike ritual, which is an exclusive event, the law is a general and all—embracing system that rejects any individual regulation that does not in one way or another form a link in the chain of rights and duties, powers and responsibilities, lawful and unlawful actions. It is in this way that private, public and criminal law give themselves the power to prevent chaotic situations developing in society, claiming to provide a orderly response to them. The law contains order in itself and then proceeds to propagate it: it creates a legal order within which we can live. Among the legal scholars there may be some discussion as to whether this is what the law *wants* to establish or if it is simply its function, or whether it is a case of an order that exists within the law or one that the law itself puts into effect in society; the generally accepted notion, however, is that society is governed by law. And just as well, most people would say. Otherwise there would be nothing but chaos.

It is a mistake to think that rituals have the same characteristics as the law has, or that they fight the same struggle against chaos. Ritual does not introduce any order into a chaotic world. It invents an order — one that exists parallel to the world.[3] An order that is as exclusive as ritual itself. It is simply not concerned with the everyday world, chaotic or otherwise. In contrast to the law that institutes order in the world, ritual initiates an order that is itself a momentary world. This momentary world coincides with the performance of the ritual and takes up as much time as is necessary for the completion of the sequence of ritual acts. To initiate an order is not something that ritual is appointed to do; nor does it undertake to do so. It is just what ritual does anyway without needing approval or appointment. The order whose task is to combat chaos comes into being through the law or some other social system for establishing norms. The order that comes into being through ceremonial, on the other hand, is an pure gratuitous order; it is in all senses sacrosanct.

II.

The ritual order was a gift that even practices of ancient law had gratefully incorporated. Our ancestors, however, sensed that an incorporation like this could not be an organic one. They didn't make the mistake of thinking that the world lives a natural life and that we have to naturalize even assimilate "Fremdkörper" in order to accommodate them, while nowadays we feel troubled not being able to come up with good arguments when we have something different and unnatural at hand. It is almost as if we have to have an excuse for practicing a ritual. We have not always thought, however, that our purposes should adjust a developing, natural world. Our projects in the past can be characterized as being more mechanistic than organic, more repetitive than instinctive and — as I take from Benjamin[4] — more *emblematic or allegoric* than *symbolic*, to fill in: we were more inclined to memento mori than to terminal care. We were contemplating the momentariness of our concerns, what makes it preferable to stay a bit longer, to take our time. (Notice that there is no rush ever within a ritual.)

The difference between the organic and the ritual perspective becomes clear in the way we envisage things. When we picture a city, for instance, we think of something permanent, a body with a pounding heart, the lively city-centre. Within the city we notice a number of important institutes and institutions, which are also permanently present. Education has its schools, religion its churches, art its museums, economy its market-places, exchanges and banks. The law possesses courts, like the Hall of Justice. General abstracts — qualifying education, religion, law and the like as such — are given an enduring site in a domain that, in itself, is nothing less abstract: the city. A city like Amsterdam or The Big Apple. Only from a very high position will it be possible to see its full dimensions. From a plane, for example. However, it is impossible to behold law in its full dimensions from any point of view. This in no way prevents us from accepting the full presence of law in a city by means of a centrally located, clearly visible and recognizable monumental building. We are able to grasp the concept of a social institution or a city and we are able to connect this to a general image; the image of a surrounded unit where social life takes place. This image of a city or a social institution did not always exist.

The typical character of a city was not always pictured in the sense of a municipal society. Our ancestors knew that a bird's-eye view of a city only resulted in a map. The cartographer's craftsmanship pointing out the striking features of each individual building, as on a map a building can only be identified by its specific features. The map itself can be the striking feature by laying it in the hands of the patroness of the city, as oil paintings or statues show. For many generations "Amsterdam" for instance was this female, surrounded by her attributes. She played a vital part and took a central role at special occasions and she always headed any procession. She was the city. She created the city anytime she described her in a solemn procession.

What applied to the city also applied to the law, the church, the annual fair. They were not there; for a specific moment they were either drawn in a procession or circumscribed. Annual fair-parades, silent religious processions, the escort of guests of honour or exiles, the solemn processions for peace and quiet, they all marked the streets. The image of law was created by the bailiff's fortnightly processions.

In Amsterdam this privilege of the bailiff consists of four so called "Loospandingen" (to be translated as "Empty Pawn") including a Major Empty Pawning ("Grote Loospanding") followed by one "Eigenpanding" ("Proper Pawn"). Their route is fixed and they are extensively described in the 17th century handwritten *Book of Ceremonies of the City of Amsterdam.*[5] Bankholidays excluded, processions took place throughout the year. It is obvious that the bailiff not only circumscribes or describes the law in his processions, but he also circumscribes the year because the successive "pandingen" (pawnings) determine the legal calendar in which four independent cycles are gathered round feasts.

The first three regular processions include a small cortege. After the opening ritual in the main square ("de Dam"), the bailiff, escorted by three officials, walks down the central street towards the mouth of the river ("Amstel"). Then he walks upstream, along the main street on the other side of the river. He crosses the river again returning to the city hall in a semi-square in order to close. In the square he performs the final ritual. The fourth procession, "Grote Loospanding" (the major one) has the same cortege and the same route but is spread out over four days and divided into four sections.

Those four processions seem to be the manifestation of the standard formula of the bailiff's "een — one, twee — two, drie — three and four times — ende vierwerf". A formula similar as to the auctioneer's "going, going, gone". Comparing the bailiff's formula with the auctioneer's, it is almost inevitable to think that the first, second, third and fourth "panding" are building up, in a similar way, towards "Eigenpanding": the fifth and last procession. One could assume that this final pawning is the proper, actual distraint. However, in the Book of Ceremonies there is only a description of a walk, a procession or the performance.[6] Barels, an 18th century jurist, who not only researched these processions but also witnessed them regularly, stresses this fact.[7] He also posed the question why this legal procession was called "panding" although no pawn is taken in and no demands are satisfied. It is most remarkable that this question is unique in legal history. Jurists and historians interested in the right of distraint normally concentrate on the actual contents of the rules.

Rules referring to formalities are usually only briefly mentioned in notes.[8] Until the civil revolution at the end of the 18th century, however, legal processions were a common sight. Therefore it may not be a trivial matter to find an answer to the question why our ancestors spent so much time and money in order to see the judicial authorities parade or go round every fortnight.

Looking for an answer Barels has argued that it would be incorrect to assume that throughout the centuries the link with giving and taking a pawn has faded and therefore only an empty and baroque event lasted. The actual privilege of 1411 already proves that organizing a procession as such is different from valuing or taking goods. Furthermore, it seems rather illogical to grant such a privilege when it turns out to be a empty custom. It is also unlikely to think that the term "panding" was wrongly applied. First of all, Barels tried to find an etymological explanation. The word "pand" may have its roots in the word "band" or "ban", which means bond or spell. The relation between the parties involved may be seen as a mutual bond of trust, and willingness to give a pawn in due course and waiting to take in a pawn when the appropriate time arrives. Barels next step was finding an explanation for the actual *Loos- & Eigenpanding*. The fairness of the duration of three months, created by the fortnightly ceremonial parades, can be explained by the fact — according to Barels — that during the privilege anyone could have returned within three months from his travels with the prosperous Amsterdam merchant fleet to the Baltic. Barels proclaims this fairness to *Loos- & Eigenpanding* and the meaning of the ancient privilege. Amsterdam would be granted the favour to be exempted from distraint temporarily, contrary to the general custom of immediate pawning. The fact that the timespan from the moment of the final ceremonial of the "Eigenpanding" to the actual valuation and acquiring may take another six weeks, does not do justice, as Barels argues, to the whole sequence of solemn parades. In his opinion this extra provision of six weeks should not be allowed to vow or object, lest after the ceremony of the "Eigenpanding" the hammer actually comes down. Barels, guided by fairness, wanted to include something general in the scope of the right of distraint to the exceptional "panding".

However, Barels jumped to conclusions by looking at the ceremony of panding as being in the same scope as the right of distraint. He interpreted the ceremony too symbolically, as if the ceremony functions as a particular sign or form, that expresses a deeper and more general meaning. Such a symbol easily subordinates to the general explanation.[9] As opposed to either Barels or Goethe's poet, we could regard the processions as something general and ordinary in which the exceptional character of *Loos- & Eigenpanding* becomes visible. In other words, we should treat the exceptional characters merely as allegories or emblems which specify rather than symbols which generate.

In the early days when this privilege was granted, the city of Den Briel had a similar ceremonial to Amsterdam. However, the actual term "panding" was not used. The word "procession" was current.[10] Proof that our ancestors did not distort the concepts of "panding" and "procession" could be found in the Dutch word "klooster*pand*" or synonym "klooster*gang*". The Dutch word "kloosterpand" means "cloister" and includes the cloistral corridor ("kloostergang"). The word "gang" means "cloister," "gallery," "ambulatory," as well as "passage" and "procession." Not only the Patroness goes round in a procession, but also the holy Monstrance, Christ and the Virgin Mary. The ceremonial procession gives the opportunity, or rather the privilege of appearance. When the cross heads the procession, Christianity appears. Likewise appears Law when the Verge of Justice[11] is used.

In order to be present, the court has to outline the law. It is a privilege indeed, to mark the territory of law. The route covered by the bailiff draws a square, the *four*square, and he even draws this square four times since he organises four loospandingen. The fourth loospand is held in four days in addition to which the procession itself is divided into four sections and is repeated with the full cast in order to fulfil one of the four sequences of the ritual legal calendar.

According to the bailiff's formula "een — one, twee — two, drie — three and four times — vierwerf", lines were set in the streets of Amsterdam. Lines can fade out. Thus the lines of justice fade as well and will only re-appear when the square is drawn again: it is the "vierschaar" (foursquare)[12] and the bailiff's privilege to outline its territory.

III.

In our present law practices and justice administration we have banned these types of rituals or ceremonies, although still some rites are in request, those we use at the beginning of an undertaking, for instance. You cannot just start without, - that is to say you can, but then you do the ordinary thing. You might as well need a sign to begin with, with something exceptional, with a solemn affair. Three times hammering, the bailiff chants: "Oyez, oyez, oyez! All persons having business before the honourable, the Supreme Court of the United States, are admonished to draw near and give their attention, for the Court is now sitting. God save the United States and this honourable Court." Or even a less extensive chant: "All rise, the Superior Court of X County, the Honourable Jane B. Smith presiding, is now in session." Like the processions were general events to became special — each in its own way — by the attribution of well-demarcated gestures, walks, formula and objects, the formal beginnings are general. To become exceptional and in our example to make known the Supreme Court of the United States or the Superior Court of X County, the beginning is in need of a well-described even entirely prescribed (and rehearsed) beginning ritual.

The capability to provide visibility, to make known and even exclusive, seemed to have been the reason why we installed rituals. Paradoxically these very skills, which rituals are using to perform and which involve at least the repetitive, superficial and meticulous techniques, are constantly threatened with extermination these days. Under the regime of the comprehending view, which surreptitiously turns every sign into a symbol rather than into an emblem, we are purifying ritual activity until it is as good as extinguished.

In the Netherlands for instance there is an ongoing debate concerning the oath taking for more than a century. The question is not whether we have to abolish the oath, as you might have expected. The consideration is rather to purify the oath, to protect the value of the oath in itself.

At the end of the nineteenth century the hypocritical situation in which the law required a nonreligious person to take an oath, saying: "I swear by Almighty God that the evidence I shall give shall be the truth, the whole truth and nothing but the truth," led to questions in Parliament. For disbelievers the oath must be meaningless. But also the debate surrounded the fact that in the eye of a religious person the oath became worthless when disbelievers swore by God. Allowing an alternative formula, like a promise or declaration, gave a solution to this problem. First, in the Act of 1916, the promise and the declaration were secondary options, but is was only in the Act of 1971 they were considered to be equivalent to the oath. The religious sense was preserved.

Recently the debate about the oath reopened. The fear of the oath being meaningless then concentrated on the fact that on some occasions the oath is taken repeatedly. This is the case when experts appear in court for the second time or more, or when a judge has to be inaugurated again because of his change from district or type of court. So, in specialist publications and literature the "devaluation of the oath" is subsequently discussed: the oath taking becomes "pure formality," sounds the regret, "it degenerates to ritual acts."[13] The projected solution is only to administer one oath. Once the oath is taken people have to be released from further oath taking.

Obviously, the oath itself is not being discussed. On the contrary, the oath has to retain its meaning and its central point. So, it must be striped of embellishments. Could we conclude that the settlement of the dispute lies in abolishing the ritual aspects that are stuck to the oath? No, that does not turn out to be the case. They discuss the mechanic, repetitive or emblematic use of the oath, but they want to "prevent that the ceremony of oath taking will loose its impressive importance."[14] Since the ritual impresses, it is needed. Thus, on the one hand ritual embellishment is required, on the other hand it could be disposed of.

IV.

It is not by chance that this paradox appears. It is inherent to the judicial world, whose essence is rationality. The jural discourse rationalizes every inch of its domain. The oath is part of its territory. To determine the rationality of the oath taking two strategies are to be employed. Firstly jural rationalism has to fight the meaninglessness, try to exorcise all that exists without any sense or meaning, i.e. fight the absence of meaning. This strategy results in the abolition of oath taking. Rationality will take the seat that became vacant, introducing — as we have seen — the promise and the declaration or extending the effect of the original oath. Secondly jural rationalism has to conquer senselessness or irrationality, i.e. fight the presence of nonsense. Not by its exorcism but through discipline and control. This strategy tends to lock up the oath in itself or to hold it in asylum, where irrationality lives. In that case the oath belongs to the realm of sacred, religious, magic, supernatural phenomena.

Rationalism which appeals to sense and meaning, introduces the paradox first by fighting absence of meaning. So reformists claim that we must abolish ritual. But within the same rationality they grant ritual to exist on level of irrationality and subjectivity — the same level where we find God and the truth. The judicial world is unable to eliminate this level. The judicial process is the very process of finding the truth. It is forced to allow the subjective truth to speak, and benefits from a combination of subjective truth with the irrational belief in celestial powers or the Almighty. Not for long times, Rationalization must, after all, maintain its dominance. Therefor when Truth had spoken, Law resumes immediately.

The interruption or necessary breakthrough of the irrational within the rational process is the reason why the ceremony of oath taking cannot be abandoned. Law and the judicial order are in need of a controllable form or sign at least that expresses the subjective and the irrational. A symbolic form is what they prefer. Ritual is perfectly suitable to serve as such, because of its visibility and observance. If we confine ourselves to the jural discourse and its logic, we might conclude that ritual give an objective expression to the sense of the truth and the Almighty. Ritual in general and the oath in particular serve as heralds of rationality. And we can clear the paradox: ritual characterized as meaninglessness has to be abandoned, but ritual identified as a objective form that gives expression to the irrationality has to be preserved.

V.

Ritual is capable of providing objectivity, but does it express anything particular? Does the raised hand express the truth, the whole truth and nothing but the truth? Or a request to God? We would love to say "Yes," like the elderly woman in the following anecdote. Despite the obligation to raise the two fingers of her right hand — as required in the Netherlands — a elderly aged women swore with one finger. To the reprimand of the judge she replied: "No, your Honour, one God, one finger!"

The meaning of the typical gesture of the oath taking has frequently been researched. Christian reasons have been proposed. Like Overdiep summarizes, the gesture with fore and middle fingers (current in several European countries) could represent the two natures of Christ (truly God and truly Human). The gesture with thumb, fore and middle fingers outstretched (valid in the same countries mentioned above) could be a representation of the Holy Trinity.[15] In case of the whole hand, however, the possibility to refer to Christ runs out on the number 5. We could evaded to the fact that in case of the whole hand the right hand is obliged. Antoine Garapon claimed that "The right hand is the hand that takes; it is the hand that symbolizes life, force, good, purity. This representation is almost universal. (...) Right is the light, the truth, left is unspeakable and obscure. Right is the height, the heaven and the peace, and left is all the opposite!"[16] It is curious to find this two incomparable explanations of the oath taking gestures, while the religious and cultural tradition is the same, namely Christianity and Europe. Overdiep was looking for an religious meaning denoting the number of outstretched fingers. Garapon tried to find a religious meaning within a peculiar mixture of all kinds of connotations. To maintain at least one of the explanations we have to find a denotation of the number 5 or else we must consider the prescribed custom to raise the two front fingers as an exception — impossible, actually, because the custom is not confined to the Netherlands at all. Moreover, in many countries, where the raised hand is imposed, many people nevertheless swear with two fingers raised.

The same incomparability between interpretations exists towards the hand raising element of the gesture. On the one hand we have the idea that there is some kind of force or energy within man, that must be released in order to move upwards. It is offered. "If the hand is closed, the energy can not go out and is driven back inside man. The image of a clenched fist evokes the idea of recycling the force for himself, the idea of a ferment. The open hand releasing his force expresses the idea of an offer, an offering, even. It brings an symbolic exchange into action. This interpretation also explains why this energy is directed upwards, to the heavens. (...) Moreover the act of raising the arm is a positive gesture; it proposes something: it is a commitment."[17] On the other hand we have the idea of an divine or magic force that comes from the up high and decends into the man who had called upon the celestial powers. The superstitious practice of undoing the oath by crossing or holding two fingers of the left hand down behind the back — as it were a lightning-conductor — should support this interpretation. Here the gesture is considered to represent an external force, and not long ago the same gesture was considered to be presenting a inhabiting power.

Under the symbolistic and rationalistic perspective, the oath taking gesture is polyvalent and polyinterpretable: not a good sign for its rationality. So the gesture must be irrational, then. It is always irrationality that glooms at the horizon of rational explanations. In rationalizing its practices the jural world is confronted with the irrational.

VI.

The ritual is acting as a double entendre. It serves as an objective form of expression, and as we have seen, this means that ritual appears as herald of the king, called Rationality. A herald superintends ceremonies. Well then, which ritual is not in favour of being master of ceremonies and acting this role out?

Ritual observes rules, and these rules prescribe precisely how the ceremony of oath taking is done: how to perform the swearing. The rules do not find the law along their side, but they find a brother-in-arms in every individual who has to testify or is to be installed. Everyone knows or relies on the Coroner, the oath administering officer, who knows how it should be done and why you can not leave the hand raising gesture out. If you don't make the gesture, you have not sworn. You can declare, state or testify at any point, but taking an oath you cannot do without the gesture.

The explanations given of the oath taking rules are not determinative towards the ceremony. These explanations do not affect the ritual event: they are indifferent to ritual. This indifference explains also the fact that ritual is not affected by time. That does not mean that we have consider ritual as a thing of the past which is now just a part of our heritage. Tradition is in fact closely related to time, while ritual resists time. In the same way it resists the law or the legal prescriptions. It is not even concerned with the aspirations of morality.[18] With conspiracy it conforms as well. After all the oath complies with legal society as well as with the illegal association, with the sacred, the secret or even the profane. No matter how, forswearing is swearing. Indifferently what the function of the bond, the syndicate or the confederation might be, the oath serves as ritual.[19]

The carelessness is accompanied by the most attentive care. The initiate deeply respects the ritual precision and ceremonial sequence. During the performance, one is not concerned with anything but the prescribed order of the event, with the perfect reproduction of everything that has been rehearsed: a specific gesture, an appropriate movement, a recitation that can go on for days, a mimed act that can undergo a moment-by-moment metamorphosis. All the techniques that the human body has at its disposal can be employed to give form to a ritual activity.

Ritual, however, does not treat perfection as a compensation for or a struggle against existing imperfections. It is not engaged in the dialectical struggle with which we are familiar. In the context of dialectics perfection is distilled out of imperfection, a process that leads to the idealizing of the perfect, so postulating its impossibility... so that once again what is actually realized is something that is imperfect. Through this dialectical logic we are confronted with a commonplace that in the meantime has been elevated to the status of a piece of worldly wisdom: even though we strive for perfection, we know that it cannot be realized. This is not the wisdom that is taught in ritual.

It is perfection that prevails in ritual. This is why the adjective "perfect" is effectively obligatory for the initiate in the ritual: the perfect body, the perfect human being, perfect harmony, the perfect way, the perfect transaction and even perfect order. We tend to regard the perfection we find in ritual as being a compensation for the imperfection of everyday life, without however quite being able to believe that the compensation is adequate (because we have postponed perfection to the afterlife). Not just that, it even overthrows dialectics by setting it against itself, by reversing the banality of commonplace wisdom. Instead of stating that we should strive for perfection while at the same time accepting that we cannot escape imperfection, the ritual itself states that everything in the ritual is perfect — while at the same time it is fully aware that imperfections can creep in. That is why the one-finger swearing woman don't have to worry, nor does the reprimanding judge have to (and didn't, in fact). The imperfections within a ritual performance are not referred to the afterlife and the Judgement of God, nor are they abandoned to fate. Imperfect ritual transactions are just as much respected as those that are perfect: they are always ritualized.

"Having reached the age of thirteen, the time of puberty, and thus the religious age of majority (Bar Mitzvah) the youth goes up in synagogue for the first time as one of the required number of persons called up for the Torah. He then reads his *parashah* (portion) to the congregation. You realize, of course, that this has been thoroughly rehearsed beforehand. (...) The person who has the honour of reading the final portion of the Holy Law on Simchat Torah (Rejoicing of the Law) and the person who on that same day has the honour of starting afresh with Genesis, they too are permitted to read their portion from the Scroll of the Pentateuch. (...) Yet these texts are read a second time by the reader (koré), *in order that nobody should be put to shame.* For a person's reading may be so bad and so full of mistakes, that an expert reader would be required to reread the whole portion. So this is how it is done: whether the recitation was good or bad... the koré always rereads the portion."[20]

The ritual rule, which begins with the formula, "This is how it is done..." provides for an element of imperfection in a ritual act even if this did not occur: the reader reads the text over again. In the case of taking an oath a similar rule is followed, one with a reversed order. First the court officer who is trained and has rehearsed, reads the formula with no error. After that the witness, or the person who is to be installed, starts to stutter, makes mistakes[21] or confines himself to a simple and firm "Yes, I do." It is not a question of exorcizing any elements of imperfection. There is no fear of a lack of completion, of a perfection that is not realized. We have already seen that ritual is also not afraid of an imperfection that is not realized. It is therefore a mistake to see, as Freud does, a connection between ritual and neurosis. Neurosis is a result of a fear of reality; ritual is quite simply not concerned with reality. Whether or not there actually is imperfection, it deserves to be respected; and respect means ritual. This is the way of accounting for the "long series of expiation rites for mistakes that might have been committed" that follows on the performance of a large-scale and elaborate ritual such as the Agnicayana as described by Frits Staal.[22] It also explains why *third time is lucky*. We may ask whether after the third (imperfect?) occasion we really can be sure of a good outcome. One thing, however, is certain: from the point of view of the ritual, once it has been done three times it has been done in a fitting manner.

VII.

Because the perfect order of ritual is completely independent of reality, you are not supposed to believe in it. This is because you can only believe in something that in the end turns out to be true, perhaps after a long and deep enquiry into the present or else into the afterlife, into nirvana or an original paradise. Anyone who puts his faith in the perfection of a ritual will expect the initiate to perform a ritual in its original setting, sticking as closely as possible to the tradition, or he will expect the ascetic eventually to transcend into higher realms. In this way ritual is turned into a myth — a myth, incidentally, in which many anthropologists put their faith. Every unorthodox performance of a ritual is classified as imperfect or impure; every attribute that is "forgotten" will be treated as an omission, every substitute as a stain on the whole. The result of faith of this kind is an attitude of permanent suspicion of any given performance of a ritual.

Suspicion like this, however, is mutual. Ritual does not depend on believers, it relies exclusively on its practitioners. Believers have to cope with a contradiction between a perfect and an imperfect ritual; the practitioners are only aware of an opposition between a perfect ritual and no ritual at all.

Perfect ritual: when the Haftarah is recited because the reading of the Pentateuch is forbidden by religious crusaders, when — later when the prohibition is removed — together with the recitation from the Torah, the reading from the text from the Prophets also continues to be used.[23]

Perfect ritual: when people who have abstained from swearing — not willing to invoke celestial powers or the Almighty — raise their hand and declare or promise either to speak the truth or to obey the code that comes with their profession.

Perfect ritual: when 14 atas replace the goats, if there is opposition to the animal sacrifice.[24]

Perfect ritual: when the ritual is performed with plastic mats instead of bamboo, Coca-Cola tins instead of traditional clay vessels and even if the music comes from a tape-recorder and the participants are dressed in jeans.

A ritual is perfect when it creates an order that is offered to chaos, when Chaos is honoured and therefore also proves to be ritualized.[25]

VIII.

So how is it done nowadays? In our modern culture the fate of the perfect ritual order is an poor and impoverished fate, and would seem to resemble that of the Map of the Empire that Borges tells of in his *A Universal History of Infamy* under the heading, *Of Exactitude in Science*:

> In that Empire, the craft of Cartography attained such Perfection that the Map of a Single province covered the space of an entire City, and the Map of the Empire itself an entire Province. In the course of Time these Extensive maps were found somehow wanting, and so the College of Cartographers evolved a Map of the Empire that was of the same Scale as the Empire and that coincided with it point for point.[26]

This artificial reproduction of the real Empire by the cartographers (that resembles the artificial repetition or reproduction by ritual of a banal event) bears no relation whatsoever to the dream of the Colleges of Sociologists, Anthropologists and Jurists, who, at least by implication, also pretend to offer some sort of map of the world. With the full force of their scholarship they attempt to uncover the world so that the world can be discovered. The Cartographers, on the other hand, have spread their parchment over the world like a veil, so achieving the opposite result: they have not discovered it; they have *covered* it. They preserve the distinction between the meticulous map of the world and the world itself, their Empire. And the Empire hides behind the decorative motifs of this topography. In the same way the world finds its hiding place behind the ritual sequences of walks, steps and recitals of formula, of seasonal festivals and special days in the calendar.

In their constant urge to ask questions about the useful use of everything, the modern human sciences have an ally in the sequel to this history. In the case of Borges it was with the succeeding Generations that this question originated:

"Less attentive to the Study of Cartography, succeeding Generations came to judge a map of such Magnitude cumbersome, and not without Irreverence, they abandoned it to the Rigors of sun and Rain. In the western Deserts, tattered Fragments of the Map are still to be found, Sheltering an occasional Beast or beggar; in the whole Nation, no other relic is left of the Discipline of Geography."[27]

Just as successive Generations will in the end have to live with the tattered Fragments of the Discipline of Geography, our succeeding generations — once the use of ritual has been questioned — must live with the scattered Traditions of the Discipline of Ritual.

IX.

Once we are familiar with Borges' history of infamy, we will know that this outcome is by no means certain any more. Fortunately an element of suspense plays a part now. We might as well live with the thought that on the surface of the Empire there will still be an open scroll of parchment, one that has been covered with a second layer of writing like a palimpsest. The script that now covers the surface is the script of the genuine, the real and the natural; it is written on top of the script of the Cartographers which, even though it has been scratched out, remains partially legible. The same feeling of suspense might induce us to think that the surface of the world must also be a palimpsest consisting of descriptions of functional, practical and ideal relations which cover the still visible fragments of ritual script. Inevitably these ritual fragments also shelter everything that is inhuman (it is a fact that human beings prefer to dwell in the Juridical and Sociological Disciplines).

The Inhuman Disciplines are no longer situated in desert places. One comes across them in the busiest and most crowded parts of modern society and recognizes them from features that remind one of ritual. Perfection above all is prevalent in this world, the world of the computer, of advertising, of fashion and of art. It is a perfection that is for sale; you are the recipients of its reflected glory; you no longer need to strive for it. These worlds also have in common with ritual the fact that they are averse to everyday fuss and bother and everything that has to be merely usefully useful, even though this may have been the reason why they were originally created. The advertisements for computers, for art, for fashion and even the advertisements for advertising promise to free us from our everyday cares. They generate a sort of holiday spirit in us. The goods that they recommend also land up in this realm: Van Gogh is to be enjoyed like a Sunday trip to a teahouse; a dress is accompanied by a picture of a tropical beach; a Philishave is like a motor "on the road;" nowadays even Moscow has its M for McDonald's.

Advertisements and the goods they promote are no longer concerned with reality. Fashion, for instance, is no longer concerned with designing clothes that provide protection against the weather, as lifestyles no longer with life. Fashion is also not concerned with deciding what is beautiful and what is ugly any more; all it is interested in is knowing what is "in;" even if that is something that is as uglier than ugly. Through edicts that oscillate between short or long, tight or wide, dark or light, smooth or pleated, underwear or overwear, it "fashions" non-stop a fascinating world, a temporary rage.

Specialists in the social sciences and the law need to be *au courant* with the latest trends in the younger generation or with patents, and they have a hard job keeping up with all these crazes. But the scholars are just as likely to be caught out by their sudden end as their unpredictable rise. For a short while crazes create an order that is purely obligatory, consigning to the attic everything that was perfectly normal up till then. Of course the specialists in these fields are aware that there must be some kind of undercurrent beneath these fashions, an undercurrent on which all kinds of caprices can surface only to vanish once again. They will however never get to know the principle underlying this trend. Because on the surface of transcendent regularity, the ordering of the world, the immanent code of ceremonial has, in fact, been wiped out.

*Associate Professor of Legal Sociology and Anthropology, Universiteit van Amsterdam.

Notes

1. Cf. G.C.J.J. van den Bergh, 1956, "Poëzie in het recht." 56 *RM Themis* 157–205 esp. 173–174.

2. Cf. Suzette Haakma, 1989, "Inleiding," Pages 7–10 in Suzette Haakma (ed.), *Rituelen*, Utrecht: Bureau Studium Generale, Rijksuniversiteit Utrecht, 8. The same function described as "symbolic modeling of the social order," is observed by Bell in the work of Geertz, T. Turner, Douglas, Lukes (see Catherine Bell, 1992, *Ritual theory, Ritual practice*, New York/Oxford: Oxford University Press, 175). In the chapter *The Ritual Body* Bell also summarizes: "In this way, ritual dynamics afford an experience of "order" as well as the "fit" between this taxonomic order and the real world of experience (Id., 104)."

3. Huizinga attributes the same feature to ritual act comparing play and ritual. See Johan Huizinga, 1938 (7th. ed. 1974), *Homo Ludens. Proeve eener bepaling van het spel-element der cultuur*, Groningen: Tjeenk Willink, 10 in conjunction with 19–20; English Trans. by R.F.C. Hull, 1949 (1980) *Homo ludens: A study of the play-element in culture*, London: Routledge and Kegan Paul.

4. See the chapter "Allegorie und Trauerspiel" in Walter Benjamin, 1925 (2nd ed. 1982), *Ursprung des deutschen Trauerspiels*, hrsg. Rolf Tiedemann, Frankfurt am Main: Suhrkamp 138–146; English Trans by John Osborne, 1977, *The origin of German tragic drama*, London: NLB, esp. 159–167.

5. In the Book of Ceremonies every corner, every street and every alley was meticulously indicated. The book contained furthermore regulations and instructions of ceremonies, like the elections, the oath taking, the promulgation of statutes and laws, and the sentencing of both capital- and minor crimes. Cf. *Ceremoniboek van de regeering der stad Amsterdam*, several handwritings, in print approx. 1736, esp. 54–59.

6. The description of the last and fifth ceremony ("Eigenpanding" i.e. "Proper Pawn") is almost the same as the fourth and mayor "Empty Pawn" ("Grote Loospanding"). The Book of Ceremonies prescribes an extra announcement ceremony in church, acted out by an court herald, at the Sunday Mass the day before the actual procession starts. Furthermore, the solicitors appear for the first time at the beginning of the third day. They bring their pawn tickets in order to present them solemnly. Still no pawn is taken or given. The extensive cortege is the third and last difference between "Eigenpanding" and "Grote Loospanding." Besides his court officer the bailiff is normally assisted by two aldermen. In case of "Eigenpanding" he is accompanied by all nine aldermen and by one of the four mayors that Amsterdam possessed at that time.

7. Jeronimo Mattheus Barels, 1774 (1780), "Onderzoek over de pandingen binnen de stad Amsterdam, als nogh gebruikt wordende." Pages 79–227 in J.M. Barels, 1774, *Aenmerkingen over eenige onzer aloude gebruiken in de rechts-oeffeninge*. Amsterdam: Hendrik Gartman.

8. M.C. van Hall, 1838, *Regtsgeleerde verhandelingen en losse geschriften*, Amsterdam: Van der Hey, Ten Brink & De Vries, 179 note 1; Hans Planitz, 1912, *Die Vermögensvollstreckung im Deutschen Mittelalterlichem Recht, Erster Band Die Pfändung*, Leipzig: Engelmann, 572 note 37, 38; R.P. Cleveringa, 1949, *Revisie en beroep te Groningen*, Groningen: Wolters, 192 note 1, 224 note 3, 225 note 2.

9. Barels is a contemporary of Goethe, no doubt: "There is a great difference between a poet's seeking the particular from the general and his seeing the general in the particular. The former give rise to allegory, where the particular serves only as an instance or example of the general; the latter, however, is the true nature of poetry: the expression of the particular without any thought of, or reference to, the general. Whoever grasps the particular in all its vitality also grasps the general, without being aware of it, or only becoming aware of it at a late stage (Goethe as quoted by Benjamin, op. cit. note 4, 161)."

10. Jan Matthijssen mentionned "processions" around 1400 in *De rechten en costumen der Stad Brielle en landt van Voorne*. Reprinted as third chapter in: Jan Matthijssen, 1880, *Het rechtsboek van den Briel*, Den Haag: Nijhoff, 150.

11. In Dutch the Verge is called "Roede", which could also mean "rod." Contrary to what a rod assumes, the Verge does not have the appearance of a scourge and an instrument of punishment. It is a branch of an ash whose silhouette figures a twisted staff. According to the 16th century allegorical dictionary by Cesare Ripa, a judge has to be represented with a staff, the emblem for judicial authority, with a snake writhed around it, as the emblem for prudence. Cf. Cesare Ripa, 1644, *Iconologia of Uytbeeldingen des Verstands*, Amsterdam: Dirck Pietersz. Pers (Reprint, 1971, Soest: Davaco); English Trans., 1779, *Iconology*. London: G. Scott (Reprint, 1979, New York: Garland Pub.). Ancient pictures show, that in Court the Verge of Justice nearly always seems to be present, either on the mantle-piece, in a vase or stuck to the wall. Sometimes the bailiff even took the verge in his hand. Whenever he proceeded in the procession through the city, the Verge of Justice was carried by a preceding court officer. See Agnes Schreiner et al., 1991, *In de ban van het recht*, Amsterdam: Duizend & Een (with pictures and English summ. "Captured by justice"); Agnes Schreiner, 1994, Recht-Spieghel, 16/4 *Tableau. Fine Arts Magazine* 91–96 (with pictures and English summ. "Mirror of Justice").

12. Originally, justice was administered in the open-air. For this purpose, a centrally located, noticeable place was marked by stretching ropes in a square, a foursquare. In Dutch this is called "het spannen van de

vierschaar," which means "stretching" or "spanning the foursquare." "Vierschaar" became synonym for the appearance of the judge: the court.

13. E.J. Anneveldt, 1981, "De devaluatie van de eed," 56/24 *Nederlands juristenblad* 626

14. Id.

15. G. Overdiep, 1986, *Ons eedsgebaar*, Arnhem: Quint Gouda, 43–45.

16. Antoine Garapon, 1985, *L'âne portant des reliques, Essai sur le rituel judiciaire*, Paris: Centurion, 113.

17. Id., 114.

18. Cf. G.E. Lagerwaard, 1977, "Het eedsbegrip," 7 *Algemeen Politieblad* 155-161, esp. 156.

19. Yet is the administration of justice not indifferent as well? The oath taking is nothing more than pure formality, an obstacle that hinders the due course in court, an obstacle that has to be taken as fast as possible. Beyond the harassing breakthrough of irrationality the judicial world is only interested in a sworn statement as evidence, and in the persuit of a perjure, if the lie occurs. In this sense, i.e. within the perspective of the law only, we are able to call the ceremony of oath taking a "rite of passage": the legal procedure needs an overpass to bridge the abyss of irrationality continuing the road rationality takes.

20. Rabbi S. Ph. de Vries, 1927–32 (7th ed. 1988), *Joodse riten en symbolen*, Amsterdam: Arbeiderspers, 23–24.

21. Some people make a mistake that results in a forswear or a curse even. For instance, Dutch people often change the (archaic) oath formula "Zoo waarlijk helpe mij God Almachtig" to "Zoo waarlijk helpe mij, god al*le*machtig." The last part is normally a cry of despair or fear, like "O, My goodness!" People mostly do not notice this slip of the tongue at all. No matter how, the oath is considered to have been taken. Th.M. de Jongh, 1979, "Eedsgebaar en eedsformulier I&II," 5482–5483 *WPNR* 344–348; 367–371, 370 note 52.

22. Frits Staal, 1989, *Rules without meaning. Ritual, Mantras and the human sciences*, New York/Bern: Peter Lang, 135.

23. Rabbi de Vries Mzn, op. cit. note 20, 25.

24. Frits Staal, 1983, *Agni*, Vol. I & II, Berkeley: Asian Humanities Press, 303 (I), 465 (II).

25. Zhuang Zi, chapter 7, in Burton Watson, 1968, *The complete works of Chuang Tzu,* New York: Columbia University Press, 97; Kristofer Schipper, 1987, *Le corps taoïste.* Paris: Fayard, 157.

26. Jorge Luis Borges, 1935, *Historia universal de la infamia*, Buenos Aires: Emecé Editores; English Trans. by Norman Thomas di Giovanni, 1972, *A universal history of infamy*. New York: E.P. Dutton & Co.

27. Id.

Chapter Eight
Si(g)ns of the Flesh: Law, Violence and Inscription upon the Body

Christopher Stanley*

Introduction:

Inside-Outside (The Body and the Sign)

This essay was prompted by two statements. The first was made by Nietzsche in *The Genealogy of Morals:* "Only that which goes on hurting will stay in the memory". The second was made by Foucault in *Mental Illness and Psychology*: "It might be said that all knowledge is linked to the essential forms of cruelty."[1] Adopting these statement as a governing motif the ensuing analysis considers the relationship between the nature of imagination in the foundation of the legal order and the process of inscription in the establishment of the authority of that order as an order of violence and force. In addition to the primary motif that these statements provide the essay also utilizes the figure of the body as both subject and object ("the irreducible element in the social scheme of order").[2] There are two bodies here. The body of the law and the body of the individual. Both bodies operate within a matrix of order and desire, disorder and repression. They are both, therefore, sites of power and as such, in terms of interpretation, sites of value. The purpose of this essay is to analyze in a particular figurative form the process of inscription in operation between and within these two sites.

The relationship between order and desire can also be understood as the relationship between pain and pleasure. The nature of inscription will therefore be discussed both as an event of writing *and* as an event of marking in the determination of pain *and* pleasure. Therefore this analysis is concerned with the symbolic *realm* of law as opposed to positive law. The symbolic in this frame of analysis is the external realm of the order of law as opposed to the imaginary of the internal realm of the desire of the self. Unifying both these realms in terms of their operation is a construction of violence and it is violence, to refer back to the statements made by Nietzsche and Foucault, which serves as the causal link in the ensuing analysis. Specifically what is at issue is the play of violence in the organization of the law of desire and the desire of law.[3] It is a violence which crystallizes the allegorical and the metaphorical into the physical and thus reflects the actuality of the force of positive law.

In introducing the paradox of the inside-outside in terms of the dynamic of the internal and external of force-violence in the articulation and distribution of desire (pain and pleasure) it is possible to convey the specific nature of this particular semiotic account of law. In a critical sense, a semiotics of law can provide an analysis of the various means by which a system of law institutes a specific life and a specific body. A semiotics of law can further depict the implicit rationalism of legal method and can instance the relationship between the legal gaze (the order of the external) and the imaginary (the desire of the internal), that which is subject to the gaze and which is constantly silenced and frozen in the name of logical schemata. Such is the project of Enlightenment-Cartesian reason which constructs the world from the outside and which then is left with the categorization and surveillance of an internal space inhabited by *others*.[4]

It is the relationship between the body of law and the body of the individual determined by violence that is the basis of analysis here. The law as a structure of material life, as an institution, is a system of images, and it is through its symbolization of authority and through its signs of power that the law dwells within the subject. "The law is in that sense nothing other than its image, no more and no less a sign; it is the spectacle of the scaffold, the aura of judgment, the sense of the normal."[5] The idea of the image of law *as* law can be understood through the nature of its mythology as a construction or reflection of that which is not law: that which is not of the symbolic but of the imaginary. The power of the sign of law therefore subsists through its determination of the space that is not law, that which is *other* to law. Through determining that which it is not, it becomes that which is. This is the desire of law. It is the desire of the negative, the absent and the dead. Goodrich notes that a semiotics of law can thus show us some of the forms of dying.[6] The ideational unity of law is maintained through the process of transmission of the image, the constant re-representation of an appearance of authority. To interrupt this process—as a *political* interruption— is to grasp the essential nature of the representation that is always the memory of death in its reproduction of a previous experience as opposed to that of lived experience. The revolution of the form of law is the masque of death, and we are the dying. That which inherits the past and determines the future, the dead (non) space, is that which ignored and escaped death, a pointless immortality without foundation, an engulfing choking web of the repression of life as lived experience.[7]

A determination of jurisdiction through absence is part of the cruelty of the law. It is cruel because it is impossible to respect because its subjection of ethics and logics occurs through its denial and disavowal of them in its very declaration of them. Law thus escapes logics and ethics through its compulsion of them to be within the schema of an empty (dead) sign. Thus the subject entering the juridic arena as a desiring person (the ethical) is offered only a particular circumscribed discursive subject-position within which to take up residence in order to engage in acceptable juridic narrative and to participate in juridic communication.[8] The field of the sign of this external discursive juridic realm is a field of closure in which the desire of the subject is silenced and frozen. As Cover powerfully reminds us: "Legal interpretation takes place in a field of pain and death."[9] Therefore, as a narrative practice, it is one which is incomplete without violence. The main if not exclusive function of many judgements is to legitimize and trigger off past or future acts of violence. The word and the deed, the proposition and the sentence, the constative and the performative are intimately linked. The sentence is both literal and metaphorical; the entrance of desire ('How does it work?') submitting to the sentence of the juridical ('What does it mean?'). Legal interpretations and judgements cannot be understood independently of this inescapable imbrication with violent action. In this sense legal interpretation is a practical activity, other-orientated and designed to lead to effective threats and violent deeds.[10]

Imagination: The Field of Desire and the Phantasm

To pursue a particular semiotic analysis whilst simultaneously maintaining and playing with the encompassing image of violence, it is possible to regard the relationship between external law (the symbolic) and internal desire (the imaginary) as one coalescing around the issue of power. The desire of law and the law of desire are both expressions of a *will to power*. Law and Desire, Foucault notes both rely upon "common representations of power."[11] Foucault follows Freud in his conceptualization of a positive-affirmative desire as a free-flowing energy source that animates the psychic apparatus. In *A Thousand Plateaus*, Deleuze and Guattari attempt to discover the language that gives it form.[12] Their purpose is to re-conceptualize this determining power relation and to open it up to the possibility of affirmative as opposed to negative utilization. The territorialization of desire (the linguistic structuring of desire), fixed early by the Oedipus complex, produces subjects of utility and docility in a political economy. The juridic subject is the effect of juridico-semiotic production and of subjects inserting themselves, or being inserted in, discursive subject-positions within the sphere of a juridico-semiotic circulation. This condition occurs within Deleuze and Guattari's notion of a *regime de signes* in which they argue that context is a critical determinant that stabilizes meaning. In following Lacan, they suggest that each signifying regime produces signs which spiral outward from the centre of its production,, intruding first into the speaking subject (the producer of the utterance) and ending in the subject of the statement (the grammatical *I*). In the *post-signifying regime* (the authoritarian code of social formation), signs travel along this path culminating in statements by subjects in conformity with the dominant reality, irrespective of a clearly materialized omnipotent centre. No longer is it necessary to police the process. The domination of the subject's internal mental structures become congruent with the externalized statement so that "(t)he enslaved are their own producers of a discourse that further enslaves them."[13] The imagination (desire) of the individual becomes trapped as soon as the individual enters the symbolic order of determination and becomes the alienated juridic subject. This process reflects that suggested by Foucault with regard to ideology in which political consent is secured insofar as it legitimizes a given type of domination in the minds of those who are subjected to it.[14]

The violence of the repression of desire that constitutes legal subjectivity manifested in the production of the juridic subject is a violence worked into the psychic apparatus, through the dual techniques of interpellation and suture. The juridic field determines the discursive subject-position within which the *I* can inhabit. The grammatical *I* is the subject which takes up residence in a discursive subject-position is but a presence of an absence. It is no longer the *I* as desiring-subject but as determined legal subject.[15] In Lacanian terms the imaginary (that which the self imagines in order to sustain and expand itself) has succumbed to the symbolic (that which is forbidden, distinguishable and thinkable).

The question becomes, in terms in the transition in the organization of social relations, of the arrival of a humanistically orientated replacement discourse, one that liberates desire and which takes place in a political economy which offers far-from-equilibrium conditions in which both order and disorder is produced. The strategy of emplacement for such a critique involves interruption, interrogation and inversion. One possible path in such a critique and the emplacement of an emancipatory discourse is to analyze the relationship between law and desire in which law becomes reliant upon desire in the establishment of the parameters of its repression (the distribution of pain and pleasure). To formulate the nature of the desire of law may then elucidate the nature of the force of law and the possibility of a strategy of critique which realizes the de-determination of individual desire within the frame of legal subjectivity without merely organizing a further frame of that subjectivity. The point has been made by Taylor:

> "The law wishes ...." What is *the* law that wishes? How can the law wish? What does the law want? What is the want of the law? What does (the) law desire? What is the law of desire? .... Law and desire appear to stand in an antithetical or dialectical relationship to each other. Law struggles to control, direct, or repress desire, and desire attempts to express itself by eluding the strategies of lawful control. This agnostic relation between law and desire is, in effect, a play of forces.[16]

Again there are insides and outsides. There are those with-in law and those without-out law. Something dead containing something alive. There is ecstatic passion within the twitching corpse. Fish has argued that the determination of what is 'inside' will always be a function of whatever 'outside' has been assumed. If what is 'inside' is a function of what is 'outside', then the 'outside' is 'inside' and the 'inside' is 'outside'.[17] When not interpreted dialectically, this inversion of interiority and exteriority illuminates the interplay between the desire of law and the law of desire. The internal which appears 'outside' the law becomes an 'inside' as an 'outside' that cannot be properly be inwardized. If law is force then force is law. It is therefore wrong to consider that desire is repressed because it is law that constitutes both desire and the lack on which it is predicated.[18] Where there is desire the power relation is already present, a power relation that is multiple, immanent, affirmative and violent. As such this internal desire is the desire that denies the fundamental law of reason. Desire (life) becomes the site of authority of Law (death). To reiterate Foucault's earlier remark:

> (Law and Desire) both rely upon common representations of power which, depending on the use made of it and the position it is accorded with respect to desire leads to two contrary results: either the promise of a 'liberation' if power is seen as having only an external hold on desire, or, if it is constitutive of desire itself, to the affirmation: you are always-already trapped.[19]

To follow a Nietzschean-Deleuzian conceptualization of desire (desire as a *will to power*) in the formulation of an emancipatory critique in terms of the violence which is in operation here, it is possible to read internal desire as that encompassing the realm of the imaginary, or that of the *phantasm.* In introducing the 'figure' of the phantasm as a specific expression of internal desire, it is possible to achieve some sense of the nature of the *other* which is subject to the determination and juridico-semiotic production of external (symbolic) Law. The figure of the phantasm also serves to introduce an alternative image into the matrix of order-disorder, internal-external, that of the nomadic subject: that force which is subject only to de-determined power and violence.

The phantasm read as a moment of imagination topologizes the materiality of the body—it maps out the otherwise mute animal instincts and drives. Outwardly in modern societies, bodies might appear to be docile. But inwardly bodies and souls boil and seethe, their secret dreams of mastery without mercy "isolated, intensified and incorporated." Driven inward and cut off from the old links of the public spectacle of atrocity and cruelty, the soul turns from "jousts to phantasms".[20] As Deleuze notes "What appears in the phantasm is the movement in which the ego opens itself to the surface and liberates the acosmic, impersonal, and preindividual singularities which had been imprisoned. It literally releases them like spores and explodes as it gets unburdened."[21] Thus the capacity to fantasize—to give expression to the phantasmagoric element of the imagination—grants the individual "disturbing nocturnal powers".[22] No matter what civilization (the external realm) may dictate, this dream world remains beyond good and evil, beyond reason and rationality and outside of discipline. It is a state akin to madness, a secret frenzy with all the "ambiguity" of "chaos and apocalypse". Given any "healthy, normal and law-abiding adult", it is, according to Foucault, possible to bring out the chaos within—"the nakedness of desire as the lawless law of the world"—by asking "how much of the child he has within him (*sic*), what fundamental crime he has wished to commit?"[23] Foucault urges that "Phantasms should be freed from the restrictions we impose upon them, freed from the dilemmas of truth and falsehood and of being and non-being ....;they must be allowed to conduct their dance even though the results are cruel."[24] After Sade "violence, life and death, desire and sexuality will extend below the level of the representation, an immense expanse of shade, which we are now attempting to recover, as far as we can, in our discourse, in our freedom, in our thought."[25]

> I instantly re-enter the night of a lost child, and enter the anguish, in order to prolong rapture with no end other than exhaustion and no exit other than fainting. It is the joy of torture.[26]

The image of the phantasm as pursued (both literally and metaphorically in the life and work of Michel Foucault) is one of a dangerous capitulation to internal forces. It is dangerous because it is the violence of refusal. That which is refused may also refuse and become *Other*. The moment of the phantasm is thus the moment of the *Other*, that which is other to law, a moment in the alternative network of the transpolitical, the transverse (the linear as opposed to the hierarchical) and the *heterotopia*, that space of refusal which is the becoming beyond the limit of the border. In a Heideggerian sense, the boundary or border is not that at which something stops, but from which something begins its presenting. It is a beginning—an origin of truth—an opening out onto the world and a prerequisite of becoming. Recognizing the limit that the boundary marks is the frontier that forms a point of passage. At this threshold—the interstice—the inside and the outside join to form an undecidable play of perpetual displacement.[27] The phantasm here is that moment of the *Other* articulated as that which has been forgotten and suppressed, that which undercuts the opposition between signifier and signified on which the representative structure of signification (juridico-semiotic production) invests. The dissolution/disruption of these rigidities/boundaries fractures the ideational unity of legal discourse as the primary site of power relations in the value of interpretation. It is a moment of the recognition of the phantasm, of the interruption of the transmission and the interrogation of value. It is a moment of the sign of the *heterotopia* and of *nomadic governmentality*. The heterotopia has been described by Foucault thus:

> There is also, probably in every culture, in every civilization, real places—places that do exist and that are formed in the very founding of society—which are something like counter-sites, a kind of effective utopia in which the real sites, all the other real sites that can be found within that culture, are simultaneously represented, contested and inverted.[28]

This is the site/sight of the phantasm, the interstice of excess in interruption as a condition of possibility and as a political technology. Its identification and recognition as the site of the *Other* becomes a strategic mechanism with which to grapple with the otherwise subconscious and unthinkable aspects of negative (dead) experience. As the foundation of a philosophical critique it thus lays bare the "nonsense of the will to know" and the purely negative freedom of the individual. In terms of a politics it is the becoming of *nomadic governmentality*. The site of the phantasm as liberated imagination becomes an assemblage of experiences, emotions and bodies on the edge of transformation. It can be imaged through the figure of the *body without organs*. As Artaud says "When you have made your body without organs, then you will have delivered him (*sic*) from all his automatic reactions and restored him to his true freedom."[29]

The body without organs is the locus of connection for all the machines of desire forming rhizomic structures: "non-hierarchical, horizontal multiplicities which cannot be subsumed within a unified structure (and) whose components form random, unregulated networks in which any element may be connected with any other element."[30] It is an entity of the 'desiring machines'; the desiring machines involve heterogeneous independent parts and "works only when they break down, and by continually breaking down."[31] The body without organs is the "field of immanence and desire, the plane of consistency proper to desire" on which flow "pure intensities, free, prephysical and prevital singularities."[32] It is thus the source of the nomadic subject, that point of pure intensity traversing the grid of the body without organs, a mobile locus of becoming which commingles identities as it migrates from desiring-machine to desiring machine.[33] The nomadic subject—the with-outlaw—is the occupant of the interstice, the space of *otherness*.

Thus, the nomadic subject is the inhabitant of the heterotopia. It is the embodiment of the phantasm as an alternative (de)construction of desire, a de-determined and violent (dis)order of desire set up, not in opposition, but as a necessary consequence of the preeminence of the juridic subject, a counter-force. As Miller states, armed with this Nietzschean knowledge, the genealogist of pain-pleasure is able to imagine "new combinations of impulses, new relationships of power, a new style of life—perhaps even a new game of truth."[34] And perhaps become invested with the moment of desiring production and become nomadic.

Inscription: Line of Flight and the Becoming of the Nomad

The relationship between nomadic subject and juridic subject can be illuminated through an analysis of the violence that is in constant operation here. It is the violence of the word against the mark, the expressionable against the inexpressible, the representable against the unrepresentable, the vital against the prevital. To adopt the spatial metaphor once again this relationship can be envisaged as a *line of flight*, a movement from within to without. The space of (de)determination, in which the inside and the outside join in perpetual displacement, is simultaneously the space of the gaze of the external (symbolic) and the space of escape through the internal (imaginary). It is the space of the desire of the body and the conflict between the order of singular identity and the disorder of the multiplicity of subjectivities. It is a space of force and of continuous movement and flow: the movement of desire mobilizing the psychic apparatus.

This image of the movement of desire is related to Kristeva's conceptualization of the presemiotic chora which produces affects, drives and flows of energy. This is the condition of the pre-verbal organization of power. The semiotic is composed of "discrete quantities of energy" moving through the body, "a nonexpressive totality formed by the drives and their states .... articulated by flow and marks"[35] which subsequently becomes ordered through the symbolic. Once expression and representation is given through the violence of language then the nomadic subject becomes the juridic subject, captured within the imposition of the structure of determination and particular subjectivity but always, however, undermined by the bodily scream.[36] The instinctual drive becomes caught in syntax, in the rules of language. At this stage the subject is established above the semiotic chora and so commences the repression of physical origin. It is only in dreams that the space of internal desire is assumed, the moment of that which has been previously disavowed. Here we mark the return of the repressed through the excess of language and the inevitable corresponding lack in the absence of the all-mastering subject, it is the moment of the involuntary admission, the echo of the voice of the other—those traces imposed through the structure of language itself.

What Deleuze and Guattari attempt is a politicized manifestation of this original (psychic and somatic) state of the instinctual distorted by the symbolic, utilizing the energy flow of the presemiotic chora. They develop the figure of the *line of flight* which can be envisaged as that which connects multiplicities as the movement of the *phantasm* in the migration from the ordered of the external to the disordered of the *nomadic governmentality* of the internal. The line of flight is of the surplus to value, of the excess, the unrepresentable and constantly interruptive. These are the lines along which desire flows and by which the subject takes flight.[37] The hierarchical structure of symbolic desire through the internalization of language and the territorialization of the body can be contrasted to the linear structure of imaginary desire through the displacement of language and the de-territorialization of the body. The former is a process of displacement of the real away from original of disallowed expression (mnemic traces). The latter—the line of flight—is that of excess in language, or what Lecercle calls *delir* ("involuntary admissions, echoes of other voices, traces imposed by the structure itself, distortion and displacement").[38] *Delir* as the articulation of the phantasm in its movement as the line of flight is the subversive, destabilizing force, "only potentially steps removed from a fully articulated oppositional discourse."[39] But every moment or recognition of the possibility of the *line of flight* (the flash of lightning in the night) is but a fleeting moment of imagination cystalizing in practice and temporarily captured as the discourse of the legislative guerilla on the margins of the centre. As Milovanovic comments "Political economy induced gaps and the subsequent mobilization of desire assures the perpetual pursuit of plenitude, jouissance, which always, in the end escapes us."[40]

In terms of narrative we search for the 'molecular' plot between the anarchic play within language and beyond the paranoiac 'molar' narrative of relentless repetition. In terms of space we transcend that of the *other* and enter the space of multiplicity (of subjectivities as opposed to the singular subject) and that of the interstice, the most dangerous deterritorialised space of the intermediate and the hybrid (the space of *otherness*). No longer the hierarchical but the linear. But to liberate the phantasm and allow it to pursue the line of flight and become nomadic means overcoming the constraints of the institutional violence of juridic language and practice. With each possibility of recognition there appears a further site of repression, a further field of external order and discipline. It is a force that reaches the very grain of the individual, touches the body, intrudes into the gesture, the attitude, the discourses: it is the determining narrative of alienated existence.[41] The site of this conflict is the body and the figure of the body as a site of power will be analyzed through the process of the violence of inscription. As Lecercle states: "A body, then, can be see as territorialized, crisscrossed by lines of flight .... what is inscribed on the body .... is not letters but unordered, unstructured lines, without beginning or end."[42] Lecercle and Deleuze both rely upon the assimilation of the phantasy with the Stoic *lekton*, that which is the significate, of the incorporeal, the attribute which dwells *upon the body*. The body without organs, that figure of the desire of the undetermined *mark* of inscription, in opposition to the singular body of determined desire of juridic inscription, the determined *word* of the law.

"Only that which goes on hurting will stay in the memory"

> The sulphur was lit, but the flame was so poor that only the top of the skin was burnt, and that only slightly. Then the executioner, his sleeves rolled up, took the steel pincers, which had been especially made for the occasion, and were which about a foot and a half long, and pulled first at the calf of the right leg, then at the thigh, and from there at the two fleshy parts of the right arm, then at the breasts. Though a strong and sturdy fellow, this executioner found it so difficult to tear away the pieces of flesh that he set about the same spot two or three times, twisting the pincers as he did so, and what he took formed at each part a wound about the size of a six-pound piece.[43]

> But how quiet he grows at just about the sixth hour! Enlightenment comes to the most dull-witted. It begins around the eyes. From there it radiates. A moment that might tempt one to get under the Harrow oneself. Nothing more happens than that the man begins to understand the inscription, he purses his mouth as if were listening. You see how difficult it is to decipher the script with one's eyes; but our man deciphers his wounds. To be sure, that is a hard task; he needs six hours to accomplish it.[44]

Here are two images of violent juridic inscription. They represent the extreme. But they also serve as useful reminders—in dramatized form—of the Force of Law In the foundation of modern social order. As Sarat and Kearns note "Modern law is built upon representations of aggression, force and disruption."[45] It is a violence which is visible, vivid and disembodied. It speaks loudly, arouses indignation and, as a result, its representations threaten to overwhelm reason. The problem of representing this violence is that of disciplining the force of the representation. In siting the descriptions of juridical violence by Foucault and Kafka as a preface to a discussion of the violence of law In the moment of its inscription upon the body what is achieved is an unmasking of the dupe of the rationality of the reasoning which purports to justify these acts, to expose the representation In its original violent state.[46] An analysis of this system of violence enables us to determine the variants and the different speeds and rate of the machine that makes bodies thc site of the inscription of the text of the sentence and the punishment and to ask ourselves for what Eye/I this writing, which cannot be interpreted by its supports, In intended.

The systematically coercive nature of this force is central to Law. The first passage expresses the sovereign will of a king which is addressed to the flesh:

it is savage, spectacular and revolting. The second passage expresses the modern rule of law which evinces a certain degree of discretion: it is methodical, austere and numbing. The Kafkian delirium seems In this case somewhat anticipatory: an allegory prefigures contemporary reality. Both descriptions are of the inscription of the sentence and punishment under the due process of the law upon the body of the individual. In the modern period there has occurred a literal enforcement of the sentence of law to the allegorical enforcement of the sentence of law. The key determinant is language: the force of the word of law. It is the immemorial effort to place the body of the individual under the law of writing.

The Body Politic founded itself through the operation of the inscription of its memory upon the Body of the Individual. The Body of the Individual was thus forced to become part of the Body Politic, becoming part of the external and symbolic Realm as opposed to remaining part of the internal and imaginary realm. It was through participation at public displays of cruelty that a social memory and the sphere of legal obligation was first brought into existence. "Blood, torture and sacrifices" were the means through which the Body Politic created itself and was the source of founding order of structure on the community.[47] The authority of law resides In its memory: the memory without origin which founds its mythology.[48] It is a social memory subscribed to or invested In through the originating act of violence (the murder of the Father) and it is a memory inscribed upon the body. Repression thus becomes the inevitable price of investing In this memory, of becoming part of the social: all that we allowed to remember is the Law, the mnemic trace—the *spur*—of this being the violence that is done to us. The voice of the law says "Give me your body and I will give you meaning." In *The Social Contract* Rousseau expressed the fear that not only would authority grow tyrannical but also that punishment would be needed to sustain repression, the subject forced to conform to 'wills that are not his own'.[49] It was/is only through the establishment of a repressive realm of alienated and external desire (for punishment for the mythical originating act of violence) that the Body Politic and the institution of the Juridical Body could/can maintain its autonomy and authority over the Body of the Individual. The Law assumed the monopoly of punishment and compliance through inscription of its word upon the body. The point is made by Certeau thus: "There is no law that is not inscribed on bodies .... This machinery transforms individual bodies into a body politic."[50]

From birth to mourning after death, the law takes hold of the body In order to make it text. The body is transformed into the table of the law, a living tableaux of rules and customs.

The spectacle of execution—the public arena in the creation of memory through cruelty—was also a site of truth. The punishment, In the enactment of which the will of the sovereign as incarnation of the Body Politic, also determined a relationship of power, not of object to a knowing subject, but rather an ambiguous relationship that was the pleasure of being recognized, of being an identifiable and legible word In a social language, of being changed into a fragment within an anonymous text and of being inscribed In a symbolic order that had neither owner nor author.[51] Death by torture enabled 'the condemned' a momentary saturnalia, where nothing was prohibited or punishable. The predicament of the condemned became a 'lightning-existence' of transcendence which harshly illuminated the ambiguity of the justifiable and the situation of the out-lawed.

But when cruelty is abolished as public spectacle then two transformations occur. The first occurs, necessarily, In the process of the violence of law. In terms of punishment the effect becomes its inevitability rather than its visible intensity. (Although there might be said to be a violence of the visibility of surveillance, either through direct incarceration or restricted movement or through the out-lawing and proscribing of particular activities). It is the certainty of being punished and not the horrifying spectacle of public punishment that must discourage the 'crime' of being *other* (*our* violence against *them*).[52] It is directed toward representing a common purpose aimed against the anomic savagery lurking just beyond law's boundaries. Once again, the violence which is actually inside the law is portrayed by law as being outside the law. The elaborate rituals and procedures of 'due process' demonstrate the care with which law now traffics In violence. The procedures and purposes of law are emphasized while its instrumentalities and wounding effects are kept In the background. While the violence outside the law is unnecessary, irrational, indiscriminate, gruesome and useless, the finesse of law's violence becomes described as rational, purposive and controlled through values, norms and procedures external to violence itself. But as Sarat notes:

> Even when we realize the way law itself often exaggerates the threat of violence *outside* law, we can never ourselves imagine that law could ever finally conquer and undo force, coercion, and disorder; its promise is a promise to substitute one kind of force—legitimate force—for another.[53]

This force is the perfection of power which renders useless any countervailing exercise of individual power In the determination of identity and existence.

In its effort to hide its violent structure through bureaucratization and technologization modern law ushers In a second transformation. For when cruelty is abolished as public spectacle it becomes a private event. In addition to its role as social sacrifice In the embodiment of memory the spectacle of the scaffold also offered a cathartic purpose. The spectacle might provoke nausea, disgust and revulsion but it also engaged a perverse fascination In its slow, meticulous ceremony: it was a kind of pornography, a release of rage and expunging of the bad humours. The removal of the spectacle through its transformation from literal to allegorical force engenders a denial of this cathartic function for the individual and therefore a rupture In the external foundation of individual identity. This cathartic purpose reappears as shadowy psychotic obsession fueled by phantasies of butchery, death and domination which finds expression In a kind of delirious murmuring, increasingly garrulous language that discovers In the most murderous impulses both an unlimited fascination and "an infinite void that opens beneath the feet of the person it attracts."[54] Here we mark the return of the phantasm In the margins of the law, that constructed by law as the violence of the outside, but which is In fact the violence of the within, when the soul turns from "jousts to phantasms".

"It might be said that all knowledge is linked to the essential forms of cruelty"

> Count 14: This was an allegation against Jaggard of assault occasioning actual bodily harm. The victim had hot wax dropped into the urethra of his penis. The penis was burned with a candle flame and then a syringe needle was inserted. Count 15 was an allegation against Jaggard of aiding and abetting assault occasioning actual bodily harm. Jaggard aided and abetted by taking a video film whilst a co-accused pushed a safety pin through the head of "L's" penis. Count 17 alleged unlawful wounding against Lucas and Jaggard. Atkinson, a co-defendant, had his penis nailed to a bench. He was caned, hit and rubbed with a spiked strap, then cut with a scalpel by Lucas.[55]

> 1) You may tie me down on the table, ropes drawn tight, for ten to fifteen minutes, time enough to prepare the instruments; 2) One hundred lashes at least, a pause of several minutes; 3) You begin sewing, you sew up the hole In the glands; you sew the skin around the glands to the glands itself, preventing the top from tearing; you sew the scrotum to the skin of the thighs. You sew the breasts, securely attaching a button with four holes to each nipple. You may connect them with an elastic band the with button holes—*Now you go to the second phase* ......I have not mentioned the burns, only because I have a medical exam coming up In a while, and they take a long time to heal .... *This is not a fantasy, it is a programme.*[56]

"All instincts that do not discharge themselves outwardly *turn inward.*"[57] The shaming of instinct In the modern stifles the cruel and murderous impulses until the individual becomes "calculable, regular, necessary"—a subject of civilized reason and morality.[58] But cruel impulses do not disappear altogether. The *internalization* of cruelty and the convergence of pleasure and pain occurs. As Miller notes "The idea of 'self-chosen torture' becomes the key In Nietzsche's *The Genealogy of Morals* to interpreting a host of intertwining phenomena: guilt; the bad conscience; and above all, the triumph of asceticism In Christianity."[59] The phantasm, now forced inwards, pursues not a line of flight but the line of resistance In the face of ensuing technological forms of punishment and the rationalization of the force of law. The individual—denied the direct spectacle of the force of law—becomes enmeshed In "tremendous clockwork, composed of ever smaller ever more subtly adapted gears" In which there is an ever-growing superfluity of all dominating and commanding events, In which the individual represents "minimal forces, minimal values".[60]

How might the cruel banality of the contemporary force of law be resisted? How might that violence of the *with-out* law be utilized In confronting the violence of the *with-in* law? In part, the contemporary processes of closure and silencing suggests the inevitability of the implosion of the myth of the internally coherent authority of law through its perfection of power so that its exercise becomes useless. All that is left becomes the will to power. The removal of the visible physicality of law has ushered In a myriad of unorthodox pleasures and desires, held In delicate balance between a multiplicity of regulatory procedures of allowance and licence, restriction and closure, capture and counter-capture. It is the implosion of order and the explosion of desire ('the lawless law of the world') that Deleuze and Guattari exploit In their agenda of resistance through the unleashing of the phantasm along its line of flight from the juridic subject to the nomadic object.

It is a resistance which can be analyzed In its form as reversal and inversion.[61] Hence In part an explanation of the prosecution of the private events of particular sexual practices (for example In the case of *R v Brown*). The prohibition of consenting acts of sado-masochism reveals the threat posed to the symbolic legal order through the process of inversion of inscription which is In operation during this act In which the word-sign of law becomes the mark-sign of desire. In addition the prosecution reveals the ironic reversal of violence In which the pleasure In the distribution of pain is received In the ecstasy of pain as the liberated pleasure of desire. Thus the violence of the *with-out* becomes central In the determination of the pleasure and excludes the violence of the *with-in* . Rather than succumbing to the violence of the external symbolic order of law In which individual desire is repressed and alienated In the process of the formation of the juridic-subject within the body politic, what occurs is the abandonment of the external referent through the extension of the contract and its ritual enforcement to an absurd logical conclusion.

The example suggests the power of the mark of desire (pleasure) In foreclosing on the inscription of the word of the law (pain). The event is without writing. And it is an event of suspended inscription In which gratification is obtained through the temporal moment of delayed inscription. The instruments of inscribing which the law possesses become merely props employed In the satisfaction of individual desire. The body as the site of memory can recall both the violence of law and the violence of desire. The event of writing points to the existence of a separate despotic law of the body politic.[62] The event of the mark encompasses the memory of the ecstasy of pain as opposed to the fear of pain. As a moment of the phantasm as an element of resistance, the mark is a symbol of opposition In which the body becomes the site of the heterotopia, that which is beyond the name of law, that which is of 'the time out of mind' of internal desire rather than of 'the time immemorial' of external order. As Clastres notes:

> The mark on the body, on all bodies alike, declares: You will not have the desire for power; you will not have the desire for submission. And that non-separate law can only have for its inscription a space that is not separate: that space is the body itself.[63]

In terms of the violence in operation in the consensual sado-masochistic relationship three points can be ventured with regard the inversion of the operation of the violence of law:

1) The first inversion concerns the singularity of the body. The law strives to construct docile individual bodies—alienated bodies. Here the bodies are alienated but not In submission to law but rather In submission to desire and therefore the individual body becomes a site of power without reference to determination by external law. The Law cannot see sado-masochism even though it is brought within its gaze.

2) The second inversion concerns the construction of legal relations. As identified by Deleuze, sadism is institutional and masochism is contractual.[64] The unifying element is that of trust. The existence of the contract marks the determining element of trust In this particular sexual liaison. In being so contracted the external is vanquished In that symbolic law has no role to play. The violence of the law is disavowed and becomes an order of desire In which the violence of pain becomes the guarantor of pleasure. The abandonment of the external referent of law which determines identity occurs through the logical extension of the form of law In its contractual nature and the satisfaction of identity through the fulfilment of imagination.

3) The final inversion of the violence of law occurs In the construction of a humanistic critique of law premised upon the philosophical foundations of sadism and masochism. For the sadist, following Sade, s/he is merely giving expression to instinctual-anarchic nature, reveling In the exhortation to "Be Cruel" and transcend the tyranny of the violence of law by becoming the administrator of one's own law of violence. Sade mocks the law by erecting a superior principle of absolute evil that institutes a kind of lawless super-law. For the masochist, following Masoch, the letter of the law which is re-written provides the subverted resistance. By

scrupulously applying the law the masochist demonstrates its absurdity and provokes the very disorder that it is intended to prevent. The law which forbids the satisfaction of desire under threat of subsequent punishment becomes a law which demands the punishment first and then orders that the satisfaction of desire should inevitably follow.

Conclusion: Anarchy of the Body and the Sign of Desire

The satisfaction of alienated internal desire through the peculiar intimacy In the administration of pain and pleasure engenders sensations and experiences which are unrepresentable, In excess and beyond the name, In which dreams, memories and aspirations assume on a new balance against the external order. These are the sensations when the phantasm pursues the line of flight. The intensity of pleasure through pain causes the momentary disorganization of self, disturbed by the sensations of affective processes 'beyond' those connected with the psychic (repressed) order. Such an affirmative disorganization points to the release of the caged power In which the self is exuberantly discarded:

> There is a creation of anarchy within the body, where its hierarchies, its localizations and designations, its organicity ...... is In the process of disintegrating .... This is something "unamenable", "useless", outside of all the programmes of desire. It is the body made totally plastic by pleasure: something that opens itself, that tightens, that throbs, that beats, that gapes.[65]

Foucault praised sado-masochistic activities for "inventing new possibilities" through the "eroticization of power".[66] The limit-experience, of which sado-masochism and the utilization of sexuality, is but one example, becomes a technology to grapple with otherwise subconscious and unthinkable aspects of negative experience, turning the dead gaze of the law upon itself as the self utters a fateful "YES" of affirmation. The nonsense of the "will to know" and the purely negative freedom of the individual are laid bare. Pain and pleasure experienced as the merging of boundaries becomes a series of reversals and revelations In which guilt becomes joy, pain becomes pleasure and torture becomes ecstasy.

Through such exercises of excess the arc of desire transcends the boundary marking the limit of the internal-external paradigm and gives expression to the unspoken of the violence of the Phantasm as it arrives as the figure of the nomad traversing a line of flight of a desire without law. As Bataille notes, such an act of excess ruptures the discontinuous individualities that constitute the confined and fragmented condition of individual existence. These acts of excess challenge institutional codes In the sense that these relations cannot be validated through an external order. These acts short-circuit and introduce alternative arenas of action where there is supposed to be only L-law.[67]

* 119B Evering Road, Stoke Newington, London N16 7SL ENGLAND

Notes

1. F. Nietzsche *The Birth of Tragedy/The Genealogy of Morals* (New York, 1953) p.192. M. Foucault *Mental Illness and Psychology* (London, 1976) p. 73.

2. As suggested by M. Foucault *The History of Sexuality Volume One: An Introduction* (1979) pp. 137–138, p. 143. The human body enters a spatial machinery of power that explores it, breaks it down, and rearranges it allocating to each person a place, and to each place a person. In this "grid" each position is coded as a value so that distribution of functions is transposed into relations fixed in this structured grid. The success of this arrangement thus depends on the coding of this space.

3. See M. C. Taylor "Desire of Law, Law of Desire" (1990) 11 *Cardozo Law Review* p. 1269.

4. P. Goodrich *Languages of Law: From Logics of Memory to Nomadic Masks* (1990) pp 251–52.

5. Goodrich *supra* 210. Hachamovitch writes with regard to the image of law and the institution of law *in* the body: "Images are instituted: they honour an imperative to produce and reproduce the text of material life, so as to transmit, again and again, the heritable sense of an origin. The history of the image is the history of the conversion of the origin by law: one law on the other: *utrumque ius*, Roman law, canon law. It is the history of fealties such conversions imply. A history of law would be on other words nothing other than a history of faith, a history of faith in the body itself, but also and at once of an absence of faith in the body, a history of Christian repression of sensation in the name of law." Y. Hachamovitch "One Law on the Other" (1990) *International Journal for the Semiotics of Law* III/8 p. 190.

6. Goodrich *supra* p. 254

7. Drucilla Cornell notes that the violent foundation of law is allegorical rather than metaphorical in that in the Law of the Law is only 'present' in its absolute absence. The 'never has been' of an unrecoverable past is understood as the lack of origin 'presentable' only as an allegory. The Law of the Law, in other words, is the figure of an initial fragmentation, the loss of Good. It is an allegory which is inescapable because the lack of origin is the fundamental truth. See further: D. Cornell "From the Lighthouse: The Promise of Redemption and the Possibility of Legal Interpretation" (1990) 11 *Cardozo Law Review*, 11 p. 1689.

8. D. Milovanovic *Postmodern Law and Disorder: Psychoanalytic Semiotics, Chaos and Juridic Exegese* (1990) p. 34.

9. R. Cover "Violence and the Word" (1986) 95 *Yale Law Journal* p. 1601.

10. C. Douzinas and R. Warrington "A Well-Founded Fear of Justice: Law and Ethics in Postmodernity" (1990) 2 *Law and Critique* 2 pp. 115–147.

11. M. Foucault *supra* n.2, p. 83.

12. G. Deleuze and F. Guattari *A Thousand Plateaux* (1987) p. 111–48. Minson in his commentary on Foucault's analytic of power notes that "(power) produces too ... productive of a range of intended and unintended effects." See J. Minson *Genealogies of Morals: Nietzsche, Foucault, Donzelot and the Eccentricity of Ethics* (1985) p. 44.

13. Milovanovic *supra* n. 7 pp. 89–91. I have drawn from Milovanovic's account of the Deleuze and Guattari thesis in addition to the explication original. In addition see the accounts provided by R. Bogue *Deleuze and Guattari* (1989) and J. Lecercle *Philosophy Through the Looking Glass* (London: Open Court, 1985).

14. See Minson *supra* n. 11.

15. See P. Bourdieu "The Force of Law: Toward a Sociology of the Juridical Field" (1987) 38 *The Hastings Law Journal* p. 831.

16. M. Taylor *supra* n.3, p. 1269.

17. S. Fish quoted by Taylor *supra*, p. 1271.

18. M. Foucault *supra* n.2, p. 81.

19. *Supra*, p. 83

20. M. Foucalut *Discipline and Punish* (1975) p. 193.

21. G. Deleuze *The Logic of Sense* (1990) p. 213. Deleuze employs the image of the inside and the outside in his description of the nature of the phantasm: "Neither active, nor passive, neither internal nor external, neither imaginary nor real—phantasms have indeed the impassibility, they inspire in us an unbearable waiting" *passim*, p. 211. Therefore the defining 'characteristics' of the phantasm can be described as a) a pure event, neither imaginary nor real, neither internal nor external, neither active nor passive; b) an "acosmic singularity"; c) a verbal existence but only as nonsense or paradox.

22. M. Foucault "A Preface to Transgression" in *Language, Counter-Memory, Practice: Selected Essays and Interviews by Michel Foucault* (1977; ed. D. Bouchard) p. 170.

23. M. Foucault (1975) *supra* n.20.

24. M. Foucault (1977) *supra* n.22.

25. M. Foucault *The Order of Things* (1970) p. 211. I have relied upon the biographical work of James Miller in my consideration of the nature of the phantasm. See J. Miller *The Passion of Michel Foucault* (1993) especially ch.7 and J. Miller "Carnivals of Atrocity: Foucault, Nietzsche, Cruelty" (1990) 18 *Political Theory* 3, 470. One of Foucault's major writings on the phantasm, apart from those already noted, is "Dream, Imagination and Existence" (1984–1985) XIX *Review of Existential Psychology and Psychiatry* 1, 31. Reference should also be made to Deleuze *supra* n.21, pp. 210–223.

26. G. Bataille *Inner Experience* (1988) p. 43.

27. G. Deleuze *Difference et Repetition* (1972) p. 55. On the construction of waste-refusal as an alternative metaphor in the organization of societal order see Goodrich *supra* n.4. Goodrich discusses the image of refusal in relation to Thomas Pynchon's novel *The Crying of Lot 49* (1967). Goodrich notes that "(T)he refuse may also, however, refuse. It may form its own network of communication, and it is largely in the name of the other, of that which remains, that the heroine Oedipa pursues the signs and the dross outside the contractual network". See also P. Goodrich "Contractions: Rousseau in the Year 2000" in *Post-Modern Law* (1990; ed. A. Carty). Here Goodrich pre-figures the entrance of the figure of *nomad*. See further G. Deleuze and F. Guattari *On The Line* (1984).

28. M. Foucault, "Of Other Spaces" 16 *Diacritics* (1986) 22.

29. A. Artaud "To Have Done With The Judgement of God" in *Selected Writings* (1988; ed. S. Sontag) p. 571.

30. R. Bogue *supra* n.13, 107. See also G. Deleuze and F. Guattari *supra* n.12 and J. Lecercle, *upra* n.13. Also M. Hardt *Gilles Deleuze* (1993).

31. G. Deleuze and F. Guattari *Anti-Oedipus: Capitalism and Schizophrenia* (1984) p. 8.

32. G. Deleuze and F. Guattari *supra* n.12, p. 191 and 58.

33. R. Bogue, *supra* n.13, p. 95.

34. J. Miller, *supra* n.25, p. 277.

35. J. Kristeva *Revolution in Poetic Language* (1984) p. 26 and 41.

36. See D. Milovanovic *supra* n.8, p. 111.

37. J. Lecercle, *supra* n.13, p. 177. Deleuze and Guattari, *supra* n.12, p. 21.

38. *Ibid*., p. 50.

39. Milovanovic *supra* n.8, p. 114.

40. *Ibid*. p. 111.

41. As Baudrillard suggests. See, for example, J. Baudrillard *In the Shadow of the Silent Majorities* (1983). See also the useful commentary on this position (the impossibility of de-determination) M. Gane *Baudrillard's Bestiary: Baudrillard and Culture* (1991).

42. J. Lecercle, *supra*.

43. M. Foucault *supra* n.20, p. 3.

44. F. Kafka "In the Penal Colony" in *In The Penal Colony: Stories and Short Pieces* (1961) p. 204.

45. A. Sarat and T.Kearns "A Journey Through Forgetting: Toward a Jurisprudence of Violence" In *The Fate of Law* (1991; eds. A. Sarat and T. Kearns) p. 211.

46. See further A. Sarat "Speaking of Death: Narratives of Violence In Capital Trials" (1993) 27 *Law and Society Review* 1, 21. See also A. Sarat and T. Kearns *supra*. Also Cover *supra* n.9, R. Dworkin *Taking Rights Seriously* (1977) p. 15 and P. Fitzpatrick "Violence and Legal Subjection" (*Unpublished Manuscript, University of Kent, 1991*). The association of law and violence is linguistically present In the ease and comfort with which we speak about enforcing the law. As Derrida notes: "The word 'enforceability' reminds us that there is no such thing as law that doesn't imply In itself, *a priori* .... the possibility of being 'enforced', applied by force. There are, to be sure, laws that are no enforced, but there is no law without enforceability, and no applicability or enforceability of the law without force, whether this force be direct or indirect, physical or symbolic." J. Derrida "The Force of Law: The 'Mystical' Foundation of Authority" (1990) 11 *Cardozo Law Review* 921 at p. 925.

47. F. Nietzsche *supra* n.1, p. 193

48. On the memory of the law see Goodrich *supra* n.4, pp. 32–53.

49. J-J Rousseau *The Social Contract* (1969) Book IV, II.

50. M. de Certeau *The Practice of Everyday Life* (1988) p. 139.

51. *Ibid*, p. 140.

52. Foucault *supra* n.43, p. 9.

53. Sarat *supra* n.46. p. 54.

54. Foucault *supra* n.2, p. 48.

55. *R v Brown* (1992) 94 Cr. App. R. 302 (CA) per Lord Lane at 306, (1993) 2 ALL ER 75 (HL). See also C. Stanley "Sins and Passions" (1993) 4 *Law and Critique* 2, 207.

56. G. Deleuze and F. Guattari *supra* n.12 p. 150. Or In the words of Lou Reed "Taste the whip, In love not given lightly" from the lyric of "Venus In Furs" on *The Velvet Underground and Nico* (1967).

57. Nietzsche, *supra* n.1, at II, 16.

58. *Ibid*, II, 1.

59. Miller *supra* n.25, p. 476. See also Nietzsche *ibid*, III, 11.

60. Nietzsche *supra* n.1, II, 11. It will be recalled that Nietzsche's speculations lead him to conclude that within nothing more to be afraid of, there is no longer anything left In the self to despise, no longer able even to enjoy the self-infliction of pain. At the end of this path lies the "last man", the docile denizen of the world.

61. I am aware of the dangers of employing inversion as a primary mechanism In the establishment of emancipatory critique since it is possible to suggest that at the point of inversion there exists merely a further site of legal subjectivity In that the identification of the inversion allows another order of subjectivity to come into existence: that the inversion comes within the gaze. However, it is possible to suggest that In the process of the inversion the ironic nature of the reversal subverts the mechanism of this subjectivity through its extension and forecloses (as In the process of inscription) on the external authority of the symbolic order through the internal maintenance of 'positive' norms of conduct. In addition, In a more directly philosophical account, I am also aware that In being reliant upon Sade as opposed to Bentham I open myself to criticism of simply hedonism and individuality as opposed to the virtue of the community.

62. P. Clastres *Society Against the State* (1987) p. 188. See also R. Girard *Violence and the Sacred* (1977).

63. Clastres *ibid*.

64. G. Deleuze "Coldness and Cruelty" In *Masochism: Coldness and Cruelty/Venus In Furs* (1989) p. 134.

65. Foucault quoted by Miller *supra* n.25 p. 274.

66. Foucault *supra* n.20 p. 34.

67. I am grateful to my colleague Deborah Cheney for our discussions on the subject of inscription and imagination. This essay was presented as a paper to the Ninth Colloquium of the International Association for the Semiotics of Law, Hebrew University, Jerusalem, 1993. I am grateful to those members of the Association who offered advice on the paper, especially Rolando Gaete, Francois Ost and Katharina Sobota. My thanks also to Lynne Williams.

Chapter Nine

Legislating Religious Rituals: How Communion is Regulated in Some Protestant Denominations

James H. Ware Jr.*

I.

Enactments of rituals by their very nature involve the exercise of power. The enactment of religious rituals involves the exercise of power with regard to that which is considered by a community to be the ultimate source of human meaning. This power in the hands of irresponsible persons is dangerous, especially when it is used to define or establish human meaning and destiny.

Although a case can be made for a much wider understanding of the term "religious rituals," in this paper it is limited to a rather traditional meaning, i.e., ritual use by self consciously religious institutions. The line between sacred and secular is in some cases clearly marked and in other situations blurred and ambiguous. The purpose of this paper is not to develop a general theory of ritual, but to deal with a particular set of ritual practices which occur in Protestant Christianity in North America.

Institutionalized religious rituals incorporate many different types of ritual genre which can be determined by the speech acts and dramas which they incorporate and their ritual usage. Within Christian institutions some rituals are used to legislate the institution's practices; some are designed for the worship of God; some are structured for interpersonal bonding; some are shaped as enabling or healing acts; some are used to constitute "reality;" some prioritize the world in which we live; some function as reenactment of definitive events in the history of the tradition; others are designed for self expression; still others are used to reinforce beliefs and explanations. Often these different uses are intertwined in a given ritual enactment.[1]

The speech acts and dramas of any given ritual are directly related to the function of the ritual itself. Both are symbolic behavior contextualized by their usage within the ritual. The manner in which the terms of the language and elements of the drama relate to their referents and the significance, force, or impact which the use of these "tokens" have are framed by the intentional function of the ritual.

The term "liturgy" will be used in the following discussion to refer to institutionalized ritual practices which have as their primary purpose the worship of God; this is in contrast to legislative rituals and language which create, order, and prescribe institutional behavior.[2] Some institutionalized liturgies require strict conformity both in language and in enactment to a pre-established pattern or patterns. This gives rise to a second meaning for the term "liturgy," i.e., the formalized texts and instructions which are enactment in worship. In some traditions there are institutionalized liturgies which do not have specified texts or detailed instructions for the celebrant; they allow the celebrant considerable latitude in the use of language and the process of enactment. These traditions often think of themselves as non-liturgical because they do not have normative texts and detailed instruction for enactment. However, some so called "non-liturgical" denominations do prescribe directly or indirectly the manner in which their particular worship practices are enacted. Insofar as they have legislated or traditional, normative understandings of their rituals and these rituals are representative of their particular style and consensus, they have a form of liturgy.

The worship of God cannot be separated from the form it takes, i.e., the form of its liturgy. What distinguishes one denomination's liturgies from another are the forms they take. Each separate form is not only based on a root paradigm, but it is an embodiment of that paradigm.[3] Different forms of liturgies not only determine how God is reverenced, but those forms are also the major means for shaping the realization of the present meaning and future destiny for those who participate in them. Through worship a religious community prioritizes its "world," defines its identity as a community, and attempts to achieve its ultimate end or destiny. Since the form of the worship determines how the worship fulfills its functions, the form of the liturgy is crucial to the realization of the ends of worship. Consequently, the proper uses or misuses of liturgy's form is not a trivial matter in the life of a religious community.

Legislative control is one way in which a community can assure that liturgies are properly enacted and properly used. However, legislative processes are themselves symbolic operations which are ritually bound. These processes are a different genre of symbolic behavior, but they are no less determinative of a religious community's behavior and the realization of the ends toward which that community is directed.

The Christian ritual known as The Eucharist, Holy Communion, or The Lord's Supper will be the focal point for looking at the relationship of legislative and liturgical ritual processes. I will try to examine how this ritual is legislated and how it is performed as worship in three North American, Protestant traditions, The Episcopal Church, The Presbyterian Church (USA), and the Southern Baptist Convention. Each denomination represents a distinctive type of legislative processes as well as a different liturgical form.

In the study of these sets of rituals it is necessary to take into account the reflective understanding of the community which engages in them. Often the reflective understanding of a community, its theology, shapes and gives insight into its rituals. However, it would be a mistake of major proportion to think that there was a one to one correlation between what an institution's reflective understanding of a ritual is, and what that ritual affects through its enactment. This will become more evident as we proceed.

II.

Among those denominations to be considered The Episcopal Church legislates its liturgies more carefully and thoroughly than the other two. In The Episcopal Church both the legislative procedures (rituals) and codes are recorded in *The Constitution and Canons*.[4] Each geographic subdivision of the denomination also has its own constitution and canons which supplement those of the denomination as a whole. When The Episcopal Church's ruling bodies meet in General Convention, they are composed of two Houses: (1) the House of Bishops composed of the ruling Bishops of the denomination; and, (2) the House of Deputies composed of priests and lay representatives from each diocese. The "ritual" handling of business in each house is set forth in *The Constitution and Canons*.

The liturgies, the written codes and language of worship, of The Episcopal Church are recorded in *The Book of Common Prayer*. The relationship between the legislative process and the liturgy stated in *The Book of Common Prayer* is clearly spelled out in Article X of the Constitution:

> The Book of Common Prayer, as now established or hereafter amended by the authority of this Church, shall be in use in all of the Dioceses of this Church. No alterations thereof or additions thereto shall be made unless the same shall be first proposed in one regular meeting of the General Convention and by a resolve thereof be sent within six months to the Secretary of the Convention of every Diocese, to be made known to the Diocesan Convention at its next meeting, and be adopted by the General Convention at its next succeeding regular meeting by a majority of the Bishops, excluding retired Bishops not present, of the whole number of Bishops entitled to vote in the House of Bishops, and by a vote by orders in the House of Deputies in accordance with Article I, Sec. 5, except that concurrence by the orders shall require the affirmative vote in each order by a majority of the Dioceses entitled to representation in the House of Deputies.
>
> But not withstanding anything hereinabove contained, the General Convention may at any one meeting, by majority of the whole number of the Bishops entitled to vote in the House of Bishops, and by a majority of the Clerical and Lay Deputies of all the dioceses entitled to representation in the House of Deputies, voting by orders as previously set forth in this Article:
>
> (a) Amend the Table of Lessons and all Tables and Rubrics relating to the Psalms:
>
> (b) Authorize for trial use throughout this Church, as an alternative at any time or times to the established Book of Common Prayer or any section or Office thereof, a proposed revision of the whole Book or of any portion thereof, duly undertaken by the General Convention.
>
> And *Provided*, that nothing in this Article shall be construed as restricting the authority of the Bishops of this Church to take such order as may be permitted by the Rubrics of the Book of Common Prayer or by the Canons of the General Convention for the use of special forms of worship.[5]

The historical reasons for the standardization of Anglican worship are given in the Preface to *The First Book of Common Prayer* (1549) which was adopted during the reign of Edward the Sixth of England. According to that Preface the "decent order of the ancient fathers hath been altered, broken and neglected," so that the entire Scriptures were not covered in the Readings, and the order of worship had become a source of contention, " some following Salisbury use, some Herford use, some the use of Bangor, some of York, and some of Lincoln."[6]

The first *Book of Common Prayer* for The Episcopal Church in the United States was prepared in 1789 and contextualizes the tradition within its new parameters. This contextualization of the traditions reflects the difference between The Episcopal Church and the Church of England from which it originated following the American War of Independence.[7] Both institutions have similar governing bodies and operate under constitutions and canons. But, the Church of England is still very much tied to the political structures of England, whereas The Episcopal Church is separated from the political structures of the United States. Nowhere is this difference spelled out more clearly than in the Preface to the 1789 Episcopal *Book of Common Prayer*:

> But when in the course of Divine Providence, these American States became independent with respect to civil government, their ecclesiastical independence was necessarily included; and the different religious denomination of Christians in these States were left at full and equal liberty to model and organize their respective Churches, and forms of worship, and discipline, in such a manner as they might judge most convenient for their future prosperity; consistently with the constitution and laws of their country.
>
> The attention of this Church was in the first place drawn to those alterations in the Liturgy which became necessary in the prayers for our Civil Rulers, in consequence of the Revolution. And the principle care herein was to make them conformable to what ought to be the proper end of all such prayers, namely, that "Rulers may have grace, wisdom, and understanding to execute justice, and to maintain truth;" and that the people "may lead quiet and peaceable lives, in all godliness and honesty."[8]

Unlike the Presbyterian Church, The Episcopal Church does not include creeds and confessions in the body of its formal constitution. Theologically the ecumenical creeds of the pre-reformation are generally held as normative. It does, however, formally recognizes two creeds in its liturgy, The Apostles' Creed and The Nicene Creed.[9] The roles of the two creeds in worship are spelled out both in the "Articles of Religion" and "Catechism" ("An Outline of the Faith"). Regarding the Apostles' Creed the "Catechism" states, "The Apostles' Creed is the ancient creed of Baptism; it is used in the

Church's daily worship to recall our Baptismal Covenant."[10] Concerning the Nicene Creed it states, "The Nicene Creed is the creed of the universal Church and is used at the Eucharist."[11]

Although "The Articles of Religion" and "An Outline of the Faith" which are statements of beliefs held by The Episcopal Church appear in the legislatively determined *Book Of Common Prayer*, they are not statements of eternal theological verities.[12] Theological statements can be and have been changed and amended, and theological diversity within its theological tradition is a given. The focus of The Episcopal Church is not on theological conformity, but on common worship. Although it has a definite theological tradition, its unity and identity as a Church depends strongly on its common liturgies.

In the legislated *Book Of Common Prayer* the Eucharist is the center and high point of worship. The normative understanding for Episcopalians is that the Eucharist is a sacrament. The "Catechism" states: "The sacraments are outward and visible signs of inward and spiritual grace, given by Christ as sure and certain means by which we receive that grace."[13] It further states, "Grace is God's favor towards us, unearned and undeserved; by grace God forgives our sins, enlightens our minds, stirs our hearts, and strengthens our wills."[14] Although The Episcopal Church recognizes seven sacraments, only the two great sacraments, that of Baptism and The Holy Eucharist, are given by Christ and are necessary. The other sacraments, Confirmation, Ordination, Matrimony, Reconciliation of a Penitent, and Anointing of the Sick, evolved in the life of the Church under the guidance of the Holy Spirit. It should be noted that in the "Articles of Religion" it is stated that these rites are not to be considered the only activity that God has toward human beings for God in numerous ways uses the material world to reach out to us.[15]

In the "Articles of Religion" there is an explicit rejection of the doctrine of the transubstantiation of the bread and wine into the body and blood of Christ.[16] The offering of Christ, once made in his death and resurrection, are not repeated in the Mass.[17] The rite is further distanced from the Roman Catholic tradition by statements to the effect that the elements of the Mass are not to be paraded or worshiped.[18] According to the "Articles of Religion": " The Body of Christ is given, taken, and eaten, in the Supper, only after an heavenly and spiritual manner. And the mean whereby the Body of Christ is received and eaten in the Supper, is Faith."[19]

The performative function of the Eucharist can "misfire" and work for the damnation of those who abuse it.[20] Consequently, as a matter of discipline, a priest is instructed to speak a private word of warning to persons who live lives that are notoriously evil, or who have wronged their neighbor, or who hate other members of the congregation. The priest may prohibit those persons from participating in the Eucharist, if they persist in their behavior and remain unrepentant. If a priest acts to exclude someone from Communion, he is to report this to his Bishop within fourteen days.[21]

The current *Book of Common Prayer* legislates two major forms of the Eucharist Rite and gives instructions for special occasions. The instructions, orders, and language for the Eucharist celebration, though allowing for some choices between alternative wording, are explicit and detailed. The principal celebrant is always a bishop or a priest; he may be assisted at the table by other ordained member of the clergy, i.e, other bishops, priests, or deacons. Lay persons may assist in reading the Lessons or in the Prayer for the People.

Most of the elements of worship included in the Episcopal Eucharist liturgy are present in Presbyterian worship and the celebrations of Communion. But what is unique about the Episcopal liturgy is the incorporation of The Great Thanksgiving to which I now turn.. About the Eucharist the "Catechism" states, ". . . the Church's sacrifice of praise and thanksgiving, is the way by which the sacrifice of Christ is made present, and in which he unites us to his one offering of himself."[22]

The performative functions of the language of thanksgiving and language of praise accomplishes two things when the "rules" of the speech acts are met. Thanksgiving speech acts are relational, bonding type statements. Speech acts of praise prioritize or exalt that which is praised; they are status granting statements.

The language of thanksgiving is not merely the expression of gratitude, that is, an expression of feelings and emotions; it is action taken in response to the giver of a gift. It is an opening up of one's self to the giver through the active acceptance of the gift. If properly enacted, giving thanks is a bonding act whereby the receiver receives the gift as a token of the giver's desire to relate and opens themselves up to the giver's initiative. Gifts imply a desire for relatedness, and responsible relatedness includes obligations. Engaging in responsible relationships and creating mutual obligation is entailed in any serious giving and receiving. Nowhere is this more evident than in Asian cultures where gift giving carries many dimensions of obligation and relatedness. What is implied in gift receiving is more clearly seen in the refusal of a gift. When a gift is refused there is a rebuffing of the giver. Serious acts of thanksgiving are speech acts which not only communicate the willingness of the receiver to relate to the giver, but also help establish those relationships.

Speech acts of praised grant status to that which is being praised. They elevate that which is praised above the common and mundane. The language of praise itself tends to be hyperbolic and even at times ecstatic because the status which is being granted is extraordinary. Acts of praise acknowledge and enhance an aura of "mysterium tremendum," i.e. a sense of the "holy," around that which is praise. It also creates and enhances within the praising person or praising community a sense of euphoria.

The speech acts which are part of Communion within the Presbyterian traditions are focused on the covenantal aspect of the rite. Covenant speech acts function as bonding statements by promissory and commissive acts and declarations rather than by statements of praise or thanksgiving. Communion for Presbyterians lacks the eucharistic and euphoric sense present in the Episcopal rite. Presbyterian Communion, as primarily a commissive or promissory act, is undertaken in the utmost sincerity and seriousness.

The legislative procedures and codes, i.e., The Constitution of the Presbyterian Church (U.S.A.), are incorporated in two parts: *The Book of Confessions* and *Book of Order*. *The Book of Confessions* is composed of eleven Creeds and Confessional, documents of the Reformed Tradition, from which the current teachings and principles of practice are derived.[23] These confessions are subordinate only to ". . . the authority of Jesus Christ, the Word of God, as the Scriptures bear witness to him. While confessional standards are subordinate to the Scriptures, they are, nonetheless, standards."[24] The *Book of Order*, in which their "Form of Governance," " Directory for Worship," and "Rules of Discipline" are contained, is based on the principles enunciated in *The Book of Confessions*. If Episcopalians incorporate their theological statements within their liturgical texts, Presbyterians incorporate their liturgical guidelines within their theological texts.

Since the confessions reflect a "living tradition," they also reflect the time and circumstances under which they were written. Consequently they do not present a monolithic statement of eternal truths but reflect a tradition of a

Reformed and Reforming Community that takes the Scriptures and the work of the Holy Spirit seriously.

The Presbyterian Church is governed by Presbyters (elders and ministers of the Word and Sacrament) who come together in governing bodies. The Session is the lowest of these bodies and governs the processes of a local congregation. It is subject to a Presbytery which is made up of the regional Ministers of the Word and Sacrament and a number of representative elders from each Church, depending upon the size of the congregation. This body not only provides general guidance for the operation of the Churches in that region, but is also responsible for the ordination of Ministers of the Word and Sacrament. The Synod coordinates and assists in a wider region the work of Presbyteries. The General Assembly is the highest governing body and is composed of an equal number of Ministers of the Word and Sacrament, and elders. The number of Commissioners, i.e., representatives, are chosen from each Presbytery according to the size of the Presbytery. This body provides the authoritative interpretations of the *Book of Order*. Constitutional changes must go through the Advisory Committee on the Constitution which then brings its recommendations to the General Assembly. The General Assembly can then amend, decline, or approve the recommendations. If the amendment is approved, it is then transmitted to the Presbyteries for approval. When the next General Assembly receives written notice that a majority of the Presbyteries have approved the amendment, it may declare the amendment to be made. If it fails to make such a declaration after the report of the approval of the majority of Presbyteries, the amendment, nevertheless, becomes affective at the adjournment of that General Assembly.

The "Directory for Worship" is the second section of the *Book of Order*. Its nature and content are stated in its Preface:

> A Directory for Worship is not a service book with fixed orders of worship, a collection of prayers and rituals, or a program guide. Rather it describes the theology that underlies Reformed worship and outlines appropriate forms for that worship. This directory suggests possibilities for worship, invites development in worship, and encourages continuing reform of worship. It sets standards and presents norm for the conduct of worship in the life of congregations and the governing bodies of the Presbyterian Church (U.S.A.). As the constitutional document ordering the worship of the Presbyterian Church (U.S.A.), this Directory for Worship shall be authoritative for this Church.[25]

The Presbyterian Church (U.S.A.) does have a service book, the *Book of Common Worship*, which it commends; but this book is not part of the constitutional structure of the denomination.[26]

Three things hang together in Presbyterian liturgy, the Scriptures, preaching, and the Sacraments. Scripture is the written Word; preaching is the Word proclaimed; and the Sacraments are the Word enacted and sealed. Each in its own particular way bears testimony to the living Word, Jesus Christ. "Through Scripture, proclamation and Sacraments, God in Christ is present by the Holy Spirit acting to transform, empower, and sustain human lives."[27] Whenever Communion is celebrated it should be preceded by the reading of Scripture and the preaching of the Word.

It is the responsibility of the session of each congregation to see that Communion is observed in an appropriate time and place, and it is the responsibility of the Minster of the Word and Sacrament to be the primary celebrant according to the terms of his\her call or appointment. Because Communion is never a private matter but an act of the Church, elders also assist in the serving of the elements.

The ordering of worship in the "Directory for Worship" includes five steps: gathering around the Word, proclaiming the Word, responding to the Word, sealing of the Word, and bearing and following the Word into the World. The sacraments are the act of sealing the Word, i.e., "The sacraments of Baptism and the Lord's Supper are God's act of sealing the promises of faith within the community of faith as the congregation worships, and include the responses of the faithful to the Word proclaimed and enacted in the Sacraments."[28] Since Communion is an act of the Church, only those who have been sealed in Christ's covenant through Baptism should be participants.

During the celebration of Communion, The "Directory for Worship" states that three types of activities should take place: (1) thanksgiving, (2) remembering, and (3) invoking the Holy Spirit. In thanksgiving the Church is to bless God for what God has done in creation, redemption and sanctification; give thanks for God's work in the world in spite of human sin; and anticipate the fulfillment of God's kingdom and offer itself in obedient service to God. In remembering the death, resurrection, and promise of Christ's return, the Church is renewed and empowered, sustained by Christ's pledge of undying love and continued presence, and sealed in God's covenant of grace through partaking of Christ's self-offering. The Church is to invoke the Holy Spirit to lift worshipers into Christ's presence, to accept their offering of bread and wine, to make the breaking of bread and sharing the cup a participation in the body and blood of Christ, to bind them with Christ and one another, to unite them in communion with all the faithful, to nourish them into the fullness of Christ, and to keep them faithful in representing and doing Christ's work in the world. It is only through the work of the Holy Spirit that the Communion is sacramental.

Other than the reading or stating of the "words of institution" (I Cor. 11:23–26), there is no specific language prescribed for the Communion ritual. However, the Directory for Worship does state that the prayer at the conclusion of Communion should include a request that God's grace be given in order to fulfill the pledges made by the people during the Supper.

The sealing process is key and fundamental to the Presbyterian understanding of Communion. Communion is not only the process whereby God's covenant made in Christ is remembered, renewed, and responded to; it is also a seal of assurance that one participates in that covenant. To use a metaphor, it is a ritual which "nails down" one's covenant relationship to God. What is sealed in the mutual bonding of God and the Church in responsible and caring relatedness. The ritual drama and its speech acts focus on the acts and promises of God recorded in Scripture, enacted in Jesus Christ, and offered to the Church for response. Although the language includes thanksgiving and remembering, in Presbyterian liturgy it is primarily promissory and commissive language, used to seal interpersonal bonding.

Southern Baptists stand in an entirely different theological tradition of the Reformation than either The Episcopal Church or the Presbyterian Church (U.S.A.). The Reformer Zwingli and, somewhat later, members of the Anabaptist Movement ascribed to the nominalism that began with Wm. of Ockham and came to full force during the Enlightenment. Words and symbolic behavior are conventionally agreed on sounds and acts which represent particular objects of our experience; otherwise they have no force. Words, symbols, and drama are merely signs of previously experienced objects or events; they cannot create ideas or realities which we have not already experienced. Laws or Universals do not exist *a priori* in nature; they are derived by generalizations from experiences of particular objects and events.

Baptists begin with the experiences of individuals. The Church is made up of individuals who gather together to worship God; the Church does not exist as an entity apart from its gathered members. Neither the Church, its Creeds or Confessions, or its rituals have any *a priori* existence or significance apart from those individuals who gather themselves together under the initiative and guidance of the Holy Spirit to form a worshiping community. Worship focuses on creating individual experiences of God's grace and individual responses of faith. Baptist legislative processes and codes are conventions agreed upon by those who have gathered together out of common interests.

One of those things which is commonly agreed upon is the authority of Scripture. The Scriptures are the testimonies of individual disciples in the first century who were led by the Holy Spirit to witness to God's work in Christ Jesus and to the work of the Holy Spirit in their own lives. In the Scriptures the early witnesses stated that Baptism and The Lord's Supper were practiced by Christ and commanded by him for his followers. Both rites should be celebrated by individuals when they are mature enough to understand their significance.

Baptism is the definitive rite for most Baptists. Baptism is the act whereby an individual, with the ability to understand, acknowledges God's forgiveness and grace in Jesus Christ and accepts it as the determining factor in his\her life. In Baptism one pictures the fact that one dies to a life of sin and is raised to walk in a newness of life. Baptism is a picture of Christ's death and resurrection and a picture of the believer's own death to sin and resurrection to obedience to God. This burial of the old self and resurrection of the new self is best pictured by the process of totally immersing the person in water.

The individual Baptist is not bound by *a priori* Creeds, Confessions, or liturgies. The one source of authority is the Scriptures as understood and interpreted with the help of the Holy Spirit. The Southern Baptist Convention is, in this sense, not a Church but a group of people who have agreed to work together, to worship God, and evangelize the world. Historically the Southern Baptist Convention arose out of the need for cooperation between similar churches to further their missionary efforts in the world.

The Southern Baptist Convention was chartered by an act of incorporation enacted by the legislature of the State of Georgia in 1845. The legislature's act states:

> Be it enacted by the Senate and House of Representatives of the state of Georgia, in General Assembly met, and it is hereby enacted by the authority of the same. That from and after the passing of this act, That William B. Johnson, Wilson Lumpkin, James B. Taylor, A. Docrey, R.B.C. Howell and others, their associates and successors, be and they are hereby incorporated and made a body politic by the name and style of the Southern Baptist Convention, with authority to receive, hold, possess, retain, and dispose of property, either real or personal, to sue and be sued, and to make all bylaws, rules, and regulations necessary to the transaction of their business, not inconsistent with the laws of this State or of the United States — said corporation being created for the purpose of eliciting, combining, and directing the energies of the Baptist denomination of Christians, for the propagation of the gospel, any law, usage, or custom to the contrary not withstanding.[29]

The Constitution of the Southern Baptist Convention clearly states that it is ". . .independent and sovereign in its own sphere. . ." and ". . . does not claim and will never attempt to exercise any authority over any other Baptist body, whether church, auxiliary organization, association, or convention."[30] The authority of the Convention is over its own Boards, Institutions, and Commissions. This includes its mission boards, The Sunday School Board, The Annuity Board, its seminaries, and commissions.

The Convention itself is composed of messengers from missionary Baptist churches that cooperate, i.e., contribute financially, with the Convention. Each such church may send one messenger, and an additional messenger for every two hundred and fifty members or $250.00 contributed to the work of the Convention. No church may have more than ten messengers.[31] Business issues which come before the Convention are decided by majority vote. Amendments to the Constitution and its articles require a two third vote of those in attendance at the time of the vote and the approval of two successive annual sessions of the Convention.[32]

Although there are Associations and Conventions which usually draw their membership along county and state lines, these bodies have no direct relationship to the operation of the Southern Baptist Convention. Their membership is drawn from local churches which support their work. Although the constitution of these regional groups is like that of the Southern Baptist Convention, they sometimes exercise indirect influence on local churches by excluding them from membership because of some teaching or practice. Local Baptist churches are theoretically autonomous institutions which can draw up their own constitutions and ordain their own clergy.

In May of 1963 The Southern Baptist Convention adopted a statement of faith titled, "The Baptist Faith and Message" which was published by the Sunday School Board of the Convention.[33] This document did not become part of the Constitution of the Convention because it was not ratified by subsequent Conventions, but it is often incorporated in the constitution of local churches. Historically within the United States there have been other Baptist statements of faith, none of which have been binding: (1) The Philadelphia Confession of 1742 which was a modification of the English, Second London Confession of 1689; and (2) The New Hampshire Confession of 1830.[34] Most local Baptist Churches incorporate what is called a Covenant in their constitutions that is a general statement of their commonly held beliefs. One such widely used covenant is printed in the *Baptist Hymnal* of 1956.[35] None of the above documents are binding on local congregations unless they choose to make them so.

In spite of the fact that there are no mandated beliefs and practices there are conflicts over the rite of Baptism and the rite of The Lord's Supper. Many Southern Baptist Churches will not receive into their membership persons who have not been immersed in a Baptist Church. This same group of people usually consider The Lord's Supper appropriate only for persons who have been baptized by a church of the "same faith and order."[36] Immersion in a Church which holds Baptism as necessary for salvation or holds it to be sacramental is not satisfactory for some Southern Baptists. A few congregations may accept persons to membership with any form of Baptism, but they run the risk of being excluded from regional and local Baptist Associations.

Although The Lord's Supper was enacted by Christ and the New Testament Church clearly practiced and prescribed it, in Southern Baptist Churches it often does not play an important role in worship. In many conservative Southern Baptist Churches The Lord's Supper is considered a local ordinance which is not only undertaken on the authority of the local Church but is also reserved for local members only.[37]

For Baptists in general the function of The Lord's Supper is to renew in one's memory the suffering love of God on human behalf in the crucifixion and death of Jesus Christ. It is ritual which calls on memory and imagination to recreate in the worshiper's mind what God has done in Christ Jesus for him\her.

It is through this memory and the work of one's imagination picturing Christ's death that the bonding with God is deepened.

With Baptists there is no thanksgiving, nor is covenant commitment generally called for. What is called for is a personal and inward response to God's suffering that will lead to a deeper appreciation of God's love and therefore a deeper bonding with God. This is not something that can be created by a liturgy or mandated by a Church. It requires the individual's active, concentrated memory and imagination (re-picturing) to take the symbols of bread and wine and make them meaningful as he\she partakes of them.

III.

What I have tried to show in this paper is how legislative processes shape the ritual of Communion. Clearly, the legislative rituals of the three religious bodies described are significantly different. Nevertheless, they underwrite in their own way the rituals of worship which are practiced in those separate denominations. Each has its own language, order, and understanding of what it is doing that gives to it its uniqueness. This uniqueness is safeguarded in each case by making the clergy of the denomination the major celebrants.

In all three denominations the ritual of Communion, or The Lord's Supper, embodies the root paradigm of the worshiping community and determines both the manner in which God is worshiped and the way in which members of the community structure their meaning and destiny as human beings. What is remarkable is that the same basic drama with the same iconic elements (bread and wine) can be appropriated and successfully enacted with such different speech acts, understandings, and forms.

In the Episcopal Church, where liturgy is more fundamental than theology, the main thrust of the drama and speech acts of the Eucharist are governed by thanksgiving and praise. For Presbyterians theology determines liturgy, and the speech acts and the drama of Communion are basically promissory and commissive in nature. Among Southern Baptists individual religious experiences authenticate the value of both theology and liturgy, and the primary speech acts and drama of the Lord's Supper are to recall God's grace and Christ's suffering in the individual's mind. Each in its unique way is legislated to be an identity forming and bonding ritual.

* Professor of Religion, Austin College.

References

"The Baptist Faith and Message," *Encyclopedia of Southern Baptist*, Nashville, Tenn. 1971.

Baptist Hymnal, ed., Walter Hines Sims, Nashville, Tenn, Convention Press, 1956.

Bold Believers In a Broken World: 1992 Annual, Nashville, Tenn., Executive Committee, Southern Baptist Convention, 1992.

The Book of Common Prayer (1979), The Seabury Press, 1979.

Book of Common Worship: Pastors Edition, Louisville, Ky., Westminster\John Knox Press, 1993.

Constitution and Canons: For the Governance of the Protestant Episcopal Church in the United States of America Otherwise Known as The Episcopal Church Adopted in General Convention 1789–1991; Together With The Rules of Order, Revised by the Convention. 1991,(no publisher given).

The Constitution of the Presbyterian Church (U.S.A.): Part I The Book of Confessions, Louisville, Kentucky, The Office of the General Assembly, 1991.

The Constitution of the Presbyterian Church (U.S.A.): Part II Book of Order, Louisville, Kentucky, The Office of the General Assembly, 1993.

Grimes, Ronald L., *Ritual Criticism*, University of South Carolina, 1990.

Hiscox, Edward T., *The Hiscox Guide for Baptist Churches*, Valley Forge, Pa., The Judson Press.

Trinity Baptist Church Constitution, Sherman, Texas, 1992.

Turner, Victor, *Dramas, Fields, and Metaphors*, Ithaca, N.Y., Cornell University Press, 1974.

Ware, James H. Jr., *Not With Words of Wisdom*, Washington, D.C., University Press of America, 1981.

Notes

1. James H. Ware Jr., *Not With Words of Wisdom*, Washington, D.C., University Press of America, 1981.

2. The institutionalization of a particular ritual is not the same as its formalization. The ritual of The Eucharist, Holy Communion, or the Lord's Supper was institutionalized in the first century Church. The formalization of the rituals at which we shall be looking developed along their specific language and behavior patterns following the Reformation.

3. "Paradigms of this fundamental sort reach down to irreducible life stances of individuals, passing beneath conscious prehension to a fiduciary hold on what they sense to be axiomatic values, matters literally of life and death. Root paradigms emerge in life crises, whether of groups or individuals, whether institutionalized or compelled by unforseen events." Victor Turner, *Dramas, Fields, and Metaphors*, Ithaca, N.Y., Cornell University Press, 1974, Pp. 63f.

4. The full title is *Constitution and Canons: For the Governance of the Protestant Episcopal Church in the United States of America Otherwise Known as The Episcopal Church Adopted in General Convention 1789–1991; Together With The Rules of Order, Revised by the Convention* 1991.

5. *Constitution and Canons*, p. 8. In the Canons provision is made for a Standing Liturgical Commission of nine person and a Custodian of the Book of Common Prayer whose duty it is to collect and collate materials that may have bearing on future revision of *The Book of Common Prayer*. There is also provision made for special forms of service under a Bishops approval. *Constitution and Canons*, p. 55.

6. *The Book of Common Prayer* (1979), The Seabury Press, Pp. 866–867.

7. The Episcopal Church still considers itself a member of the Anglican Communion.

8. *Book of Common Prayer* (1979), Pp. 10f.

9. In the original Articles of 1571 the Creed of Athanasius is also recognized, and in the current Catechism it is also acknowledged as ". . . an ancient document proclaiming the nature of the Incarnation and of God as Trinity." (See: "Articles of Religion" and "An Outline of the Faith" in *The Book of Common Prayer* (1979), p. 869 and p. 851–2 respectively). The text of the Creed of Athanasius is also included in the "Historical

Documents" section of *The Book of Common Prayer* (1979) (See: Pp. 864–865).

10. "An Outline of the Faith,"*The Book of Common Prayer* (1979), p. 852.

11. "An Outline of the Faith,"*The Book of Common Prayer* (1979), p. 852.

12. In the 1979 edition of *The Book of Common Prayer* the "Articles of Religion," are modified statements of the "Thirty Nine Articles" first adopted by the Church of England in 1571, reaffirmed in 1662, and adopted by the Episcopal Church in the United states in 1801. They are included in the Historical Documents of the Church section which, though authoritative, carries somewhat less weight than the liturgical part of the book.

13. "An Outline of the Faith,"*The Book of Common Prayer* (1979), p. 857.

14. "An Outline of the Faith,"*The Book of Common Prayer* (1979), p.858.

15. "An Outline of the Faith,"*The Book of Common Prayer* (1979), Pp. 860–861.

16. "Articles of Religion,"*The Book of Common Prayer* (1979), p. 873.

17. "Articles of Religion,"*The Book of Common Prayer* (1979), p. 874.

18. "Articles of Religion,"*The Book of Common Prayer* (1979), p. 873.

19. "Articles of Religion,"*The Book of Common Prayer* (1979), p. 873.

20. For the manners in which a ritual may fail see Ronald L. Grimes, *Ritual Criticism*, University of South Carolina, 1990. Pp, 191ff.

21. *The Book of Common Prayer* (1979), p. 409. It would be of some interest to know how often this procedure is currently followed.

22. "The Outline of the Faith,"*The Book of Common Prayer* (1979), p. 859.

23. The Creeds and Confessions included are: (1) The Nicene Creed, (2) The Apostles' Creed, (3) the Scots Confession, (4) The Heidelberg Catechism, (5) The Second Helvetic Confession, (6) The Westminster Confession of Faith, (7) The Shorter Catechism, (8) The Larger Catechism, (9) The Theological Declaration of Barmen, (10) The Confession of 1967, and (11) A Brief Statement of Faith- Presbyterian Church (U.S.A.). *The Constitution of the Presbyterian Church (U.S.A.): Part I The Book of Confessions*, Louisville, Kentucky, The Office of the General Assembly, 1991.

24. " The Form of Government," *The Constitution of the Presbyterian Church U.S.A.: Part II Book of Order*, Louisville, Kentucky, The Office of the General Assembly, 1993, G-2.0200.

25. "Directory for Worship," *The Constitution of the Presbyterian Church (U.S.A.): Part II Book of Order*, para.(a). The Preface also states:
this directory
(1) SHALL, and IS TO BE\ARE TO BE signify practice that is mandated,
(2) SHOULD signifies practice that is strongly recommended,
(3) IS APPROPRIATE signifies practice that is commended as suitable,
(4) MAY signifies practice that is permissible but not required.
This directory also uses language about worship which is simply descriptive." Preface, para. b.

In reading the directory it is not all clear which of these categories apply to any given instruction. The ambiguity stated in opening paragraph of the directory, that is, on the one hand the directory sets standards, and on the other hand it suggests, invites, and encourages reform, extends throughout the directory for the average reader.

26. *Book of Common Worship: Pastors Edition*, Louisville, Ky., Westminster\John Knox Press, 1993.

27. "Directory for Worship," *Book of Order*, W-1.1004.

28. "Directory of Worship," *Book of Order*, W-3.3601.

29. *Bold Believers In a Broken World: 1992 Annual*, Nashville, Tenn., Executive Committee, Southern Baptist Convention, 1992, p. 4.

30. *Bold Believers In A Broken World*, p. 4.

31. *Bold Believers In A Broken World*, p.4.

32. *Bold Believers In A Broken World*, p. 6.

33. "The Baptist Faith and Message," *Encyclopedia of Southern Baptist*, Nashville, Tenn. 1971, Vol. III, Pp. 1589–1594.

34. Edward T. Hiscox, *The Hiscox Guide for Baptist Churches*, Valley Forge, Pa., The Judson Press, Pp.156–202.

35. *Baptist Hymnal*, ed., Walter Hines Sims, Nashville, Tenn, Convention Press, 1956, p.476,

36. *Trinity Baptist Church Constitution*, Sherman, Texas, 1992, Article V, para. B and D.

37. *Trinity Baptist Church Constitution*, Article VI, Sect.2, para, A and B.

Chapter Ten

Enacting Law: Ritual Performances In Dutch Political Culture

Willem J. Witteveen*

Rituals of What?

It is not at all clear that all rituals are meaningful, in the sense of their reference to symbols and myths that precede them. What is reasonably clear, however, is that ritual activity can endow meaning, that it can create useful mythologies and readable symbols. Ritual performances are 'myths in action' that find their meaning in processes of interpretation within some particular local community of performers and spectators. What is, again, unclear is *what* these rituals perform. From an internal perspective a ritual may be acknowledged to be a ritual of a particular nature, say religious or political or legal. What is the 'stuff this dream is made on'? Is it possible to differentiate spheres—of religion or politics or law—and to see these differentiations reflected in the rituals themselves? And if this is possible, perhaps we can say that the ritual refers to these notions after all? In real life, making observations from within a particular culture, it is never easy to mark these differences. Law and politics do not have graspable essences that rituals can symbolically enact (nor do religious experiences). Limiting ourselves to the domains of law and politics, rituals seem to arise exactly where boundaries between implicitly 'pure' spheres create dangers and opportunities. This paper traces four ritual performances that are regularly enacted in Dutch political culture. The separation of law and politics, but also their mutual dependence, figure prominently as recurring themes in these performances. My interpretation of the rituals will elaborate on work done in symbolic anthropology, particularly that developed by Mary Douglas.

Spheres Of Law And Politics

It has never been easy to draw a sharp boundary between a sphere of law and a sphere of politics. The effort has, of course, mostly been made in theoretical discourse. Positivism and autopoiesis are two instances of theories seeking clear demarcation lines between 'fields' or 'systems'. Opposing views, like natural law theory or deconstruction,[1] tend to deny that there are such sharp limits. Where does the legal domain end and where does the realm of politics begin? (Or, for that matter, where do these spheres give way to separate fields of morality, or economics, or religion, or ...?) But far from these familiar doctrinal discussions, people participating in political and legal practices find it sometimes equally hard to see the demarcation lines, while still feeling a need for them. Most people will experience ambiguities here. 'Pure' spheres of law and politics may perhaps not exist, not even in the mind. Yet, through a very long history, the simple picture of separated spheres, fields, domains, or systems with their own identities has remained convincing. The separation of law and politics is a deeply ingrained assumption in Western cultures.

One can escape the overriding concern with boundary-drawing by admitting that law and politics presuppose each other: they are mutual preconditions for effective functioning and clear identities. In such a view, transgressions are likely events. Actors primarily concerned with law draw strength from political background knowledge. Actors obviously engaged in political activities relate to the legal system as a precondition to such activity. Legislation and judging are both legal and political acts. A legislature is a political arena that produces legally binding texts. A court is a forum for the application of pre-established laws that is legitimated by references to the democratic process and to the political ideals of the society at large. The two spheres depend on each other and interrelate. But they do not become one diffusely conceived sphere of law-and-politics. Seeing the relation between law and politics as one of identity would be counter to important democratic ideals and would subvert the idea of law.

Thus this alternative to boundary-drawing is unlikely ever to become a dominant opinion. There is a pragmatic explanation for this. It would bring to an end important critical discussions about the quality of the political and legal processes. Keeping the differences between the legal and the political in mind immediately provides one with arguments that feed these important debates. Separating law and politics offers a standpoint from which politics can be seen invading law and law can be understood as overtaking politics. As a corollary, it is then possible to raise concern, to warn, to fight dangers. One can, for example, see sharply how political majorities use their power to enact legislation that is instrumental to politically established purposes and values. When politics thus takes on the appearance of law, when it instrumentally employs law to its own ends, this can easily lead to protestations that there are values and purposes inherent in law, in justice, in the legal system, relating to the rights of minorities, for instance, and to the legal mechanisms that are designed to protect these rights against the 'tyranny of the majority'. But one can also see how judges, under the guise of the interpretation of law, become participants in the political process by signaling to governmental agencies or other political actors their willingness or unwillingness to adapt the law to politically accepted ends. Again, such a view leads to criticism, only this time of judicial reasoning. Separating law and politics, one can attack the power of non-elected judges as encroaching on the power of democratically legitimated authorities. Such critical exercises, the truth or attractiveness of which can only be judged in the context of particular instances, are possible only when one has an underlying picture of constructively separated spheres, an idea of harmony resulting from separation and balancing of powers.

The conceptual differences between law and politics are not trivial. *Trias politica* - the Latin name for a family of theories about the ways legislative, administrative, and judicial powers are to be organized in order to preserve the rule of law and to avoid tyranny - is a deeply embedded assumption in Western cultures which, in many other respects, show great differences. Local versions of *trias politica* are continually being interpreted when changes occur in society and in power relationships. But all these local versions have some traits in common: distrust of power accumulation, the sense that legal tradition embodies values that limit the free range of political choices, the idea that democratically elected officials must determine policy within the limits of the regulative ideal of the rule of law. Fusion of the legal and political spheres, no matter how *trias politica* is interpreted, is always experienced as a constitutionally dangerous development. Montesquieu's famous warning against combined powers remains operative.[2]

The Performance Of Myth In Ritual

Rule of law, separation and balance of powers, democratic government: these terms point to the self-image of a society. We now encounter another ambiguity. Often it is thought that this self-image is contained in scientific knowledge and procedures: that we have a science of law, a science of politics. But this is a contested idea and it can never be the whole truth. Many critical scholars tend to see the self-image expressed in regulative ideals as myth, as uncritically examined operative knowledge, as habitual procedure. The ambiguity relates to the status of our knowledge of public life: we expect to find both a science and a mythology of law and politics. The same person may at one moment demand rational argument in policy articulations or in judicial decisions and be taken the next moment to understand the irrationality and emotionality of the actors involved.

In what terms can this self-image best be understood? The research language of myth and ritual, originally developed for cultures in the remote past or for the ways of life of 'savage' peoples, may be helpful here. Myth has not disappeared in the age of science, ritual has not lost its importance in modern polities (Kertzer, 1988: 8). Moreover, a semiotic perspective on society forces the observer to take myth and ritual seriously. When signs or symbols (however defined) are of central interest, myth points to coherent systems of symbols, ritual to the enactment of symbolic meanings. Let us look briefly at some statements of these relationships, randomly selected from the vast literature on myth and ritual. The selected authors adopt different theoretical orientations but converge on this crucial point.

Cassirer - for whom myth is still an earlier and different stage of thinking by comparison to science - stresses that myth and ritual are not mere symbolic representations but construct an experienced reality. Ritual is myth in action.

> Rites cannot be explained as a mere representation of beliefs; on the contrary, the part of myth which belongs to the world of theoretical representation, which is mere record or accredited narrative, must be understood as a mediate interpretation of the part which resides immediately in the activity of man and in his feelings and will. Seen in this light, rites are not originally "allegorical"; they do not merely copy or represent but are absolutely real; they are so woven into the reality of action as to form an indispensable part of it (Cassirer, 1955: 39).

Interestingly, in the semiotics of Barthes this idea of the reality of myth returns. Barthes defines myth as 'depoliticized speech'. Through myth historically produced meanings become naturalized.

> Myth is constituted by the loss of the historical quality of things: in it, things lose the memory that they once were made. The world enters language as a dialectical relation between activities, between human actions; it comes out of myth as a harmonious display of essences.

The naturalization through myth does not give an explanation for facts (it does not refer) but states them with a special authority.

> Myth does not deny things; on the contrary, its function is to talk about them; (...) it gives them a clarity which is not that of an explanation but that of a statement of fact. (...) In passing from history to nature, myth acts economically: it abolishes the complexity of human acts, it gives them the simplicity of essences, it does away with all dialectics, with any going beyond what is immediately visible, it organizes a world which is without contradictions because it is without depth, a world wide open and wallowing in the evident, it establishes a blissful clarity: things appear to mean something by themselves. (Barthes, 1972: 142–143)

His concern with signification seems to lead Barthes away from 'mythical action', but this is quickly compensated by turning to the American tradition of research into political symbolism. When the symbol is central, when politics is seen as being expressed through symbols, it becomes imperative to "understand how the symbolic enters into politics, how political actors consciously and unconsciously manipulate symbols, and how this symbolic dimension relates to the material bases of political power" (Kertzer, 1988: 3). Symbols order experience but also instigate action. Following Durkheim, Kertzer defines ritual as "symbolic behavior that is socially standardized and repetitive", as "action wrapped in a web of symbolism" (Kertzer, 1988: 9). And returning to the author this selection started with, he concludes:

> Standardized, repetitive action lacking such symbolization is an example of habit or custom and not ritual. Symbolization gives the action much more important meaning. Through ritual, beliefs about the universe come to be acquired, reinforced, and eventually changed. As Cassirer puts it: "Nature yields nothing without ceremonies." Ritual meaning not only gives meaning to the universe, it becomes part of the universe. (Kertzer 1988: 9)

This view of symbols and ritual lends itself to an analysis of the political uses of legal forms and meanings. The legal tradition does not perpetuate itself in an apolitical manner. As Fitzpatrick remarks in a similar vein:

> Law as ritual is not simply a matter of ideal standards imposed on a populace. Nor can it be equated simply with behavior. Rather, these dimensions (...) are fused by ritual into something else which is myth. Through legal ritual, people act in accordance with certain forms to create and sustain situations that have their distinct, legal identity. (Fitzpatrick, 1992: 182)

While ritual is myth in action, myth is also created through ritual.

The Myth of the Legal State in Political Ritual

Our sample of converging views on ritual and myth suggests an approach to the conceptions of law and politics in a society. We must look for beliefs about the world that are experienced as no mere representations but as (socially constructed) realities. By observing ritual performances, the contents of the myth that is seen 'in action' must become clear. We can expect that the myth being enacted has its roots in history, but that it naturalizes its historical subject matter into a display of powerful essences. In that display we should look for symbols that can and will be used for political ends. The power of the ruling mythology is dependent on its ritual enactment, since the ritual fuses the ideal standards with behavior, thereby offering the self-image of a society that understands itself as a political and legal society.

So, ritual must be the starting-point. We will now consider four rituals in Dutch society. All of them involve both law and politics. Three of these rituals are enactments of political events that are of greater or lesser significance in Dutch politics. All three of them symbolize national unity as a counterpoint to political discussion and division; they underscore the supremacy of an ideal of legal order and link this notion to very practical uses of political power. The fourth ritual is clearly legal in meaning; this ritual refers to the same symbols as the political rituals and so completes the myth the political rituals perform from the other end, from the side of the law in action. The central symbol linking all four rituals is that of the Queen. The myth being enacted will be called "the myth of the Legal State:" an implicit but firm notion that politics in all its manifestations abides by the law.[3]

The Formation Ritual

Elections for the national parliament in the Netherlands never lead to clear-cut victories for one party or one combination of parties. The system of proportional representation, in combination with the heterogeneity of political life, ensures that there will never be a governing majority on the basis of the election results alone. A cabinet can only take office after extensive negotiations between two or more political parties. For a long time this century, Dutch social life was characterized by a form of 'social apartheid' which sociologically went by the name of 'pillarization'.[4] Dutch society was basically divided along religious lines, with a segmentation of organizational life, so that, for instance, catholics and protestants would go to different schools, would read different newspapers, would listen to different radio stations, in short, would lead 'separated' lives. This pillarization was also politically significant in providing for a welter of political parties. While there was differentiation at the bottom of the internal hierarchies, there was elite cooperation at the top, however, as a result of a shared understanding that the nation would need to be governed. It led to a political culture in which running the state was conceived as a comparable undertaking as running a large business firm. Governing coalitions would typically consist of large coalitions, government policy would respect the interests of opposition parties to a remarkably large extent, and politics would be an art of compromise, through which ideological conflicts would preferably be kept out of public view and divisive issues would be 'depoliticized'. This situation changed when, in the seventies, polarization strategies were first taken up on the left and later on the right of the political spectrum. Still, a polarization strategy in election times would never lead to decisive victories; immediately after election day, the leaders of parties that had been fighting each other in the campaign would have to negotiate whether to be in or out of government. Coalitions would always include the christian democratic party or parties, since these would occupy the middle ground, and would alternate between the conservative-liberals on the right and the social-democrats on the left. The election of 1994 has brought about significant changes in voter preference away from the christian democrats. As a result, for the first time since early this century, the liberal-conservative and social democratic parties are now in government together.

The formation of a cabinet is, in these conditions, always fraught with difficulties. Perhaps this is why a ritualization of the negotiations has occurred. The danger of dissensus and the spectre of a very long period without an effective government, or even of a failure of negotiations leading to another round of elections, are widely perceived as threats to political order. The negotiations are structured by constitutional rules that allow considerable leeway to the negotiators but fix their orientation on constructive action in a symbolic focal point: the Queen. The Queen is not supposed to possess any real power. She is the Head of State, not the political leader. In fact, the doctrine of ministerial responsibility ensures that the actions and words of the Queen cannot be criticized as her own acts but must be imputed to the acting government. This means that the Queen needs the permission of the government for all her public activities and that all acts the Queen performs in public are assumed to have been approved by the government. This state of affairs dates back to the 1860s when the rules of ministerial responsibility (already embodied in the written constitutions of 1840 and 1848) were finally accepted by the King who, considering himself an enlightened monarch, had since the end of the French occupation under Napoleon (1813) played a very prominent role in Dutch political life. Nowadays, after elections the Queen is the symbolic leader of a nation that has just produced a political stalemate; no real 'winner' can, at this stage, possess a similar symbolic weight.

Such is the ordinary situation at any national parliamentary election. A ritual solution has been found to mark the passage from one well-ordered state of the political community to the next. To begin with, the symbolic space is created within which the Queen is more visually endowed with power. The government yields power. Before the election, the government of the day becomes *demissionair*, a term which indicates that the government has lost the right to adopt policy measures that are new, far-reaching, or unsupported by consensus. The Queen is constitutionally part of the government (the dignified part): she remains while the cabinet retreats. Cabinet members keep performing all tasks that are necessary in the public interest until their successors can assume their place.

The formation ritual consists of a highly formalized series of questions and answers in which the Queen, as permanent part of government, formulates the questions and considers the answers. After the election, all party leaders immediately report to the Queen to recommend a course of action. They advise on the preferred government coalition and on the person who should be in charge of the negotiations. These recommendations are often strongly diverging. The Queen, acting on this public advice (and on secret advice from her royal advisers) appoints a person - a senior member of parliament or an authoritative former politician - who must try either to form a government or to make preliminary enquiries as to its possible formation. This latter route is the usual one. The person in charge acquires an official status as either *formateur* or *informateur*. The Queen is thus clearly provided with a degree of real power: she has to make a choice. Ministerial responsibility for this act of power is construed retroactively. Upon the successful completion of a cabinet formation procedure, the incoming government assumes responsibility for all actions the Queen has performed, including those that have led to unsuccessful negotiations between different prospective coalition partners. But before this fiction can be invoked there will have been a very real instant in which, with politics at its most tense, the Queen will have made her own decision. Royal participation in the cabinet formation procedure is a delicate task. It is especially hard to do this when the coalition formation is not getting anywhere. Sometimes two, three, or four attempts must be made, with different persons in charge of the negotiations, and with different parties bargaining for power. Whenever the process gets stuck, the Queen must intervene. The *informateur* then reports to the Queen, the party leaders again give their views, the secret advisers speak, but the Queen also has to decide again. The ritual demands that politicians do not take the lead in this particularly momentous decision but submit their opinions and accept the royal intervention. With royal support a new 'informer' is in a very strong position to force the negotiating parties to overcome their differences. The ritual consultations and the royal interventions in the cabinet formation process are a repetitive performance of national importance, closely followed by newspapers and television. This may continue for a long time, sometimes more than a hundred days. The cycle of questions and answers ends when the message comes that a cabinet has been formed which can reasonably be expected to be supported by a majority in parliament. With the formal introduction of the new government, a picture session takes place showing the Queen, surrounded by the new cabinet, on the steps to the entrance of the Royal Palace.

The period of cabinet formation provides a huge contrast to that preceding it. During an election campaign the ordinary business of politics is suspended. Both the acting government and the Queen are in the background. Political parties and party leaders debate with one another and compete for voter support. In these efforts, the media are their most important primary target. The political debate is at its most public, with many critical comments by journalists and opinion leaders. After the election, the whole setting of the political spectacle changes. Politicians address one another and only incidentally appeal to the nation. There is a strong tendency to hold the most important negotiations in secret, and to supply minimal information to the press and to the general public. The interactions with the Queen are often the most public events: at least the questions she puts and the answers she receives are made public. As a result, the Queen appears as a central figure on the stage.

In order successfully to negotiate a program for a new governing coalition, the secrecy of the negotiations is indispensable. Moreover, there are, understandably no fixed constitutional rules determining the negotiation process. But in view of this closure to public scrutiny and the leeway left to political players, the outward side, the visible formation ritual, still gains in symbolic importance. When we interpret this ritual as 'myth in action', what myth is here being expressed? More will be said later about the symbolic meaning of the Queen. By way of preliminary observation, we must notice that, as a sign, she stands for the Nation as a whole. The Queen is the conventional symbol of national unity. In the context of the suspension of 'normal' politics, this symbol of national unity acquires a special significance. It underscores that power in politics is not absent while the politicians are creating new alliances of power. It visualizes continuity. The nature of this continuity is not, however, political in the sense of power politics. The Queen is not an ordinary political actor. She is 'outside' or 'above' politics. In the performance of the Queen a limit to politics is made visible: the politicians negotiate and advise, while the Queen occupies an empty space next to or above this political drama. The ambiguity of 'next' and 'above' is important. Being next to the politicians means that the Queen is not a real but a symbolic power, that she is not a source of danger to the political process. Being above politics means that the Queen is the formal device keeping the political process within its constitutionally prescribed bounds. Both from a position on the sidelines and from one above the political drama, the Queen can legitimately perform certain interventions (such as appointing an *informateur*), but her range of options is limited; she will leave the political interactions within limits but will not interfere with them.

When the negotiations are difficult, as they often are, this myth of national unity and political order becomes pervaded with the idea of law. By being the symbolic power present when real power is at an impasse, the Queen expresses the idea that the Dutch live in a well-regulated state, in a Legal State. The business of constitutional law continues. Indeed, these secret but divisive negotiations are regulated by law and made possible by law; they are themselves perfectly normal in a legal framework. When we remember the days of open public discussion of the election campaign, another dimension of the myth of the Legal State comes to the fore. During the election period, politicians address the voters, even if indirectly through the media. After the election, politicians address the symbol of national unity. The Queen now takes the place of the people, and becomes the representative of the people. The empty space next to or above politics is not entirely empty, after all: in it, the Legal State manifests itself, and in it, the Queen acts as representative of the people. Her clear interest in forming a government quickly through her chosen *informateurs*, visible especially when the process is slow, is generally interpreted as an expression of the general interest and the wish of the public.

The Opening Ritual

In ordinary times, the formation ritual is repeated every four years. It is a ritual of beginning, a performance marking a new start. Closely linked to this ritual, we can see another ritual of beginning that is enacted every year. Every summer parliament recesses, to reconvene on the third Tuesday of September. On that day, an opening ceremony is held in which the Queen figures prominently. In the course of this event, through a Royal Speech, the acting government announces its plans for the next year. After this performance, the minister of finance presents the new budget. The opening ceremonies are followed by a general political debate in the lower house of parliament.[5] In the following weeks, the budgets of all the different departments will be approved in turn.

The opening ritual shows all the visible characteristics of ceremonies of state. It is a national occasion at a fixed time and place. It is broadcast live on television, watched by millions of viewers. It is a focal point in Dutch politics, a moment of intense interest in all aspects of the political program of the government. At the same time, it is the only moment in the year when ordinary people participate in large numbers in politics by watching the ceremony unfold. The combination stands for a general democratic feeling, an experience of involvement, of citizenship.

From her palace in The Hague, the Queen embarks on a procession through the winding streets of this old city that will bring her to the *Binnenhof*, the traditional center of government, where, in a large medieval hall, a joint session of the upper and lower houses of parliament has convened. The procession consists of various coaches drawn by horses, accompanied by police officials on horseback. At the centre of the procession, there is the Golden Coach, with servants on foot walking next to it. From this coach, the Queen and her husband greet the crowds that line the streets. Many people position themselves along the royal itinerary at a very early hour, in order not to miss a glimpse of the Queen the minute she will be in view. Television broadcasts this coach tour from beginning to end. The commentators are more respectful than they would be with 'ordinary' politicians. Traditionally, much attention is bestowed on the dress the Queen is wearing. The Queen enters the *Binnenhof* while the national anthem is played, and proceeds towards the congregation. She is received by the chairmen of both houses of parliament; the members of the cabinet occupy the front rows in the hall. She then seats herself on the throne and reads the Royal Speech, a lengthy and abstract text containing the government's plans for the next budget, discussing all the departments of state in turn. The cameras will show the viewers the faces of the members of the cabinet, listening to the Queen discussing their policy area. At the end of the speech, there is usually a prayer or a prayer-like statement calling for God's blessing on parliament's work. When the Queen has finished the speech, the chairman of the upper house shouts 'Lang leve de Koningin'! ('Long live the Queen') and all those present reply by screaming 'Hoera!' ('Hurray') three times. The Queen then leaves the hall, and returns to the palace, again being cheered by the crowds. For most people, the climax of the proceedings is the royal appearance on the balcony of the palace afterwards, when she is closer to view than from behind the windows of the Golden Coach. The Queen and her family wave to the people. The live broadcast continues.

Shortly after these symbolic events, the minister of finance enters the hall where the lower house usually convenes in order to present to the chairman a white briefcase, bearing the words *Derde dinsdag in september* (Third Tuesday of September). This small ceremony offers another photo opportunity to the press. It marks the moment that the government budget, which has been under an embargo, can be publicly discussed by politicians and the press. After this moment, normal politics resumes: politicians and journalists discuss the import of the government's plans, comment on proposals, and announce their views in anticipation of the parliamentary debates to come. Representatives of social and political interests also give their comments. On television, but also in the newspapers, there is created the occasion for a rare forum of all opinions from all quarters and about all topics of public policy.

The opening ritual can be read in the same key as the formation ritual, since the Queen is in both instances the performer of a rite of passage in which one condition of political life changes into another, even though the Legal State is as permanent as ever. The legality of the performance of the Queen is even more pronounced in the opening ritual, because the text that is being read to parliament has a constitutional status as an act of the government that prefigures the policy measures and the legislative program that the cabinet will present to parliament in the course of the next session. Here, the symbolic power of the Queen is shared with the government, as appears clearly in the television coverage alternating between shots of the Queen reading and the ministers listening to what are, in fact, their own words. After the ceremony, the debate will start, and the opposition parties will have their say, but the ritual celebrates national unity shared between the Queen, the cabinet, and the united parliament. (The hall also includes a small number of specially selected ordinary citizens, as representing the national audience.) The different status of the government pursuant to the opening ritual by comparison to the formation ritual emerges clearly when it is considered that in the former there is no need for any confrontation between the Queen and the political leaders. There is only one voice speaking, not a formalized game of questions and answers. The general interest need not be represented by the Queen to the politicians; on the contrary, the general interest is now presented to the citizens. The Queen still symbolizes the nation, but now the focus of the act of representation is changed: she is not addressing politicians on behalf of the people but addressing the people on behalf of politicians.

The harmony of this ritual, underscored by the cheering crowds, cannot obscure an important friction (that does not have a counterpart in the formation ritual). The Queen is seen reading the speech the cabinet has produced, in her own voice, in her own unmistakable, slow style, giving every sentence an equal weight to all the others, thus not favouring any topic over another: we are surely in the realm of national unity where equality does not only reign between citizens but also between government departments. We can witness everything as citizens. Thanks to television, we are there. But the text that is being read is full of generalities that never become clear messages, full of obscurities that have meaning in limited political circles only, full of political and economic jargon that does not interest the ordinary person, full of selective information. It is a speech that omits most of the contents of government policy, that mentions measures in euphemistic ways, that contains an overdose of appeals to a mentality of common responsibility. This text, ostensibly about the tasks of government and the responsibilities of all citizens in a changing world, is illegible for the active citizen who wants to know what the government is doing. Though everything is in view, the content of the symbolic performance is a closed book. The Queen speaks the words she has been given, but her lips are sealed.

The Enactment Ritual

The third political ritual involving the Queen occurs with great frequency as part of the ordinary political process. It concerns the 'passing' of legislation. Statutes are the result of the lawmaking cooperation of three actors: the government (which usually takes the initiative and introduces a proposal), the lower house of parliament, and the upper house of parliament. The lower house can make amendments, the upper house can only confirm or reject. This formal structure is, in practice, supplemented by the participation of various legal and quasi-legal actors. A statute is in preparation for a long time under the auspices of one or more government departments. Pressure groups have their say, empirical research into its implications is sometimes conducted, official documents are exchanged in a slow process of opinion formation. The official advisers then intervene, most notably the Council of State; they have a weighty voice in regard to the legal aspects of any proposed statute. When the government accepts a proposal and introduces it into parliament, the same discussions that have been ongoing, sometimes for many years, resume in both houses of parliament, usually among a small group of specialists from the various political parties. Sometimes, the matter is of wider interest and the press will report controversies about it. Finally, the legislative proposal comes to a vote. If adopted, the statute must then become law. This change in the legal status of the legislative text is the moment when the Queen again performs her symbolic role by signing the text, which can consequently be published in the official records and can become effective vis-à-vis the citizens.

The royal participation in the enactment procedure is much more limited, much less visible than her participation in the rituals discussed above. Here, she personifies the law. Her signature validates the law. The statute opens with a royal message stating succinctly the purpose of the law in question. The Queen speaks on behalf of the legislature, no more, no less. Symbolic power seems to be firmly subjugated to political power. The Queen is part of the government under Dutch constitutional law, as we have noted. This means she will be consulted before the final stage of the adoption of legislation, that she can make her views heard. But this consultation process never becomes public. There is no way of knowing whether the Queen has debated a statute with the government and whether she has perhaps influenced the text, for instance by threatening not to sign it. We cannot bear witness to these secret conversations preceding the royal message and the signature on the document. Officially, they were never there, they do not leave a trace.

Yet, this preponderance of the political power over the symbolic power marks the exact point at which the political will becomes the legal command. The Queen's involvement in the legislative process occurs precisely at the boundary between the political and the legal domains. This confirmation of the boundary is again an act proclaiming the myth of national unity. Here, the national unity refers to the idea of the general interest, of general lawmaking. In Dutch constitutional theory much weight is traditionally given to the views of Montesquieu and Rousseau on this point. Especially Rousseau's idea that the statute is the perfect and logical expression of the general will - and in this way differs fundamentally from the tainted expressions of particular wills, of specific interests - lends itself easily to symbolization through royal involvement. The signature is a confirmation of the quality of the statutory text; it authenticates it (like a notary authenticates a will).

But again, a friction is discovered. The enactment of legislation is a formal process that does not concern the content or quality of the regulation. The signature is not a guarantee that all the interests that arise in the matter have been duly considered and that the one rule or regulation has been formulated which best captures the general will. Indeed, much legislation can be severely criticized precisely on these grounds. The symbolic power of the Queen, put to work in the ritual of enactment, often lends legitimacy to statutes that are not perfect, logical, obvious, or useful. The symbol of national unity, in its interpretation as symbol of the general will, is a polluted, manipulated symbol. Its practical impact in society is small. Here, we see a side of ritual that does not associate it with effective action in society, but with the maintenance of formalities and the guarding of boundaries that form the horizon within which 'normal politics', 'ordinary lawmaking' take place.

The Application Ritual

In these three political rituals, we see a gradual shift from performance to text, and from ritual to myth. In the legal application ritual, the royal involvement is even less pronounced; in it, the Queen is not an actor but only a visual symbol, a virtual presence in the setting of the stage. The application ritual is the most familiar in legal practice and it has been studied extensively in various legal cultures (Hoefnagels, 1970; Goodrich, 1990: 179–208). In courtrooms, the law has to be applied to cases that are brought to the judges notice. The idea of an 'application' of law is historically charged with significance: it connotes to the initiates of law's empire that the law is not of the judges' own making. The judge at most interprets the law, but does not invent law. All law, written or unwritten, in some sense already 'exists' before the actual conflict arises in which recourse must be had to the categories and remedies of legal language. This doctrinal expectation is well attuned to what the lay participant or observer in court proceedings is made to feel: that all actors knowledgeable in law act in the firm belief that to every legal problem the answer is in some sense already given (if only one can come to agree upon this 'right answer'), that the laws are waiting silently in the books to be found, read, understood, in a word, applied. In the medieval imagery of the law as a living organism, the judge was often portrayed as *bouche de la loi* (mouth of the law), a phrase which has become famous through its insertion in Montesquieu's description of the English legal system. Court ritual is one very effective way of conveying the impression of the pre-existence of the law to all concerned.

Nowhere is the separation of law and politics as clearly marked as in a court procedure. The judge is in appearance not a political actor. He or she dons a robe that is obviously the sign of professional authority as well as a symbol of a central value inhering in law: impartiality. Whereas politicians speak, judges listen. Whereas politicians speak on behalf of their own partisan stand, judges listen to both sides of any issue without prejudice. Judges are often shown listening to counsel, occupying an elevated position behind the table. When judges finally read their decisions, these readings are acts of authoritative statement. No interruptions are allowed. When judges speak the law, everybody listens (including the politician). These familiar notions are all illustrated in the ritual proceedings in the courtroom. The roles the law allows in its dramatization are all clearly delineated in advance (in line with the pre-existence of a right answer to any problem). The people actually engaged in controversy are only there in a very specific and limited capacity, for instance as witnesses or as parties to a suit, or as suspects. Their legal part will mostly be played on their behalf by representatives: lawyers who also don robes. The legal argument takes place between representatives of the parties and the Representative of the Law: the judge. So much for the application ritual itself. Though the details may vary somewhat in different kinds of procedure, the overall structure is the same.

How does the Queen figure in the application ritual? The terms of legal theory point at an oral connection: the judges pronounce their decisions *in the name of* the Queen. This formula used to be part of every judicial opinion. The historical reference can be connected with the history of the idea of the judge being the mouth of the law. The judges are the representatives of the King and are responsible to the King for their words (sentences, verdicts, opinions). This oral connection of subservience of the courts to the Court has often been unmasked as a myth of the Legal State. It does not accurately reflect historical developments. For instance, it does not show the perpetual conflicts between judges as members of a professional group and the ruling authorities that politicize law. Even the expression 'bouche de la loi' can be understood in another meaning. Whoever is the mouth of the law is not a puppet but is the one who decisively states what the content of law is (Schönfeld). This interpretation squares with Montesquieu's own political standpoint in the controversy between the court and the aristocracy in France: he believed in moderation exerted by a middling aristocracy, especially in judicial matters. The orality of the application ritual is still supported by allusions to the law as king, a personification of the exclusive power of the law within its own domain (empire).

In actual court proceedings, however, the Queen is, first of all, a visual symbol of the Legal State. Above the presiding judge, there is always found the official portrait of the Queen dressed in a royal robe. The picture used most frequently is the one that was made at the time when she took office. *Vive le roi!* (It is a portrait that reminds one of the automatic response of calling *Hoera!* after the Royal Speech at the opening of parliament.) Two features are important: one is this officiality, the ostensive wearing of official symbols of royal power and national unity; another is the gaze. There is a hint of a smile, of taking in a situation in an open mind and yet of not being committed to comment on this situation. The Queen smiles like the judge could smile, if there was still any need to affirm his independence and impartiality. And above the smile the Queen's eyes stare straight at the viewer. In Orwell's 1984 it is remarked that the official portrait of Big Brother was composed in such a way that from whatever point of view you looked, the eyes would always stare at you. *Big brother is watching you.* The Queen's gaze is not as all-knowing and not as penetrating. But the eyes can be seen from anywhere in the room and the portrait sees everything that is happening there. This seeing stands for an obvious metaphor: literally the Queen is absent, metaphorically she is overseeing the proceedings. The law unfolds in the presence of the royal power, which again refers to the unity of the political community.

Royal involvement in the daily business of the application of law is so slight as to appear entirely as a surface phenomenon. Here involvement is merely symbolical, surely? But this alerts us to Barthes's remarks on the naturalization effected in mythologies. The naturalized reality of the myth of the Legal State obscures its history. But it does not obscure its theoretical importance to the legal initiates. The Legal State may be visible on the surface, but one needs legal doctrine in order to read its significance. Of all the rituals under consideration, only this one evokes strong theoretical considerations. The word 'theory' may be somewhat misleading. It is not intended to refer to a set of interrelated arguments that are explicitly formulated in a form that can be brought to bear on empirical reality or that can be used to provide normative coherence in a legal system. The theory of the Legal State is a 'theory in use' (Argyris and Schön, 1978). It takes the form of a combination of elements that together form a story about the proper relationships between the actors in the process of making and applying the law. It is a doctrinal story (Witteveen, 1993) that reminds its users of 'what the law means'. Separation of powers is the doctrinal story most congenial to the ritual of application and the accompanying mythology of clearly demarcated political and legal spheres. It prescribes to the actors in court how general statutes precede, not only temporally but also normatively, their application in concrete judgments to particular facts. It legitimizes an attitude of deference to the legislature and orders neutrality and textbound interpretation on the part of judges. Political decisions by judges are forbidden. Interpretation that is a form of invention, 'creative interpretation', is a very dangerous activity. Such is the theory restating the mythical contents of the application ritual.

But this theory in use does not account for all that takes place in court practice. Strong pressures have made judges less reluctant to take an active part in lawmaking. Especially in private law, but also in administrative law, Dutch judges can sometimes be very activist. This attitude is usually accepted by legislators, public authorities, and the legal community. So prevalent has judicial activism become, that the terminology of 'applying the law' and the doctrinal story of the separation of powers are often experienced as not matching reality and as not being adequate to provide normative orientation. It is in many instances more accurate to say that judges balance interests than that they apply rules. The idea of balance of powers, which is seen as an American invention, is slowly becoming more attractive as theory in use. Sometimes judges explicitly refer to ideas that cannot be squared with the doctrinal story of separation of powers. This enmeshing of theories of proper judicial behavior can remain implicit most of the time. But sometimes a case comes before the courts that is perceived - by the judges themselves but also by a wider audience, such as the press - as involving political aspects. This is when the symbolic power of different doctrinal stories can be tested. Up until now, the separation story has won over the balance story. Supreme Court decisions tend to use strong, principled, concise language when it comes to demarcating the legal from the political. Judges will not apply human rights law, which technically they can enforce against legislation, if they think that this course of action would limit the options of the legislature to find a politically acceptable solution to the problem at hand. The formula employed is always the same. It is repeated again and again; it is a ritual within the text. The formula states that there are limits to judicial activism, relating to 'the position of the judge in the constitutional order'. In the Dutch phrase, the idea of the judge being the mouth of the law, the one who is subordinated to a higher order, reverberates. Montesquieu's words easily come to mind. The ritual performing this myth is an abstract one: the repeating of formulaic expressions. The law is applied, not explained, shown, not thought. Within the text of the judicial decision similar gestures are made as those performed daily in the courts.

The Potency Of Disorder

In each of the four rituals which have been summarily described, the Queen figures differently. In the formation ritual, she is an active performer, the person initiating new acts in the drama of cabinet formation following an indecisive election. In the opening ritual, she is the central performer, speaking on behalf of the government to a symbolically united nation. The enactment ritual shows only traces of the royal presence in the signature and the royal message appended to new legislation. For the players in the application ritual, the Queen is a visual symbol that metaphorically oversees the performance. In all four rituals, the myth of the Legal State lies at the heart of the performance. All four rituals show a clear concern with order. Yet, at the same time, the order postulated by the ritual acts is not very explicit. It does not have the quality of a clear and public script that has to be played according to invariable and established rules. The formation ritual, especially, takes place as a rite of passage in which a new phase in the political process is entered by all participants; their status as leaders of political parties and members of a cabinet-to-be is uncertain, some of their ordinary functions are temporarily suspended. Even the Queen is in an ambiguous position when she has to take real responsibility as a symbolic political actor. The opening ritual has a fixed choreography but the text being spoken varies; through the Royal Speech with its clearly recognizable stylistical features, one glimpses at the new directions the cabinet wants to take: order shows openness towards the future but also concern, anxiety, apprehension. In the enactment ritual, the status of the Queen as part of the government proposing and enacting legislation is unclear. Her agreement can only be inferred negatively, while the statute is promulgated under her signature. The application ritual brings an imposed order to the conflicts of real life. It is certain what the outcome will always have to be: the right answer will be given. But, at the same time, it is also open to the vicissitudes of rhetoric, to the struggle between positions that occupy the space afforded by the procedural rules. Here, the outcome is uncertain: rhetoric promises that the most convincing argument will win, not that it will produce the best or even the only true answer. Behind the authority of judicial application of law, there lurks an indecision as to the true role of the judge in settling, interpreting, perhaps inventing law. When law is in danger of being perceived as politics by other means, ritual formulas underscore the ruling mythology of the Legal State.

One would like to give an interpretation of these rituals that is not only concerned with order, with the organization of social experience, but which also recognizes disorder, the perception of dangers and powers beyond or behind symbols and performances. In this, the anthropological work of Mary Douglas on rituals relating to pollution proves very rewarding. In this symbolic anthropology, disorder is the necessary counterpart to order.

> Granted that disorder spoils pattern; it also provides the materials of pattern. Order implies restriction; from all possible materials, a limited selection has been made and from all possible relations a limited set has been used. Disorder by implication is unlimited, no pattern has been realized in it, but its potential for patterning is indefinite. This is why, though we seek to create order, we do not simply condemn disorder. We recognize that it is destructive to existing patterns; also that it has potentiality. It symbolizes both danger and power. (Douglas, 1966: 94)

If order and disorder show this mutual dependency, it is clearer why, behind the fixed rituals of the application of law in the courts, there is also a very real appreciation to be found of the advantages of disorder, of creative lawmaking by judges. Indeed, the judicial art symbolizes both danger (to the established order of the separation of powers) and power (the perspective of achieving true justice in the case under consideration and in like cases). Douglas draws attention to ritual dealing with disorder.

> Ritual recognizes the potency of disorder. In the disorder of the mind, in dreams, faints and frenzies, ritual expects to find powers which cannot be reached by conscious effort. (Douglas 1966: 94)

This ritual recognition of the power inherent in disorder must take many forms. In our modern societies, judges do not enter a trance in order to 'see' the Law, as if it were the Command of God. But specifically as regards the requirement of doing justice, one often hears that emotion, intuition, and the appeal of principles play their part. The foremost Dutch writer on judicial reasoning writes about the 'leap' the judge has to make when confronting the solutions his logical mind has extracted from the materials in the case with the intuitive insight emerging from his conscience (Scholten 1931). When it comes to the rhetoric of the lawyers, the potency involved in their verbal struggle, which at the minimum offers two appealing solutions to the issue, is clear for all to see. And so is the danger that the wrong side will win through verbal trickery. Dressing both contestants in the same black robes and subordinating them visually to the judge (seated above them), who is also dressed in a black robe, is a recognition of this potency and this danger: those who bring irreconcilable solutions and threaten to propose a wrong decision are wearing the same dress as the person who will weld all this material into the one unassailable Right Answer. The similarity in colour suggests that all actors are really after the same good, while the elevated position of the judge shows that justice will in the end always win over sophistry.

The implicit doctrinal stories that can be gleaned when law is in danger of becoming politics indicate that in such a clear instance of danger, there is also potency in disorder, the potency of turning towards an alternative myth of the Legal State which, perhaps, better captures its regulative ideals. When these theories in use come to the fore in texts, such as judicial opinions, the speakers try to issue a message about their message, they speak a meta-language, recognizing that a problem of communication has arisen and that it is in everybody's interest to explicate the demands of the social order. Thus, the ritual affirmation of order is a reaction to the experience of both the power and the danger of disorder.

> By ceremony, speech and gesture (people) make a constant effort to express and to agree on a view of what the relevant social structure is like. And all the attribution of

> dangers and powers is part of this effort to communicate and thus to create social forms. (Douglas, 1966: 101)

What 'potency of disorder' is present in the case of the three political rituals? The formation ritual and the opening ritual are interesting, first of all, as rituals in which dangers are tamed: the danger of dissensus, of prolonged misunderstanding, of damage to the general interest through factional politics. But these are dangers that are connected to powers, to the promise of power in an Aristotelian sense of the word: the possibility to act (Arendt, 1958: 175–207). When a coalition is formed and a program is discussed, the danger of failure is very closely associated with the chance of seeing and realizing new potentialities. Both the coalition partners and the plan of action are seen to be decisive for the future of the nation. At least, this is how participants in the negotiations will come to perceive the situation. That understanding makes the twin dangers that the preferred coalition fails to materialize and that even the best program has to be compromised at once so real and threatening. When the stakes are low, the process can be more relaxed and the chances of a positive outcome may be higher. But, as it is, coalitions are always formed under great stress. The emerging cabinet thus has already withstood its first crisis by the time it takes office; the ritual of formation creates the energy for the new start. The opening ritual is a clear reflection of the need to come to terms with both the danger and the promise of political rhetoric. Before everybody ventures into public discussions with the prospect of new, well-founded policies and the danger that the policies will not be adequate to their purposes, the opening ritual reflects the awareness that the discussions will take place against a background of shared understandings, in a context of equal citizenship. That is not the last consideration, however. The ritual is clearly to the advantage of the government that can give its program central importance. There is no neutrality in political ritual. So the constructive, power-recognizing aspect of this ritual is complemented by the emergence of a new danger: that of partiality to the pretensions of the government. Even in this strongly structured ritual, there remains the potentiality of new disorder.

The enactment ritual is a structuring activity *par excellence*. In new legislation, the social world is renamed, reorganized: new relationships are perhaps created. The power aspect seems to be all there is. But this is not true. Statutes are powerful when someone with sufficient knowledge and in the right frame of mind takes them seriously. Statutes are texts and they need readers to be understood before they can be acted upon. Only then can they be obeyed, and achieve some of their aims. The dangers in the act of legislating are to be found in the pitfalls of the legislative communication process. Without readers, the text will be a dead letter. When the attention of the right audience has been gained, it may misunderstand the statute, it may interpret it in a different manner than the framers had foreseen, it may consciously disobey its commands. These are the dangers the ritual seeks to tame by inserting the royal presence. Who would refuse to listen to the Queen or who would fail to obey her every wish? But surely, these dangers are potentialities too. Because the audience may not need the statute, it may have good reasons for interpreting it the way it does; it may be justified in evading its prescriptions. And, because the royal presence in the statute is so limited, so symbolic, so abstract, it is possible that these ways of reacting are actually also legitimate because the Queen—as a symbol of national unity and the general interest—cannot be supposed to wish her subjects to act against their best reason.

Law In Politics and Politics In Law

If we needed any proof of the existence of culturally differentiated domains of law and politics - and assuming we would not know how constitutional law and political theory conceptualize these domains - the four rituals of the Legal State would provide that proof. Ritual being myth in action, we can see in these ritual performances involving the Queen as symbol that the boundaries are delineated and that conceptions of boundaries are necessary for their interpretation. Crossing the boundary is a dangerous activity. Being in both realms simultaneously is a special status that no ordinary mortals can achieve. Following Douglas, we can also recognize the potentialities in these ritual performances, the power they evoke, represent, and put to work. But, as soon as we see this, and remember that the boundaries are apparently not so clear as to offer a space free from danger, the image of domains, fields, or spheres that are separated from each other is no longer convincing. (At this moment, the divide between law and politics loses its naturalized aspect.) Rather, the situation seems to be more complex. While there are differences that serve important functions, named by theories of *trias politica*, the spheres are not exactly autonomous in their functioning: they need to be linked to each other in certain ways in order to function at all. The rituals combine at every moment political and legal aspects. This imbrication gives us a clue to a situation of interdependence of law and politics. In order to guarantee that democracy asserts itself through the powerful but dangerous episodes of the formation of cabinets, the start of parliamentary debates, and the passing of new legislation, the Legal State has to be projected ritually as the encompassing background within which political action is possible and meaningful. There is law in politics because the strength law provides is important to effective political action. However, the application ritual and its mythical and theoretical assertions show how politics, in the sense of the well-ordered democratic process, is the precondition for all mundane acts of 'application' of the law; through the royal picture, politics is present symbolically in law. In the statements by judges naming the legitimate place of the judiciary in the political order, this dependence on the power of politics is repeated, facing the dangers that a fusion of law and politics would also generate. Again, politics lies in the background as part of the framework. And again, the political legitimation of acts of the judicature lends these acts an authority and a power they would not otherwise possess.

This acknowledgment of interdependence must not lead to diminished concern for the different identities of law and politics. The liberal art of separation has brought liberties to those operating within the demarcated spheres and it has also made for more equality between people (Walzer, 1984). As Walzer argues, political liberalism can be conceived as a movement that redrew the map of the social and political world. Liberal theory and practices from the Enlightenment have carved the organic and integrated whole of society. As Walzer puts it:

> Church and state, church-state and university, civil society and political community, dynasty and government, office and property, public life and private life, home and shop: each pair was, mysteriously or unmysteriously, two-in-one, inseparable. Confronting this world, liberal theorists preached and practiced an art of separation. They drew lines, marked off different realms, and created the sociopolitical map with which we are still familiar. The most famous line is the "wall" between church and state, but there are many others. Liberalism is a world of walls, and each one created a new liberty. (Walzer, 1984: 315)

These liberties also establish new forms of equality. As an example, Walzer points to the effects of religious liberty on the coercive power of political and ecclesiastical officials, creating a priesthood of believers "in which all believers are equally free to seek their own salvation." Religious freedom from the state creates pressures towards more power for laymen in the churches. The context of Walzer's remarks is his political theory. The art of separation provides guidelines for distributive justice. "A modern, complex and differentiated society enjoys both freedom and equality when success in one institutional setting is not convertible into success in another." (Walzer, 1984: 321)

The "spheres of justice," so conceived, suppose a separate political sphere. How does this sphere relate to the sphere of law? Walzer never addresses this question directly. Perhaps he feels that within the legal system only instrumentalities of justice are at stake; that this sphere is a translation machine that authorizes in legal form the divisions of social goods that are governed by principles of distribution particular to other spheres (such as religion or politics). The relation between law and politics is at stake indirectly, however, when Walzer discusses the need to protect the political sphere proper issuing from infringements from one of the other spheres.

> On the liberal view, men and women are not free in the state so much as from it; and they are equal under the law. So they are protected from political power (...) But if we turn from individuals to institutions, it is clear that political power itself requires protection - not only against foreign conquests but also against domestic seizure. The state is unfree when power is seized and held by a set of family members, or clergymen, or office-holders, or wealthy citizens. (Walzer, 1984: 326)

The liberal solution should be to extend the process of separation, so that the state is separated from all other institutions. But what exactly can this mean? To Walzer, democracy is the answer:

> A state that is in the hands of its citizens generally - just as a free church is in the hands of believers, a free university in the hands of scholars, a free firm in the hands of workers and managers. And then citizens are free in the state as well as from it (...); and they are equal in the making of the law and not only under the law.

Being 'equal in making the law' means being equal in a political way. Apparently, this extension of the art of separation, leading to ever greater liberty and equality, does not firmly separate politics from law ('being equal under the law'), but politicizes the law in the sense of making the citizens its master. So, whereas Walzer is utterly consequential in following the logic of liberal political theory, even this logic ends when the political sphere has been conceived as a separate one and threats to its independence must be curbed; the picture then becomes one of mutual interpretation and interdependence of law and politics (in fact, the picture loses its clarity, it becomes blurred). Walzer has brought his logical reasoning to a point where the art of separation confronts another kind of boundary: the place where it is seen that politics and law need each other to gain strength and affirm their identities.

* Tilburg University, The Netherlands

References

Andeweg, Rudy B. *Dutch Voters Adrift: On Explanations of Electoral Change 1963–1977.* Leyden: Leyden University, 1982.

Argyris, Chris and Schön, Donald. *Organizational Learning.* Amsterdam: Addison-Wesley, 1978.

Barthes, Roland. *Mythologies.* St. Albans: Paladin, 1973.

Cassirer, Ernst. *The Myth of the State.* New Haven and London: Yale University Press, 1946.

______________. *The Philosophy of Symbolic Forms: Volume 2; Mythical Thought.* New Haven and London: Yale University Press, 1955.

Cornell, Drucilla. *The Philosophy of the Limit.* New York and London: Routledge, 1992.

Cotterrell, Roger. *The Politics of Jurisprudence: A Critical Introduction to Legal Philisophy.* London and Edinburgh: Butterworths, 1989.

Daalder, Hans. "The Netherlands," in: Henig, S. (ed.), *Political Parties in the European Community.* London, 1979, 175–208.

Douglas, Mary. *Purity and Danger: An Analysis of the Concepts of Pollution and Taboo.* London and Henley: Routledge and Kegan Paul, 1966.

Fitzpatrick, Peter. *The Mythology of Modern Law.* London and New York: Routledge, 1992.

Goodrich, Peter. *Languages of Law: From Logics of Memory to Nomadic Masks.* London: Weidenfeld and Nicholson, 1990.

Hoefnagels, G.P. *Rituelen ter terechtzitting*. Deventer: Kluwer, 1970.

Kertzer, David I. *Ritual, Politics, and Power*. New Haven and London: Yale University Press, 1988.

Lijphart, Arend. *The Politics of Accomodation: Pluralism and Democracy in The Netherlands*. Berkeley: University of California Press, 1975.

Montesquieu. *The Spirit of the Laws*. Translated and edited by Anne M. Cohler, Basia C. Miller and Harold S. Stone, Cambridge: Cambridge University Press, 1989.

Scholten, Paul. *Algemeen Deel*. Zwolle: Tjeenk Willink, 1931.

Schönfeldt, K.M. *Montesquieu en "La Bouche de la Loi"*. Leyden: New Rhine Publishers, 1979.

Teubner, Gunther. "A Constructivist Epistemology of Law," *Law & Society Review*, Volume 23, Number 5, 1989: 727–757.

Walzer, Michael. "Liberalism and the Art of Separation." *Political Theory*, Volume 12, Number 3, 1984: 315–330.

Witteveen, Willem J. "Doctrinal Stories." *International Journal for the Semiotics of Law*, Volume 6, Number 17, 1993: 179–202.

Notes

1. An insightful analysis of the political side of legal philosophy, treating positivism and natural law, but also relating to interactionism, legal realism and critical legal studies, is Cotterrell, 1989. Teubner, 1989 relates autopoiesis to concurring epistemologies. An interesting effort to use Derridean deconstruction as an ethical message about law and legal thinking, is provided in Cornell, 1992.

2. Montesquieu writes: "When legislative power is united with executive power in a single person or in a single body of the magistracy, there is no liberty, because one can fear that the same monarch or senate that makes tyrannical laws will execute them tyrannically. Nor is there liberty if the power of judging is not separate from legislative power and from executive power. If it were joined to legislative power, the power over the life and liberty of the citizens would be arbitrary, for the judge would be the legislator. If it were joined to the executive power, the judge could have the force of an oppressor. All would be lost if the same man or the same body of principal men, either of nobles, or of the people, exercised these three powers: that of making the laws, that of executing public resolutions, and that of judging the crimes or the disputes of individuals." (Montesquieu, 1989 (1748), 157)

3. The notion 'the Legal State' both draws upon and differs from that of Cassirer, 1946. Cassirer traces the idea of the Legal State to its roots in platonism, where not the best but the ideal, perfect, permanent state is first articulated. Plato, in doing so, moves away from the ruling myths of the Homeric world. This notion that there exists a pure form of the state that is at the basis of all empirical manifestations and, as it were, implied by them, has in later times itself become a myth, however. In speaking about the Legal State, reference is not made to explicit, theoretical platonic interpretations but to an unruly, implicit idea of the well-regulated legal nature of all political forms. So, in the terms employed by Cassirer, the Legal State is now a myth rather than the antithesis of myth.

4. Ground-breaking research into the political aspects of pillarization was published in Lijphart, 1975 (*The Politics of Accommodation*); many empirical and normative studies have followed in its wake; see, for instance, Daalder, 1979 and Andeweg, 1982.

5. The Dutch and the English parliamentary system differ in important respects. Though there are an upper and a lower house of parliament, cooperating with the cabinet in the enactment of legislation, some defining differences are: proportional representation (in practice leading to the impossibility of a majoritarian government), separation of persons (cabinet

members cannot be members of parliament), individual responsibility of ministers (being more important than collective responsibility of the cabinet), weaker position of the prime minister within the cabinet and in respect to parliament.

Index